THE
CHEATING CHEF'S
SECRET
COOKBOOK

517 Delicious Dishes
in 4 Steps or Less

SURPRISING TECHNIQUES!
EASY SHORTCUTS!
HIDDEN INGREDIENTS!

Reader's
digest

New York / Montreal

Project Staff

EXECUTIVE EDITOR
Elissa Altman

SENIOR ART DIRECTOR
Edwin Kuo

COVER DESIGNERS
Rich Kershner
Rose DeMaria

WRITER
Sharon Bowers

COPY EDITOR
Lisa Andruscavage

ILLUSTRATIONS
Harry Bates (how-to)
Norm Bendell

INDEXER
Cohen Carruth Indexes

RDA Content Creation Team

VP, EDITOR IN CHIEF
Neil Wertheimer

CREATIVE DIRECTOR
Michele Laseau

EXECUTIVE MANAGING EDITOR
Donna Ruvituso

ASSOCIATE DIRECTOR, NORTH AMERICA PREPRESS
Douglas A. Croll

MANUFACTURING MANAGER
John L. Cassidy

MARKETING DIRECTOR
Dawn Nelson

ISBN: 978-1-60652-977-5 (hardcover)

ISBN: 978-1-60652-241-7 (paperback)

We are committed to both the quality of our products and the service we provide our customers. We value your comments, so please feel free to contact us.

Reader's Digest Trade Publishing
44 S. Broadway
White Plains, NY 10601

Printed in China

1 3 5 7 9 10 8 6 4 2 (hardcover)

9 10 8 (paperback)

For more Reader's Digest products and information, visit our website:

www. rd.com (in the United States)

www.readersdigest.ca (in Canada)

THE CHEATING CHEF'S
SECRET HANDSHAKE

I WILL always strive to cook delicious dishes that are delectable, quick, and inexpensive.

—⁓—

I WILL proudly use under-the-radar "secret" ingredients that will make my dishes absolutely yummy!

—⁓—

I WILL use clever and surprising shortcut techniques that will save tons of time and barrels of money.

—⁓—

I WILL share the fruits of my cooking with family and friends everywhere.

—⁓—

I WILL understand that part of being a CHEATING CHEF means that I WILL be lighthearted and joyful about the process of cooking, and that the pursuit of creating wonderful meals quickly and inexpensively is as delicious as it is fun!

CONTENTS

Shhh...The Chef Knows a Secret!

Why is it that when you buy a cookbook from a famous chef and follow every instruction to the letter, your version of the dish doesn't taste the same as what you ate in his restaurant? You probably thought it was your fault, and that you'd missed something or didn't buy the exact same kind of flour or took it out of the oven a little too soon.

Wrong.

The answer is simpler than that: Chefs never tell you everything.

Let's face it—if you knew all their secrets, you wouldn't spend your money in restaurants and professional cooks wouldn't have jobs. In that respect, restaurant chefs are like your Great-Aunt Ethel, who'll be happy to give you her classic coconut cake recipe, only she'll conveniently forget to add a few details. So yes, you'll have a tasty cake, but it'll be missing that certain something. Aunt Ethel probably figures it'll keep you coming back for more at family reunions, and also keep her magic intact as the family baker. Imagine how astonished you'd be to discover that your family's favorite cook actually uses a white cake mix, tarted up beyond all recognition by soaking each layer with cream of coconut before assembling the tiers. That's not difficult! But it certainly seems that way if nobody ever told you about it!

In this book, we're going to lay bare all the tips and tricks that separate the pros from the amateurs and let you in on the sly little secrets that every chef knows and prefers not to share. Do chefs use a lot of butter and salt? Well, yes and no—they know that a bit of fat and salt, used judiciously, can dramatically improve flavor without adding an unhealthy element to a dish. But there are other tricks to making cooking easier and making dishes taste better and fresher that can be as simple as a few knife flicks. You don't have to go to culinary school to be the talk of every potluck or picnic. You just need a few aces up your sleeve to take everyday dishes from simple to downright spectacular. Those aces are right here!

EVERYDAY FOOD

While you, too, can cook food like a chef, what this book won't teach you to do is cook chef-like food. If you're cooking at home, for family and friends, you're much more likely to be putting a tasty dish of pork chops and applesauce on the table, not a Pan-Seared Medallion of Milk-Fed Suckling Pig with a Butter-Apple Coulis and Horseradish Foam. That kind of stuff definitely has its place: in restaurants, and that's where it should stay. Home cooks and eaters want home-cooked food, not a pale imitation of a fancy dish that required four chefs to make it. Home cooking is its own admirable art, and we're all in favor of it. What we want is the chef secrets that make any type of cooking more enjoyable, and that's what we're giving you here...in 4 steps, or less!

But even chefs have to cook for their families sometimes, and when they do, you can be sure they're not in the kitchen for hours on end making foams and emulsions. In fact, when you ask chefs about their favorite foods for their days off, the answers may be surprising: "gooey mac and cheese," "a really juicy hamburger," "moist chocolate cake." When chefs are in their home kitchens, just like the rest of us, they tend to like simple and savory. They like the kinds of food their mothers and grandmothers used to make. They don't want to spend a lot of money. They don't want a recipe to take too long or have too many steps.

But unlike us, they usually know a few more things about achieving those ends with ease and flair. They know how to cull the most flavor from the least expensive cuts of meat. They know how to work a dough to keep it tender and flaky. They're not afraid of seasoning, and they know that sometimes, a little bit of fat goes a long way to improving flavor in the final dish.

By culling the top tricks and techniques from the pros, you too can make simple meals into something special, each day, and your family

YOU DON'T HAVE TO GO TO CULINARY SCHOOL TO BE THE TALK OF EVERY POTLUCK OR PICNIC.

and friends will say WOW, HOW DID YOU DO THAT? And now, the secret is yours!

THE SCRUMPTIOUS SECRETS

In putting this book together, we searched far and wide and spoke to chefs from all over the world about the little touches that make their food fabulous; we tested every recipe thoroughly and hit on innumerable tricks that make those recipes outshine every other. And in the end, we wound up with more than 517 brilliant dishes made great with what the French called "kitchen trucs"—those ingredients, gadgets, and everyday items and cheffy secrets that we'd otherwise overlook as they sit gathering dust in our pantry or kitchen cabinet.

In truth, most of the secrets that chefs keep to themselves come straight out of their noodle (so to speak); the power of ingenuity never ceases to amaze us. Why use a meat pounder when you can use the bottom of a sauté pan? Why use a special lemon zester when you can use a regular vegetable peeler? Did you know that cilantro mimics the flavor of lime so if you're among the 50% of the population who can't tolerate the herb, you can use lime and you won't know the difference?

The fact is that chefs everywhere know the truth: that there are secret tweaks, ingredients, techniques and downright tricky tricks that can turn a good dish into a fantastic one...if you know what those tricks are. And most of us don't...until now!

EVEN VEGETABLES TAKE ON NEW LIFE WHEN YOU DO IT THE CHEF'S SECRET WAY.

What makes a beef stew rich and velvety? Anything from the addition of instant coffee to a piece of a storebought chocolate bar.

How do you give a little bit of lift to tomato sauce? You could use a drop of lemon juice, buttermilk and even a small dollop of yogurt. Ora dash of that kitchen cabinet favorite, white vinegar.

Rolling out some dough but don't have a rolling pin? Why, you can use a wine bottle!

Need to use that brown sugar but it's hard as a rock? Slip a piece of white bread in the bag and watch it soften like butter!

Tossing pasta with cooked vegetables? Cook the pasta in the same water as the vegetables and watch the flavor jump right off the charts!

Want to make stuffed peppers but they always topple over? Roast them in a muffin pan!

Love roast chicken but yours always comes out dry? Roast it upside down!

The fact is, you can beg chefs everywhere for the little secrets to their cooking that make a big, big difference in the quality of what's on the plate, and they'll never tell you... until now!

COME AND GET IT: RECIPES HOT AND FRESH

All this knowledge would be no use to you without some fabulous new dishes to practice on until these techniques become second nature. Any pro in any field knows that it's a lot easier to learn by doing. So what you'll get here are literally hundreds of new recipes, for dishes ranging from American down-home classics to dinner-party dazzlers, each helping to clarify or illustrate a chef's sassy secret. Roast beef that's perfectly pink at the very center and crispy brown outside, cook vegetables so succulent and sweet that you'll think you've never tasted a green bean before, and make the mashed potatoes of your dreams.

Even vegetables take on new life when you do it the chef's secret way. Turns out the secret to perfect boiling is in the amount of salt and the amount of water you use. Roasting a vegetable like they do at your favorite bistro requires much higher heat than you might have expected, and even serving veggies raw reveals new info on the way chefs slice and prep.

Even breakfast is not immune from the tinkering and techniques of the pros. Make muffins with perfectly raised golden crowns just like in a bakery, and finally see why the perfect omelet is the mark of a true French chef.

We've even gotten pastry chefs to spill the (vanilla) beans when it comes to serving up sweets that are a unified success. Make homemade cakes that are blissfully moist and flavorful, with an even crumb and a high rise, without needing any of the chemical emulsifiers and preservatives of a cake mix. Get ready to become known in your neighborhood as the greatest chocolate chip cookie baker of all time, thanks to one simple secret that professional bakers were keeping to themselves.

A LASTING IMPRESSION

The final results couldn't be more satisfying: You'll be a better, more confident cook, one who

can take on any dish—and take it to the next level. You'll be surprised how quickly you become the cook who wows friends and relatives at the stunning ease with which you toss off casual tips and culinary creations. From your knife skills when chopping herbs to the magnificence of each juicy burger you flip off the grill, knowing a few chef secrets is like knowing the password to the world's greatest culinary club.

Never again will you fear a raw artichoke, a yeast-raised loaf of bread or a package of chicken waiting to be fried. Learn to spurn the store-bought version of everything from hummus and guacamole to chicken noodle soup and cupcakes, because your homemade versions are so much better.

If it's true that an army marches on its stomach, with *The Cheating Chef's Secret Cookbook*, you've just been promoted to the rank of general. Lead on!

1 BREAKFAST TREATS
THAT CAN'T BE BEAT

Guess what? Breakfast can be tastier, cheaper, more satisfying, and far better for you when it doesn't come out of a package. You can even do a little cooking in advance to get the meal ready on short notice. Once you get the rhythm down, cooking breakfast on a regular basis is really just as fast as smearing cream cheese on a bagel. When you make muffins and hearty, natural cereals at home (homemade muesli is so delicious!), you won't get that prize in the cereal box, but you'll feel fortified and happy for the day ahead. What better prize is there than that?

Bran Raisin Muffins

These moist and hearty muffins will stay fresh from Monday to Friday. Bake them in paper cupcake liners and keep them in an airtight container. If the muffins are getting tired toward the end of the week, split and butter them and pop them in the toaster oven for a few minutes, or microwave for about 30 seconds, no longer.

2 eggs

1/2 cup vegetable oil

1/2 cup milk

1/2 cup brown sugar or honey

2 cups all-purpose flour

1/2 cup wheat bran

2 teaspoons baking powder

1/2 teaspoon cinnamon

1/4 teaspoon salt

1/2 cup golden raisins

Sugar for topping (optional)

PREP TIME: 8 minutes • **COOK TIME:** 20 minutes • **MAKES** 12 muffins

1 Preheat the oven to 400°F. Line a 12-cup muffin pan with paper liners.

2 Beat the eggs, oil, milk, and sugar or honey in a medium bowl. Add the flour, bran, baking powder, cinnamon, salt, and raisins and mix just until combined. (You can do this in a food processor, blending the wet ingredients first and pulsing in the dry ingredients just until combined; add the raisins after the pulsing is done.) If the raisins are large, chop them lightly before adding.

3 Fill the prepared cups three-quarters full. Sprinkle a little sugar, if using, on top of each muffin. Bake for 20 minutes, or until golden brown.

DID YOU KNOW?

If your muffins emerge from the oven flat instead of puffed into a dome, you're probably overbeating the batter. Resist the impulse to beat it smooth. Add the dry ingredients to the wet all at once and turn the batter over from the bottom with a wooden spoon or rubber spatula, not a whisk. Several brisk stirs should do the trick. When you can still see a few streaks of unincorporated flour, that's the time to spoon the batter into the prepared muffin pans.

TOP SECRET

When chopping dried fruit, such as dried apricots or dates, spray both sides of the knife lightly with cooking spray. It will prevent the dried fruit from sticking to the knife, allowing you to cut smaller pieces quickly and more efficiently.

Carrot Muffins

Like a plump, warm piece of unfrosted carrot cake— but healthier and perfect for breakfast! With this heavy, carrot-filled batter, it's especially important that you take care not to overmix.

2 eggs

1 cup milk

1/2 cup vegetable oil

3/4 cup brown sugar

1 3/4 cups all-purpose flour

1/2 cup rolled oats

2 teaspoons baking powder

1 teaspoon cinnamon

1/4 teaspoon salt

2 carrots, peeled and grated (about 1 cup)

1/2 cup raisins

1/2 cup chopped walnuts

Sugar for topping (optional)

PREP TIME: 10 minutes • **COOK TIME:** 20 minutes • **MAKES** 12 muffins

1 Preheat the oven to 400°F. Line a 12-cup muffin pan with paper liners.

2 In a medium bowl, blend the eggs, milk, oil, and sugar. Stir in the flour, oats, baking powder, cinnamon, and salt, just until combined. Add the carrots, raisins, and nuts and stir very briefly, just to distribute throughout the batter.

3 Spoon the batter into the prepared cups until three-quarters full. Sprinkle a little sugar, if using, on top of each muffin. Bake for 20 minutes, or until golden brown.

VARIATIONS

Zucchini-Gingerbread Muffins

Add 1/4 cup unsulfured molasses when blending the egg and milk mixture. Substitute zucchini (1 medium or 2 small) for the carrots. Add 1 tablespoon ground ginger and 1/4 teaspoon ground cloves to the dry ingredients along with the cinnamon. Replace the raisins with golden raisins and leave out the walnuts.

Chocolate Carrot Muffins

Add 2 tablespoons semi-sweet chocolate chips to the dry ingredients.

TOP SECRET

Once you have a basic muffin recipe that works, you can swap like ingredients for like ingredients to get new flavors every time you bake. Replace carrots with apples or zucchini. Replace the raisins with chopped walnuts, pecans, or almonds. Use ground ginger in place of the cinnamon, or add 1/4 teaspoon freshly grated nutmeg instead. Replace no more than 1/2 cup of the flour with up to 1 cup rolled oats. Replace up to half the flour with whole-wheat flour.

Irish Whole-Meal Soda Bread

In its purer form, this fast-mixing, fast-baking bread is moist and flavorful, almost like a tender-crumbed cake. In Ireland, it's the traditional accompaniment to smoked salmon, but sliced thick for breakfast and spread with butter and jam, you'll go out the door whistling "When Irish Eyes Are Smiling."

1 1/2 cups stone-ground whole-wheat flour

1/2 cup all-purpose white flour

1/4 cup wheat germ

1 teaspoon baking soda

1/4 teaspoon salt

1 egg

1 1/4 cups buttermilk

PREP TIME: 7 minutes • **COOK TIME:** 40 minutes • **MAKES** 1 loaf

1 Preheat the oven to 400°F. Grease a baking sheet.

2 In a large bowl, stir together the flours, wheat germ, baking soda, and salt. Beat the egg and buttermilk together in a small bowl.

3 Make a well in the center of the dry ingredients and add the egg mixture all at once. Stir to combine, then turn the dough out onto a floured surface and knead briefly, shaping into a disk about 3 inches high. Cut a cross about 1/2 inch deep on the surface.

4 Bake for about 40 minutes, or until it sounds hollow when you thump the base. Cool on a rack and wrap tightly to store. To slice, break into four quarters along the lines of the cross on the surface. Slice the quarters thickly and serve with butter and jam or marmalade.

VARIATION

Seeded Irish Raisin Soda Bread

Add 1 tablespoon fennel seeds and 1 tablespoon golden raisins to the dry ingredients.

DID YOU KNOW?

Steel-cut oats have the nuttiest flavor when made into oatmeal. Rolled oats have been flattened, so they cook much more quickly and retain a nuttier flavor. Quick-cooking oats and instant oats have been milled very finely so that they cook up in seconds, but there's a big sacrifice in flavor and texture.

TOP SECRET

The secret to making whole-meal breads moist and nutty, instead of dry and tough, is wheat germ. Adding wheat germ brings a caramel-like scent to the finished bread and helps keep it moist for days longer. For each cup of whole-wheat flour in a bread recipe, add a 1/4 cup wheat germ (and for the best bread, whole-wheat flour should never be more than 50 percent of the recipe).

Swiss Muesli

The original muesli was a wholesome mix of dried fruits, nuts, and grains developed by a Swiss doctor and intended to be eaten with yogurt and fresh fruit. You can start with a box of store-bought muesli and bulk it up to your taste with dried fruits, nuts, rolled oats, and wheat bran, or you can make your own muesli from all-natural ingredients, best bought in bulk in a health food store.

5 cups (about 1 pound) rolled oats

1 cup bran flakes

1/2 cup wheat bran

1/2 cup wheat germ

1 cup chopped dried fruit such as apricots, dates, figs, and apples

1 cups raisins

1 cup chopped walnuts

1/2 cup shelled sunflower seeds

Berries or sliced fresh fruit for topping (optional)

PREP TIME: 5 minutes • **COOK TIME:** 0 minutes • **MAKES** 10 cups

1 Mix all the ingredients and store in an airtight container in a cool place.

2 To serve, combine 1/2 to 3/4 cup muesli with 1 cup milk and 1/2 cup plain or flavored yogurt. Leave it for 5 minutes before eating to allow the grains to soften. Top with berries or fruit, if using.

VARIATION

Crispy Almond-Banana Muesli

Replace the dried fruit with banana chips and substitute toasted whole almonds for the walnuts and sunflower seeds. Use 2 cups corn flakes in place of the bran flakes, and add 1 cup unsweetened coconut flakes. Serve with papaya or mango yogurt, or with plain yogurt and cubes of fresh papaya or mango.

TOP SECRET

Delicious yogurts are available at the grocery store, but the classic way to eat muesli is with plain, unsweetened yogurt, which is *very* inexpensive to make and super easy, especially if you own a 1-quart Thermos. Bring a quart of milk to a boil, then immediately turn off the heat and cool the milk back down to 115°F. Stir in 2 tablespoons any kind of yogurt, as long as it has live and active cultures (the label will say so). Pour into the Thermos, cap, and leave for 4 to 6 hours. The even temperature of the Thermos will produce a yogurt that's thick, creamy, and full-flavored, not watery and thin.

Better Banana-Cranberry Bread

Banana bread is usually so heavy and dense that it's often difficult to bake it all the way through. This is a much lighter version that bakes up cakelike, and the bananas, along with the refreshingly tart bite of fresh cranberries, keep it deliciously moist and fresh for days. It doesn't even need butter or cream cheese.

1/2 cup (1 stick) unsweetened butter

1/2 cup sugar

2 eggs

4–5 very ripe bananas

1 1/2 cups all-purpose flour

2 teaspoons baking powder

1/4 teaspoon salt

1/4 teaspoon ground nutmeg

1/2 cup fresh or frozen cranberries, coarsely chopped

PREP TIME: 8 minutes • **COOK TIME:** 30 minutes • **MAKES** 1 loaf

1 Preheat the oven to 375°F. Lightly grease a 9 x 4-inch loaf pan.

2 Using a hand beater, in a large bowl, cream the butter, sugar, and eggs for 3 to 4 minutes, or until light in color and very fluffy. Add the bananas. Blend in with the beaters, leaving slightly chunky.

3 Add the flour, baking powder, salt, nutmeg, and cranberries. Mix very briefly, just to combine.

4 Pour into the prepared loaf pan and bake for 30 minutes, or until browned on top and a toothpick or knife blade inserted in center comes out clean.

VARIATION

Banana-Cherry Walnut Bread

Replace the cranberries with dried tart cherries and add 1/2 cup coarsely chopped unsalted walnuts.

LEFTOVER LUXURIES

Keep your breakfast quickbreads ready to eat all week long by storing them in airtight containers, preferably in a ziplock bag. Really moist bread with lots of added fruit should be kept in the refrigerator to discourage mold. If you definitely won't eat the whole thing in a few days, slice the cooled loaf and place sheets of waxed paper between the slices; wrap the whole loaf in a double thickness of plastic wrap and store in the freezer. When you're ready to eat, toast (frozen slices will need some extra time) until just heated through but not tough.

TOP SECRET

The secret to this light bread is the few extra moments spent creaming the butter, sugar, and eggs, so don't skimp on that, and don't make this in a food processor, which will make the finished bread flat and tough.

Milk-and-Maple Oatmeal

Everyone knows that oatmeal is good for your cholesterol levels and an excellent source of fiber. But the instant kind is low in fat, high in sugar, and doesn't taste very good. The answer is steel-cut oats or pinhead oatmeal. It can take up to an hour of attended cooking, but the technique below reduces your time at the stove to minutes and results in a tender, nutty-flavored oatmeal.

1 cup steel-cut oats or pinhead oatmeal

3 cups water

1/2 teaspoon salt

Real maple syrup, to taste

Milk, to taste

PREP TIME: 1 minute • **COOK TIME:** 5 minutes (plus sitting overnight) • **SERVES:** 2–3

1 Right before you go to bed, mix the oats or oatmeal, water, and salt in a small saucepan. Bring to a boil, stir, then immediately turn off the heat and cover. Leave overnight.

2 In the morning, turn on the heat under the pan, stir the oatmeal, and bring it to a quick boil.

3 Put some in a bowl and top with maple syrup and milk.

VARIATION

Almost-Instant Oatmeal with Peaches and Walnuts

Instead of steel-cut oats or pinhead oatmeal, put 3/4 cup rolled oats and 1/4 teaspoon salt in a pan with 1 1/2 cups low-fat milk. Bring to a boil and simmer gently for 2 to 3 minutes. While the oatmeal cooks, peel and dice a ripe peach and stir it in. Cover with a lid, remove from the heat, and let stand for 2 minutes. Give it a brisk stir and divide between two bowls. Top with chopped walnuts and a splash of light cream.

TOP SECRET

The key to perfect oatmeal every time is to not add milk until the end; otherwise, it will curdle and throw off the texture of the cereal (not to mention its flavor).

Speed-of-Light Breakfast Sandwich

Who needs pricey, high-fat breakfast sandwiches from fast-food restaurants? If you have a microwave, you can make a much tastier, cheaper, and delicious version at home. Eat it plain or with a dollop of salsa. If you don't have English muffins, use toast or—even faster—buttered brown bread.

1 English muffin

1 egg

Butter

Salt and pepper, to taste

1 thin slice American or cheddar cheese

PREP TIME: 4 minutes • **COOK TIME:** 2 minutes • **MAKES** 1 sandwich

1 Split and toast the English muffin.

2 Meanwhile, break the egg onto a saucer and beat it lightly with a fork. Microwave on high for 30 to 60 seconds, until the egg is just set and a bit puffy.

3 Butter the muffin and place the egg on the bottom half. Sprinkle with salt and pepper, then add the cheese. Add the muffin top and eat immediately.

VARIATION

Quick Breakfast Burrito

Use a warm flour tortilla instead of the English muffin. Use grated cheese in place of the slice, and spoon on a generous amount of salsa. If you like, spoon a thin line of sour cream down the middle, then fold and eat.

TOP SECRET

To avoid splatter, and for even cooking, cook bacon in the microwave. For 1 sandwich, place 1 or 2 slices of bacon on a folded paper towel and lay it in the microwave. Cook on high for 2 to 3 minutes, or until the bacon is crisp and sizzling. For more than 2 slices of bacon, lay the paper towel on a plate and increase the cooking time as needed.

Buttermilk Pancakes

This is the simplest, most foolproof pancake recipe around, resulting in cakes that rise up light and delicate. The recipe is easily doubled or tripled.

3/4 cup all-purpose flour

1/2 teaspoon salt

1 teaspoon baking soda

1 cup buttermilk

1 large egg, room temperature

4 tablespoons butter (1/2 stick), melted

1 tablespoon vegetable oil

PREP TIME: 4 minutes • **COOK TIME:** 10 minutes • **MAKES** 6 (6-inch) pancakes

1 In a medium bowl, combine the flour, salt, and baking soda.

2 In a small bowl, whisk together the buttermilk, egg, and butter. Make a well in the center of the dry ingredients and pour in the buttermilk mixture. Stir just until blended.

3 Heat a griddle or skillet over medium-high heat. Brush the surface with oil and reduce the heat slightly. Pour 1/3 cup batter, tilting pan slightly to allow it to spread to a 6-inch circle.

4 Cook for 2 minutes, or until bubbles rise to the surface and the edges of the pancake look dry. Flip and cook for another minute until just golden brown. Continue with remaining batter and serve immediately.

VARIATION
Whole-Wheat Blueberry Pancakes

Reduce the flour to 1/2 cup and add 1/4 cup whole-wheat flour. Rinse 1 cup blueberries and dry with a paper towel. When you pour the first pancake onto the griddle, immediately top it with a couple tablespoons of berries. Continue cooking as above, but be aware that the blueberries may hide rising bubbles on the surface of the pancake, so be careful not to overcook.

TOP SECRET

The best and lightest pancakes are made from buttermilk and baking soda, which together create air bubbles that are trapped by the gluten in the flour. This simple chemical reaction happens and subsides quickly, so don't wait around. Mix the pancake batter quickly (and minimally—overbeating makes them tough and flat) and cook them immediately. Discard any leftover batter.

THE BEST PANCAKE ADDITIONS

Everybody loves pancakes: They're an all-American favorite. Here are the top Cheating Chef favorites for adding to this delicious breakfast treat:

1 Bananas

2 Peaches

3 Nectarines

4 Chocolate Chips

5 Butterscotch Chips

6 Sliced Apples

7 Blackberries

8 Blueberries

9 Strawberries

10 Raspberries

11 Corn Kernels

12 Ricotta Cheese

13 Chopped Scallions

14 Sliced Kiwifruit

15 Pineapple Chunks

16 Currants

17 Raisins

18 Sliced Pears

19 Minced Jalapeños

20 Shredded Cheddar

What's the key to keeping pancakes from getting soggy when you add fruit? Cook the cake for a few seconds until it begins to bubble; add the fruit (and less is always more), wait a few more seconds, and then flip. When bubbles begin to appear on the surface of the pancake, it's time to flip it.

Sour Cream Breakfast Waffles

Rich and eggy, these dense waffles are tender thanks to all the sour cream in the batter. Serve hot with maple syrup or fruit and whipped cream or powdered sugar.

1 3/4 cups flour

1 teaspoon baking powder

1/2 teaspoon baking soda

1/2 teaspoon salt

4 medium eggs

1 container (16 ounces) sour cream

1/4 cup (1/2 stick) butter, melted

PREP TIME: 5 minutes • **COOK TIME:** 10–15 minutes
MAKES 6–8 waffles, depending on waffle iron

1 Preheat a waffle iron according to manufacturer instructions.

2 Blend the flour, baking powder, baking soda, and salt in a medium bowl. With a hand mixer or whisk, beat the eggs in another medium bowl until thick and pale. Beat in the sour cream and butter, then pour into the flour mixture, stirring gently just until combined.

3 Bake in the waffle iron according to manufacturer's directions.

VARIATION

Sour Cream Waffles with Chocolate Chips

Whether you want chocolate chips, diced bananas, blueberries, dried cranberries, chopped nuts, or anything else, stir 3/4 cup into the waffle batter. Before you spoon the batter into the waffle iron, make sure the appliance's surface is well-oiled, and stir the batter up gently from the bottom each time for an even distribution of the goodies.

TOP SECRET

Are your breakfast baked goods a little tough? Here's a secret weapon that just might help: sugar. Stir a few tablespoons of sugar in when combining the dry ingredients. Sugar helps weaken the gluten in the flour so it can't form such tough bonds. When it comes to baking, sugar is a natural tenderizer.

Crisp and Light Waffles

These waffles have far less fat than ordinary ones; the egg whites are beaten until stiff, which is the classic way to make waffles that bake up high and light rather than dense and chewy. Enjoy the waffles for breakfast if you like, but this version is even better for savory dishes, like chicken and waffles.

2 cups all-purpose flour

2 teaspoons baking powder

1/4 teaspoon salt

4 medium eggs, separated

1 3/4 cups milk

1 tablespoon butter, melted

PREP TIME: 10 minutes • **COOK TIME:** 10–15 minutes
MAKES 6–8 waffles, depending on waffle iron

1 Preheat a waffle iron according to manufacturer's directions.

2 Combine the flour, baking powder, and salt in a medium bowl. Whisk the egg yolks in a small bowl with the milk and butter and stir them briefly into the dry ingredients, being careful not to overmix.

3 Beat the egg whites in a clean medium bowl until stiff. Fold gently into the batter. Avoid beating out all the lumps or you'll deflate the egg whites.

4 Bake in the waffle iron according to manufacturer's directions.

VARIATION

Crisp and Light Pumpkin Waffles

Add 1 teaspoon ground cinnamon, 1 teaspoon ground ginger, and 1/2 teaspoon allspice to the dry ingredients. Blend 1/2 cup pumpkin with the egg yolks and milk.

TOP SECRET

If you have trouble beating egg whites until stiff, try this chef trick: Add 1/8 teaspoon cream of tartar per egg white to the whites before you start to beat them. This substance creates a chemical reaction that enables the peaks to form easily, and to hold. If you have no cream of tartar, use a drop of lemon juice instead.

French Toast

Far easier to make than waffles and even pancakes, French toast is fast enough to be a weekday morning breakfast, but still hearty and satisfying. The trick to this recipe is the simplicity. When you start adding sugar, vanilla, and cinnamon to the egg, you move into dessert territory. Maple syrup should be all the sweetness you need for this classic eggy version.

4 eggs, beaten

1/2 cup milk

8 slices bread

Unsalted butter

Maple syrup

PREP TIME: 5 minutes (includes soaking) • **COOK TIME:** 8 minutes • **SERVES:** 4

1 Beat the eggs together with the milk in a medium bowl until smooth. Soak the first 2 slices of bread in the egg mixture.

2 Heat a nonstick skillet over medium heat, and add about a tablespoon of butter. As soon as it sizzles, carefully place the soaked slices into the pan.

3 Put more bread in the egg mixture to soak while cooking the first slices, about 1 minute per side, until just set and golden brown. Lift onto a serving plate and continue with the remaining bread, adding more butter to the pan as needed to prevent sticking.

VARIATION

Panettone French Toast

For a much more elegant breakfast, substitute slices of Italian panettone, the sweetened Christmas bread studded with candied citrus. The square cardboard boxes holding panettone are ubiquitous in grocery stores around the holidays, and this is a perfect way to use up the last few slices.

LEFTOVER LUXURIES

French toast is the perfect way to come up with a great meal from a nearly empty kitchen. It can be made with nearly any kind of dry leftover bread, but avoid anything that's too savory or too soft. In fact, you need the bread to be stale to make good French toast; fresh bread can turn gummy. Egg-enriched challah and brioche both make luxurious versions, but you can also make an excellent French toast with cinnamon-raisin bread.

TOP SECRET

Ever wonder how restaurants get their French toast so brown and sweet without overcooking the middle? Here's the trick: When you melt the butter, add a pinch of brown sugar, a pinch of ground cinnamon, and a pinch of salt to the pan at the same time. When the butter begins to foam, put the bread in the pan, but do not move it around until it's time to flip!

Honey-Banana Stuffed French Toast

In this recipe, the sheer simplicity of basic French toast gives way to major indulgence. Once you get the hang of the technique, you can stuff French toast with all sorts of fillings, from a spoonful of jam to raspberries and cream cheese or blueberries and mascarpone, but this tasty banana version is a nice way to get started.

2 small bananas, diced

2 tablespoons honey

1/2 teaspoon ground cinnamon

4 slices (1 1/2-inches thick) Italian bread

4 eggs

1/2 cup milk

Butter

PREP TIME: 10 minutes • **COOK TIME:** 15 minutes • **SERVES:** 4

1 In a small bowl, combine the bananas with the honey and cinnamon. Cut a pocket about 2 inches deep into each slice of bread, and spoon in the filling, pressing the edge (but don't worry if it gapes open).

2 In a shallow dish, whisk the eggs and milk. Heat a nonstick skillet over medium heat. Lay a stuffed slice in the egg mixture, turning to coat.

3 Melt a few teaspoons of butter in the skillet and move the soaked bread to the skillet with a spatula. Cook 2 to 3 minutes per side, until golden brown. Continue with the remaining pockets. Serve immediately, either with powdered sugar or syrup.

VARIATION

Berry-Stuffed French Toast

Omit the honey, cinnamon, and bananas and instead use a few tablespoons of fresh berries—whatever is in season—that have been gently warmed in a small saucepan, with a dash of sugar.

TOP SECRET

Making a pocket in a thick slice of bread is a snap... it only looks impressive! Slice the bread about 1 1/2 inches thick, lay it on a cutting board, and, using a sharp paring knife, carefully make a 1 1/2- to 2-inch slit in the thickest part of the crust. Using your pinky, deepen the hole a bit, and there you have it! Instant pocket!

Classic Omelet

The benchmark for American chefs is the simplicity of roast chicken, but the hallmark of a real French chef is an omelet. Done right, it's puffy, creamy, and moist, without a hint of browning on the surface, and an almost custardlike texture.

2 eggs

Pinch of Kosher salt

1 tablespoon unsalted butter

Salt and pepper, to taste

PREP TIME: 2 minutes • **COOK TIME:** 2 minutes • **SERVES:** 1

1 Heat an omelet pan over medium-high heat while you whisk the eggs vigorously with a fork in a cup. Have a serving plate ready nearby.

2 Stir in a light sprinkle of salt and then drop the butter into the hot pan. As soon as it melts and sizzles, but before it browns, pour in the eggs.

3 With a heatproof rubber scraper, lift the edges of the cooked egg to let more raw egg run underneath. Shake the pan gently to dislodge the omelet.

4 As soon as most of the egg is set, but a moist layer of raw egg is still visible, pick up the pan and let gravity do the work: Roll the egg out into thirds, directly onto a waiting plate. Sprinkle with salt and pepper, and eat at once.

VARIATION

Omelet with Cheese and Chives

Have ready 1/4 cup grated sharp cheddar cheese and 1 tablespoon chopped fresh chives. Sprinkle the cheese and chives down the center just before folding.

TOP SECRET

Want a perfect omelet? Getting the egg out of the pan is the challenge. Here are some helpful hints chefs already know:

- **Heat the pan *hot!* When you pour in the egg, it should sizzle and bubble. The pan should be hot enough to cook in just moments, without browning.**

- **Use a heavyweight nonstick pan, and make sure it is spotlessly clean.**

- **Use a heatproof rubber scraper. These flexible tools, once used merely to scrape batter out of pans, have become major cooking tools with the advent of heatproof silicone blades.**

Green Pea Frittata with Parmesan

Thicker than an omelet with more substantial fillings, Italian-style frittatas have become commonplace. They're sturdier and more versatile, too, able to be served hot, at room temperature, and even cold from the fridge—more like an egg cake or crustless quiche than an omelet. They're also equally good for lunch and supper and are perfect for a picnic.

2 tablespoons extra-virgin olive oil

1 onion, minced

1 clove garlic, peeled and minced

1 cup frozen green peas

1 teaspoon fresh thyme leaves

Salt and pepper, to taste

8 eggs, beaten until frothy

1/2 cup freshly grated Parmesan cheese

PREP TIME: 5 minutes • **COOK TIME:** 20 minutes • **SERVES:** 6

1 Preheat the oven to 450°F. Heat the oil in a 12-inch ovenproof skillet over medium heat until it shimmers. Add the onion and garlic and cook, stirring occasionally, for 4 to 5 minutes, or until tender and lightly browned.

2 Stir in the peas and thyme leaves and season lightly with salt and pepper. Cook 2 to 3 minutes longer, until the peas are softened.

3 Pour the eggs over the onion and pea mixture in the skillet and cook, lifting the edges occasionally to let more raw egg run underneath but do not stir.

4 After most of the egg is set but the top is still wet, sprinkle the Parmesan evenly on top and place the skillet in the oven for about 8 minutes, until the top is set and lightly browned. Serve hot, warm, or cold.

VARIATION

Spanish Tortilla (Egg Cake with Potatoes and Onions)

Use sliced onion instead of minced. Then add the potatoes thinly sliced, and cook until the edges are just golden. Season the potatoes and onions with a little salt and pepper. Skip the peas, thyme, and Parmesan.

TOP SECRET

For an extra crispy, perfectly browned frittata top, drizzle with a light splash of extra-virgin olive oil before popping into the oven.

Hash Browns

You know it's a lazy weekend breakfast when you have an opportunity to make homemade hash browns. Whether you have leftover boiled potatoes in the fridge or you boil them specifically for this recipe, you'll be glad you did when you sit down to breakfast. Use a nonstick skillet or a well-seasoned cast-iron skillet to get maximum crispness without sticking.

2–3 tablespoons butter or oil

5–6 medium waxy potatoes, peeled, boiled, and grated

Salt and pepper, to taste

PREP TIME: 10 minutes • **COOK TIME:** 30 minutes • **SERVES:** 4

1 Heat the butter or oil in a large nonstick or cast-iron skillet over medium-high heat. Lower the heat to medium-low, add the potatoes and season lightly with salt and pepper.

2 Cook, pressing down with a spatula, until the potatoes are golden brown and crisp. After 20 minutes, turn the potatoes once, in large pieces, rather than breaking up the crisp surface too much. (You can raise the heat a bit if the potatoes are browning too slow, but don't let them burn.) Cook for another 8 to 10 minutes, or until the second side is brown. Serve hot.

VARIATIONS

Vegetable Hash
Add a few rashers of chopped bacon to the pan and render until crispy before adding the potatoes. Then add sliced onions, peppers, and mushrooms—together or alone—to the potatoes as they cook.

Home Fries
Cut the potatoes into large chunks instead of grating them. Add additional flavor by cooking some finely minced onions and/or green or red peppers in the butter for 2 to 3 minutes before adding the potatoes.

TOP SECRET

Boil the potatoes in advance and—this is the key—*refrigerate them overnight* before grating them, resulting in picture-perfect hash browns that are golden-edged and crisp. That's because cooking and chilling will crystallize the potato starch, allowing them to cook up dry and crisp, not gooey.

Country-Style Farmer's Pancakes

These hearty, stick-to-your-ribs pancakes are perfect for when there's a chill in the air. Packed with both fruit and meat, they're deceptively rich but also healthy, owing to the turkey sausage. If you're making breakfast for vegetarians, replace the turkey sausage with tofu sausage and proceed with the recipe.

4 turkey sausage links, removed from casings and crumbled

2 eggs

1 1/3 cups 2% milk

1/4 cup canola oil

2 cups pancake mix

1 teaspoon ground cinnamon

1 cup grated Granny Smith apple

PREP TIME: 10 minutes • **COOK TIME:** 15 minutes • **SERVES:** 4

1 Preheat the oven to 200°F.

2 In a large nonstick skillet over medium heat, cook the sausage thoroughly, breaking up the meat with a wooden spoon. Remove and set aside.

3 In a medium bowl, beat together the eggs, milk, and oil. Fold in the pancake mix and cinnamon until just moistened. Stir in the apples and sausage.

4 Pour the batter by 1/4 cupfuls onto a lightly greased hot griddle and cook until the top of each pancake has tiny bubbles, about 3 minutes. Turn the pancakes and cook until the bottoms are golden brown, 1 1/2 minutes longer. Transfer to a plate and keep warm in the oven. Repeat with the remaining batter.

VARIATIONS

Hearty Vegetarian Pancakes

Replace the turkey sausage with vegetarian sausage. Crumble and cook it in 1 teaspoon canola oil, drain, and proceed with the recipe.

Perfect Pear Pancakes

Replace the cinnamon with ground nutmeg and add 1/8 teaspoon powdered ginger. Use a Bosc pear instead of the apple.

TOP SECRET

While it's absolutely admirable (and often more delicious) to make batter from scratch, good-quality pancake mix saves the day—and time—in recipes: Breakfast will be on the table in a jiffy.

Super-Scrumptious Scrambled Eggs

Anyone who loves eggs loves scrambled eggs, but this worldwide favorite can run the gamut from wet and runny to dry as a bone. Here's a way to keep them satiny smooth and packed with flavor. You'll never make them any other way.

2 tablespoons unsalted butter

1/4 cup onion-flavored cream cheese

4 eggs, lightly beaten

1/4 teaspoon salt

Snipped chives, to taste

PREP TIME: 5 minutes • **COOK TIME:** 5 minutes • **SERVES:** 4

1 In a medium nonstick skillet over medium heat, melt the butter. When it stops foaming, lower the heat to medium-low, and add the cream cheese, stirring until melted.

2 Stir in the eggs, salt, and chives, and cook for about 1 1/2 minutes, stirring, until the eggs are soft and set. Serve immediately.

VARIATIONS

Garden Patch Scramble

Omit the cream cheese and instead sauté 2 chopped large tomatoes in the butter. When they've released their liquid into the pan, add the eggs.

Yummy Asian Scramble

Omit the butter and cream cheese, and instead use 1 teaspoon roasted sesame oil. Omit the salt and add 1 tablespoon soy sauce.

TOP SECRET

The secret to scrambled eggs is in the cream cheese. When cream cheese melts, it doesn't melt into a liquid; it melts down to the consistency of sour cream, which adds a velvety smoothness to this delicious dish.

Breakfast Enchiladas

This never-fail brunch favorite is terrific fare to serve to a crowd. They can be assembled (minus the taco sauce) the night before, and can be made either with flour tortillas or corn. Either way, your guests will love this dish, and you.

8 hard-boiled eggs, chopped

1 can (8 ounces) cream-style corn

2/3 cup shredded cheddar cheese

1 can (4 ounces) chopped jalapeños

2 teaspoons taco seasoning mix

1/4 teaspoon salt

8 flour or corn tortillas

1 bottle (8 ounces) mild taco sauce

Sour cream (optional)

PREP TIME: 15 minutes • **COOK TIME:** 20 minutes • **SERVES:** 8

1 Preheat the oven to 350°F. Grease a 9 x 13-inch baking dish.

2 Combine the eggs, corn, cheese, chiles, seasoning mix, and salt in a medium bowl. Spoon 1/2 cup of the mixture down the center of each tortilla and roll up tightly. Place the enchiladas, seam-side down, in the prepared baking dish. Top with taco sauce.

3 Bake, uncovered, for about 15 minutes, or until heated through. Serve with sour cream, if using.

VARIATIONS

New Mexican Brunch Enchiladas
Swap out the flour tortillas for the corn variety. Before rolling them up, dip each tortilla in warm salsa.

Very Veggie Brunch Enchiladas
Replace the eggs with crumbled extra-firm tofu, and include thawed frozen carrots, peas, and artichoke hearts along with the corn.

TOP SECRET
What is it that gives this dish its velvety creaminess? The cream-style corn! This silky smooth addition will have your guests scratching their heads as to how you produced such a creamy dish with no cream.

Old-Fashioned Skillet Breakfast

Rich, tender, toothsome, delicious...there are so many words to describe this simple dish that's long on flavor and short on time! Your family will love the hominy—dried corn kernels with the hull and germ removed. Look for it in the canned vegetable aisle of your supermarket.

1/2 pound bacon, diced

1/2 cup chopped onion

2 cans (15 ounces each) hominy, drained

8 eggs, lightly beaten

1/4 teaspoon freshly ground black pepper

PREP TIME: 5 minutes • **COOK TIME:** 15 minutes • **SERVES:** 4

1 In a medium nonstick skillet, cook the bacon until almost crisp, then drain.

2 Add the onions and continue cooking for about 4 minutes, or until the bacon is crisp and the onions are tender.

3 Stir in the hominy, eggs, and pepper. Cook and stir for about 5 minutes, or until the eggs are completely set. Plate and serve.

VARIATIONS

Spicy Breakfast Skillet
Sauté 1/2 cup cored, seeded, and chopped red bell peppers together with the onions, and add 1/4 teaspoon hot pepper sauce to the eggs.

Vegetarian Breakfast Skillet
Replace the bacon with crumbled vegetarian sausage and the eggs with crumbled extra-firm tofu.

DID YOU KNOW?
If you're on a fat- or salt-restricted diet, there's no need to suffer! There are many brands of vegetarian sausage and bacon on the market today, and they almost always can be used in place of the real thing.

TOP SECRET
Hominy, one of the most unsung ingredients there is, adds a punch of good ole Southern corn flavor to this dish. You can make it with white or black beans, but once you taste hominy, you'll understand why it's a longtime Southern favorite!

Sunny Day Quesadillas

What happens when you cross bagels and lox with a quesadilla? You get this yummy, surprising dish that marries the best of both worlds. Make sure that you use the ripest avocado you can find for this dish.

1/2 cup peeled, pitted, and finely chopped Hass avocado

1/2 cup finely chopped tomato

2 teaspoons chopped fresh cilantro

1/8 teaspoon salt

2 flour tortillas

2 tablespoons softened cream cheese

2 large slices smoked salmon

2 very thin red onion slices

2 teaspoons drained chopped capers

PREP TIME: 15 minutes • **COOK TIME:** 10 minutes • **SERVES:** 2

1 In a small bowl, combine the avocados, tomatoes, cilantro, and salt and mix well.

2 Spread each tortilla with the cream cheese. Lay 1 slice of the salmon on half of each tortilla. Separate the onion into rings and spread them over the salmon then sprinkle with the capers. Fold the tortilla over to form a half-moon.

3 Heat a large cast-iron skillet over medium heat until hot. Add the quesadillas and cook for 3 to 4 minutes per side, until lightly browned and heated through.

4 Transfer the quesadillas to two serving plates and top each with half of the avocado mixture.

VARIATION

Ham-and-Cheese Quesadilla

Replace the salmon with thin-sliced ham and the cream cheese with Swiss cheese. Omit the cilantro.

DID YOU KNOW?

If you find yourself stuck with half an avocado, keep it fresh by pressing it, flesh-side down, onto plastic wrap, and then wrap the rest of it tightly. The plastic wrap will prevent the avocado from oxidizing for a day or so.

TOP SECRET

You might be inclined to toast a quesadilla—or even a grilled cheese sandwich for that matter—in a non-stick pan. Don't do it! The best tool for the job is a dry, well-seasoned cast-iron pan. Why? The cast iron provides a hot, dry surface, which will lead to good browning and caramelization. Nonstick pans are fine for cooking, but toasting is often difficult to accomplish in them.

Healthy Parfait Crunch

Breakfast by yourself? Then this simple, healthy take on a dessert favorite is for you. Elegant, delicious, and crunchy, the granola will stay crisp, even when layered between yogurt and sautéed bananas.

1 teaspoon
unsalted butter

1 small ripe banana,
cut into 1/4-inch-
thick slices

1 tablespoon
light brown sugar

1 teaspoon dark
rum (optional)

1/2 cup plain
low-fat yogurt

1/2 cup granola

PREP TIME: 5 minutes • **COOK TIME:** 5 minutes • **SERVES:** 1

1 Heat the butter in a small nonstick skillet over medium-high heat. When it melts, add the bananas and cook for 1 minute.

2 Add the brown sugar and cook for 1 to 2 minutes, stirring occasionally, until the sugar melts and the bananas soften. Off the heat, stir in the rum, if using, then return to the stove and cook for about 15 seconds, until the rum evaporates. Remove from the heat and let stand for 3 minutes.

3 Spoon 1/4 cup of the yogurt into the bottom of a tall parfait or wine glass. Top with 1/4 cup of the granola and half of the bananas. Repeat with the remaining ingredients.

VARIATION

Maple Magic Parfait
Add 1 tablespoon maple syrup to the first layer of granola and omit the rum.

TOP SECRET

It happens: You buy (or make) granola for a pretty penny, and after a day, it begins to stick together and get soggy. To repair it, spread it out on a nonstick baking sheet, pop it into a 200°F oven for 5 minutes, and then turn off the heat. Let it sit in the oven for another 5 minutes. Remove, let cool, and enjoy the restored crunch!

HOW TO BE AN EXPERT OMELET FLIPPER

3 Steps That Will Work Every Time

Some people use a metal spatula to dislodge an omelet from its pan; some put a dinner plate over the hot pan and just invert the omelet onto the plate. What do chefs do? None of the above. These three simple, secret steps to omelet removal will have you turning out gorgeous omelets in no time.

1 When it's time to roll the omelet out onto a plate, wrap your right (or left, if you're a lefty) hand under the handle of the pan so that it sits across your palm. Your fingers should wrap around the top of the handle.

2 Tilt the pan so that the omelet begins to slide out toward the plate.

3 Use the pan to roll the omelet out onto the plate.

Spiffy Southern Cornbread

No matter where you go in the South, everyone loves cornbread, and with good reason: It's delicious. Recipes tend to be different from place to place, but the addition of sausage and cheese can make it double as a side dish as well as hearty breakfast fare. Most Southerners use pork sausage, but replacing the pork with turkey makes it a little bit lighter.

1 pound turkey sausage, removed from casings

1 large onion, chopped

1 1/2 cups self-rising cornmeal

1 can (15 ounces) cream-style corn

3/4 cup 2% milk

2 eggs

1/4 cup canola oil

2 cups shredded sharp cheddar cheese

PREP TIME: 10 minutes • **COOK TIME:** 50 minutes • **SERVES:** 8

1 In a large nonstick skillet, cook the sausage and onions together until the meat is browned and the onions are tender. Drain.

2 Preheat the oven to 425°F. Grease a 10-inch ovenproof cast-iron skillet and place it in the oven to get hot.

3 In a medium bowl, combine the cornmeal, corn, milk, eggs, and oil. Remove the pan, and carefully pour half the batter into the skillet. Sprinkle with the sausage mixture and cheese. Spread the remaining cornmeal mixture on top.

4 Bake for 40 to 45 minutes, or until a toothpick inserted in the center comes out clean.

VARIATIONS

Spicy Southern Cornbread
Omit the cheddar cheese and use Jalapeño Jack instead. Drizzle the batter with hot sauce before pouring it into the pan.

Honeysuckle Cornbread
Ten minutes before it's done, remove the pan from the oven and brush the cornbread with 2 tablespoons honey. Return to oven, and continue to bake until done.

TOP SECRET
The real secret to the best cornbread isn't in the batter; it's in the process. The hotter the cast-iron pan is before you pour in the batter, the crispier the crust will be. (Just be careful removing it from the oven!)

Super Cherry Breakfast Polenta

This favorite Italian side dish also happens to be a perfect breakfast food; it's hearty, flavorful, and warming. So when the temperature drops, break out the cornmeal!

1 1/2 cups frozen dark cherries

3 tablespoons sugar

2 cups 2% milk

1/4 cup honey

1/2 teaspoon vanilla extract

1/2 cup yellow cornmeal

3 tablespoons softened cream cheese

1 tablespoon unsalted butter

PREP TIME: 10 minutes • **COOK TIME:** 15 minutes • **SERVES:** 4

1 In a small saucepan over medium heat, combine the cherries and sugar. Bring to a simmer, then reduce the heat to medium-low and cook for 6 to 7 minutes, until the cherries are tender.

2 Meanwhile, combine the milk, honey, and vanilla in a medium saucepan over medium-high heat. Bring the mixture just to a boil, then whisk in the cornmeal in a slow, steady stream. Cook for about 5 minutes, stirring constantly, until the polenta is thick and creamy.

3 Remove from the heat and stir in the cream cheese and butter.

4 Divide the polenta among four bowls and top each with some of the cherry mixture. Serve immediately.

VARIATION

Very Berry Breakfast Polenta

Replace the cherries with 2 cups fresh or frozen blackberries and/or raspberries.

TOP SECRET

Even though it is a snap to make this dish, it works even better if it's made the night before. Cool the polenta to room temperature, then store it in an airtight container in the refrigerator. In the morning, combine 1/2 cup of the prepared polenta and 1/3 cup milk in a small saucepan over medium heat. Cook, stirring, until the polenta is hot and creamy. Serve topped with some of the warmed cherry mixture, or microwave some of your favorite jam, honey, or even maple syrup to use instead.

Luscious Oatmeal Surprise Granola

What used to be called hippie food has been reborn as a sumptuous breakfast cereal that's really perfect for snacking as well. Make a big batch on Saturday morning and watch it disappear by Sunday night.

4 cups rolled oats

1 cup coarsely chopped walnuts

1 teaspoon ground cinnamon

1/8 teaspoon ground nutmeg

1/4 teaspoon salt

1/2 cup maple syrup

1/4 cup honey

1/4 cup canola oil

2 teaspoons vanilla extract

1 cup dried cranberries

1 cup dried cherries

PREP TIME: 10 minutes • **COOK TIME:** 45 minutes • **MAKES** 6 cups

1 Preheat the oven to 300°F. Coat a large baking sheet with cooking spray.

2 In a large bowl, combine the oatmeal, walnuts, cinnamon, nutmeg, and salt.

3 In a small bowl, whisk together the syrup, honey, oil, and vanilla. Pour over the oatmeal mixture and mix well to combine. Fold in the cranberries and cherries.

4 Spread the oatmeal mixture evenly on the baking sheet. Bake for 45 to 55 minutes, stirring every 10 minutes, until the mixture is lightly golden and toasted.

VARIATION

Coconuty Granola

Add 1/4 cup sesame seeds, 1/4 cup slivered almonds, and 1/2 cup sweetened coconut flakes along with the walnuts. Omit the cinnamon and nutmeg.

FIX IT FAST

If you find that the granola is too sticky, that's okay. Let it cool completely after cooking, put it in a large ziplock bag, and break it up into pieces by hand.

TOP SECRET

Most granolas involve masses of raisins, which can get old and stodgy after a while. The secret to the delicious tang that gives this granola such bright flavor are crisp and tart dried cranberries and dried cherries.

The Best Ham 'n' Cheese Strata

Of all the one-dish breakfast treats that are ideal for big brunch parties, this ham-and-cheese strata might just be the most delicious. Traditionally, stratas include ingredients like bacon, sausage, sun-dried tomatoes, or other vegetables. Our version includes ham and a surprisingly crisp topping.

12 slices white bread, crusts removed

1 pound fully cooked ham, diced

2 cups shredded cheddar cheese

6 eggs

3 cups 2% milk

2 teaspoons Worcestershire sauce

1 teaspoon ground dry mustard

1/2 teaspoon salt

1/4 teaspoon freshly ground black pepper

Dash of cayenne

1/4 cup minced onion

1/4 cup cored, seeded, and minced green bell pepper

1/4 cup unsalted butter, melted

1 cup crushed cornflakes

PREP TIME: 10 minutes • **COOK TIME:** 50 minutes • **SERVES:** 8

1 Grease a 9 x 13-inch baking dish, then arrange 6 bread slices in the bottom. Top with the ham and cheese. Cover with the remaining bread slices.

2 In a medium bowl, beat together the eggs, milk, Worcestershire sauce, mustard, salt, black pepper, and cayenne. Stir in the onions and green peppers and pour over all. Cover and refrigerate for several hours, or overnight. Remove from the refrigerator 30 minutes before baking.

3 Preheat the oven to 350°F.

4 Pour the butter over the bread and sprinkle with the cornflakes. Bake, uncovered, for 50 to 60 minutes, or until a knife inserted near the center comes out clean. Let stand for 10 minutes before serving.

VARIATIONS

Spinach and Mushroom Strata
Sauté some sliced mushrooms and baby spinach leaves until the spinach is wilted and the liquid in the pan is mostly evaporated, then layer these on top of the ham and cheese.

Zucchini and Broccoli Rabe Strata
Sauté zucchini slices together with blanched (or even leftover) broccoli rabe until the liquid in the pan is mostly evaporated, then layer on top of the ham and cheese.

TOP SECRET

Everyone loves the crunchy bits on baked dishes like stratas and even lasagnas. The ingredient that's bound to make crunch-lovers happy is cornflakes! Sprinkle them on just before baking, and watch your family beam with delight when the dish comes out of the oven.

Hearty Farmer's Winter Casserole

This handy breakfast casserole can be assembled the night before. In fact, it's better that way because the flavors have time to blend. In the morning, just pop it in the oven, and you'll be good to go.

3 cups frozen shredded hash browns

3/4 cup shredded Monterey Jack cheese

1 cup diced fully cooked honey ham

1/4 cup chopped scallions, white parts only

4 eggs

1 can (12 ounces) evaporated milk

1/4 teaspoon freshly ground black pepper

1/8 teaspoon salt

PREP TIME: 5 minutes • **COOK TIME:** 55 minutes • **SERVES:** 6

1 Place the hash browns in an 8-inch square baking dish. Sprinkle with the cheese, ham, and scallions.

2 In a small bowl, beat together the eggs, milk, pepper, and salt and pour over the hash brown mixture. Cover and refrigerate for several hours, or overnight. Remove from the refrigerator 30 minutes before baking.

3 Preheat the oven to 350°F.

4 Bake, uncovered, for 55 to 60 minutes, or until a knife inserted near the center comes out clean. Serve hot.

VARIATION

Country French Casserole

Replace the Monterey Jack with grated Gruyère and the hash browns with 6 cubed small red potatoes.

TOP SECRET

Evaporated milk, the secret weapon in this dish, provides it with incomparable creaminess. Use it wherever you need to make a cheese sauce but don't want the fuss of creating a traditional Mornay.

2 APPETIZERS AND SNACKS
NIBBLY BITES WE ALL LOVE

Whether you're a professional chef or a home cook, nobody likes taking 2 hours to prepare a teeny snack that will be casually gobbled down in 2 minutes. So how to make the most of flavor when time, size, and budget may not be on your side? To start, dips and spreads are key, since they're simple to make, store very well, and can pack intense punch into a few small bites. With easy tricks and techniques for clean-cutting avocados and peeling garlic, you can learn to make super-savory into super-speedy, too. The recipes in this chapter will help you turn out nibblies that will impress party guests, kick a meal off with a thrill, make a perfect light lunch, or merely mellow out the midnight munchies with style.

Goat Cheese with Gremolata

Gremolata is an Italian condiment of parsley, garlic, and lemon, moistened with olive oil. It's full of bite and zest—almost like a parsley pesto. Spooned over softened goat cheese, it makes a fast and elegant accompaniment to drinks. You can serve this with crackers but it's best with little round slices of a fresh baguette so you can sop up the pesto and olive oil around the plate.

1 large bunch flat-leaf parsley

1 lemon

1 clove garlic, peeled

1/4 –1/2 cup extra-virgin olive oil

1 log (5–7 ounces) of goat cheese

PREP TIME: 5 minutes • **COOK TIME:** 0 minutes • **MAKES** about 1 1/2 cups

1 Rinse the parsley, shake off the water, and put about 2 cups of leaves in a food processor or blender.

2 Using a vegetable peeler, peel 2 or 3 strips of lemon zest lengthwise off the side of the lemon, and add these long strips to the parsley. Juice half the lemon and add the juice to the parsley.

3 Place the garlic and 1/4 cup of the oil in the food processor or blender and pulse until finely chopped. Add a little more olive oil, if necessary.

4 Place the cheese log on a serving plate and cover it with the gremolata. Drizzle the remaining olive oil around the plate.

VARIATIONS

Herbed Goat Cheese Spread

Drop chunks of a softened log of goat cheese into a food processor and pulse along with 1 minced clove of garlic, 2 to 3 tablespoons olive oil, and 2 to 3 tablespoons of a mixture of chopped fresh herbs, such as thyme, rosemary, and chives. Spoon into a bowl and serve with crackers or slices of French bread.

Peppered Goat Cheese Log

Chill the goat cheese log for 2 to 3 hours. Grind 1/3 cup fresh black or mixed peppercorns onto a plate. Remove the cheese log from wrapping, roll in peppercorns, and refrigerate, uncovered, for another 2 hours. Serve at room temperature with crackers or slices of French bread.

TOP SECRET

When you need to zest an entire lemon or orange or more, do what chefs do and use a vegetable peeler to peel long strips of zest off the fruit. Finely chop or julienne the long pieces with a knife, or pulse it in a food processor with the recipe's oil or sugar until the zest is as fine as needed.

APPETIZERS AND SNACKS

Hummus

Although hummus has Middle Eastern origins dating back many thousands of years, it has been absorbed into American culture just like pizza—we don't care where it came from, it's ours! Perhaps that's because it's so versatile. It can be a dip or a sandwich spread; it's great with vegetables or on crackers or triangles of pita.

1 can (16 ounces) chickpeas, drained

1/3 cup tahini

3 tablespoons lemon juice

1 teaspoon ground cumin

1 clove garlic

1/2 teaspoon salt

Dash of cayenne or Tabasco

PREP TIME: 5 minutes • **COOK TIME:** 0 minutes • **MAKES** about 2 cups

1 Put all ingredients in a food processor and process for 1 to 2 minutes, until smooth. If the mixture is too thick, add 1 to 2 tablespoons water. (Be careful not too add too much water or the mixture will become too thin for dipping.)

2 Taste and adjust the seasoning, adding a bit more salt or lemon juice, as needed. Serve at room temperature, and refrigerate leftovers in a tightly sealed container for up to a week.

VARIATIONS

Garlic Hummus
Add 1 clove of garlic to the food processor with the chickpeas and leave out the cumin.

Roasted Red Pepper Hummus
After pureeing the hummus, add the peeled and seeded flesh of 1 roasted red bell pepper or 1/3 cup roasted red pepper strips from a jar. Puree until completely smooth. Sprinkle with chopped fresh parsley before serving.

White Bean Hummus
Replace the chickpeas with drained canned white beans.

TOP SECRET

To intensify the flavor of spices, toast before use. Heat a dry pan (not nonstick) over medium-high heat, add the spices, and toss for about 1 minute. As soon as you smell the fragrance of the spice rising from the pan, remove and pour the spice out of the pan—leaving it in contact with the hot metal will cause the spice to scorch.

Chili Bean Dip

An old Southwestern standby, this is a hearty and satisfying dip that never gets tired. Use pinto beans for a paler dip, while black beans, spiked with extra cayenne, are zestier fare. You can leave out the olive oil for a fat-free dip, but the small amount of oil makes a huge difference in the richness of flavor. Serve with tortilla chips.

1 can (15 ounces) black or pinto beans, drained and rinsed

3 tablespoons olive oil

3 tablespoons fresh lemon juice

1/4 cup salsa

1 teaspoon ground cumin

1/8 teaspoon cayenne

Salt (optional)

2 tablespoons fresh cilantro leaves

PREP TIME: 5 minutes • **COOK TIME:** 0 minutes • **MAKES** 2 cups

1 Place the beans, oil, lemon juice, salsa, cumin, and cayenne in a food processor and puree until smooth. Taste and add salt, if using (canned beans are often salty and need no additional seasoning) or more lemon juice or salsa, if desired.

2 Add cilantro and pulse until just chopped. Serve immediately or leave covered in the refrigerator overnight for flavors to develop.

VARIATION

Mediterranean White Bean Dip

Replace the black beans with a can of cannellini beans and replace the salsa, cumin, and cilantro with 1 clove of garlic and 2 teaspoons fresh rosemary. For added fillip, use about 1 teaspoon fresh lemon zest (then you can squeeze the juice of the lemon directly into the processor—watch for seeds!)

TOP SECRET

Chefs often squeeze fresh lemons with one hand directly into their upturned other hand, held over the bowl, letting the juice trickle through their loosely cupped fingers. That way they can catch and discard the seeds. It's faster than stopping to look for a strainer, and this way, the pulp gets to go into the dish, where it can add more flavor.

APPETIZERS AND SNACKS

Bacon-Cheddar Toasts

Creamy, rich, and perfect as a snack or alongside a soup or salad, this riff on bruschetta is as crunchy as it is tender. Your guests will be amazed!

1 cup mayonnaise

2 teaspoons Worcestershire sauce

1 cup shredded sharp cheddar cheese

1 onion, chopped

3/4 cup slivered almonds, chopped

6 bacon strips, cooked and crumbled

1 loaf (about 1 pound) of French bread, cut into 1/2-inch slices

PREP TIME: 10 minutes • **COOK TIME:** 10 minutes • **MAKES** about 4 dozen

1 Preheat the oven to 400°F. Lightly grease a baking sheet.

2 In a medium bowl, combine the mayonnaise and Worcestershire sauce. Stir in the cheese, onions, almonds, and bacon.

3 Spread the bread slices with the cheese mixture. Cut the slices in half and place on the prepared baking sheet. Bake 8 to 10 minutes, or until bubbly.

VARIATION
Ham and Swiss Toasts
Replace the cheddar with grated Swiss cheese, omit the onion, and replace the bacon with 4 ounces of minced deli ham.

LEFTOVER LUXURIES

If you have friends who are regularly popping in to say hello, this dish is for you: The toasts freeze beautifully. After cooking, freeze them directly on the baking sheet until solid, about 1 hour. Transfer them to an airtight container, and freeze for up to 2 months. To serve, place the frozen appetizers on a greased baking sheet and bake until bubbly, 10 to 12 minutes.

TOP SECRET

Common sense would tell you to make "coated toasts" like the ones above with the addition of a beaten egg, which acts as cooking glue. Wrong! Mayonnaise works just as well if not better, and adds a velvety texture and a hint of flavor to whatever it is you're cooking. Combined with minced garlic and lightly brushed onto about-to-be-broiled fish, it elevates a simple dish to utterly delicious.

Creamy Shrimp Dip

Making this dip the night before will allow the sweet and mild flavor of the cooked shrimp to bloom. But if you're pressed for time, you don't even have to remember to soften the cream cheese: Set the unwrapped block on a plate and microwave it for 1 minute on high, then proceed with the recipe. Serve with crackers.

1 package (8 ounces) cream cheese

2 stalks celery, chopped

1/4 cup fresh lemon juice

1/4 cup mayonnaise

1 cup cooked, peeled shrimp or 1 can (4 ounces) cooked shrimp, drained

1/2 teaspoon hot sauce

PREP TIME: 10 minutes • **COOK TIME:** 0 minutes • **MAKES** about 1 1/2 cups

1 Place the cream cheese, celery, lemon juice, and mayonnaise into the food processor. Pulse until smooth.

2 Add the shrimp and hot sauce, and pulse just until the shrimp are chopped.

VARIATION

Hot Crab Dip

Preheat the oven to 350°F. Omit the celery and shrimp and add 6 ounces of drained canned crabmeat and 1 tablespoon of Worcestershire sauce along with the other ingredients in the food processor. Spoon into a shallow buttered dish and sprinkle with 1/4 cup grated Parmesan. Bake for 20 minutes, until browned and bubbling. Serve immediately with bread or crackers.

TOP SECRET

Most of the shrimp you buy at the grocery store is farmed, so there's no longer the necessity of deveining it the way that wild shrimp often requires. Not deveining wild shrimp can result in a gritty or bitter taste, but that's unlikely with farmed. If you can't plainly see a dark trail around the back of the shrimp, don't bother deveining—just peel and go.

APPETIZERS AND SNACKS

Faster Fondue

Fondue is back! It has long since shaken off the taint of 1970s dinner parties because it's good. Melted cheese and cubes of bread—what's not to like? What you no longer need is your enameled fondue set. With the aid of the microwave, Faster Fondue can be hastily whipped up for a snack, a party, or a casual dinner—and heated or reheated as necessary.

1 clove garlic, halved

2 tablespoons butter

1 tablespoon cornstarch

1 cup flavorful bottled beer, such as a red ale

1 pound sharp cheddar cheese, grated

1 tablespoon English or dry mustard (optional)

Dash of Tabasco

1 round sourdough loaf

PREP TIME: 4 minutes • **COOK TIME:** 7 minutes • **SERVES:** 6

1 Rub the cut side of the garlic halves all over the inside of a microwavable glass bowl suitable for serving. Discard the halves.

2 Place the butter in the bowl and microwave on high for less than a minute, just until melted.

3 Stir in the cornstarch until smooth, then add the beer, cheese, and mustard, if using. Microwave on high for 3 to 4 minutes, or until the cheese starts to melt, then stir and continue to cook until cheese is fully melted. Add Tabasco for spice, if using.

4 Meanwhile, cut the bread into bite-size cubes, then serve with the hot fondue.

VARIATION
Classic Fondue

Make this fondue on the stovetop using a nonstick saucepan instead of in the microwave. Replace the beer with 2 cups dry white wine and replace the cheddar with 1/2 pound shredded Gruyère and 1/2 pound shredded Emmentaler or other Swiss cheese. In place of the mustard, stir in 2 tablespoons Kirsch (cherry-flavored liqueur) just before serving.

TOP SECRET

Thickening a sauce with cornstarch or flour is such a standard part of every cook's repertoire that it's hard to remember that there's any other way. But if you've ever wondered why the chef's sauce is so much thicker, richer, and creamier than yours, it may well be because the chef skipped the flour altogether and thickened his sauce solely with cream. In place of 1/2 cup of sauce, you can, for an exquisite rendition of any dish but especially fondue, boil a cup of cream until it reduces by half, then season and proceed with your recipe.

APPETIZERS AND SNACKS

Caramelized Onion Jam

It will seem as if you went to far more trouble than you actually did when you serve a bowl of these onions with garlicky toasts. Chopped onions are slowly cooked in a skillet with some olive oil and balsamic vinegar. The result is a golden heap of tender caramelized onions, a sort of savory onion "jam" that can be served on sliced fresh baguette, store-bought Melba toast, flavorful crackers, or bruschetta.

6 large
yellow onions

1/4 cup olive oil

2 tablespoons
balsamic vinegar

Salt and pepper,
to taste

PREP TIME: 5 minutes • **COOK TIME:** 45–50 minutes • **MAKES** 2 cups

1 Chop the onions with the slicing blade of a food processor. They don't need to be chopped especially finely or uniformly, because the slow cooking with tenderize them.

2 Heat the oil in a large skillet over medium heat and add the onions. Cook, stirring occasionally, for 10 minutes, or until softened, then stir in the vinegar and reduce the heat to low.

3 Cook over very low heat for 40 minutes, or until the onions have reduced to a tender brown jammy mass. Season with salt and pepper.

VARIATION

Caramelized Onion Dip

Stir 1/2 cup of Caramelized Onion Jam into 1 cup sour cream and 1 cup mayonnaise. Add 2 tablespoons Worcestershire sauce and a dash of hot sauce. Serve with potato chips and you'll never look back at onion dip made with a package of soup!

LEFTOVER LUXURIES

When taking the time to cook caramelized onions, make double or triple the amount needed and store the remainder in the fridge in an airtight container up to 2 weeks, or in the freezer for up to 2 months. Add 1/4 cup to soups or sauces to deepen and enrich the flavor.

TOP SECRET

If you want to serve caramelized onions but don't have the time to let them cook over low heat for 40 minutes, do what the pros do: Add 1 teaspoon sugar and 1 table-spoon butter to the dish while it's cooking. The sugar will force caramelization, while the butter will provide the fat vehicle to melt the sugar quickly. The caveat: Keep your eye on the pan during the 20 minutes it'll take to cook it.

APPETIZERS AND SNACKS

Guacamole

The simplest guacamole—like the kind someone's grandmother in Mexico might serve—is a very pure dish designed to highlight the flavor of exquisitely ripe avocados. If you get such an item in your hand—and it must be the small, dark, nubbly-skinned Hass avocado, not the large, bland ones with smooth green skin—then this is the way to serve it.

2 ripe Hass avocados, peeled, and pitted

3 tablespoons fresh lime juice (2 small limes)

1/2 cup strained peas

Kosher salt, to taste

Warm corn tortillas

2 scallions, including green parts, finely chopped

Cilantro leaves

PREP TIME: 5 minutes • **COOK TIME:** 0 minutes • **MAKES** 2 cups

1 Mash the avocado flesh with a fork in a shallow bowl. Stir in the lime juice, peas and some salt, whipping gently with the fork to fluff the guacamole.

2 Serve the guacamole with the tortillas: Slather guacamole on the warm tortilla, sprinkle with the scallions and cilantro, then roll and eat. To serve with corn chips, stir the cilantro and scallions directly into the guacamole.

VARIATION

Party Guacamole

Add any or all of the following: 1/2 cup finely diced tomatoes, 1 finely minced fresh jalapeño, 1/2 cup diced white onion, 1 teaspoon ground cumin, and a few dashes of hot sauce. You can also skip all the extras and simply stir in 1/2 cup good-quality salsa.

FIX IT FAST

If a recipe calls for raw onion, tame its harshness by doing the following: Chop the onion as directed in the recipe, then soak it in cold water with a splash of vinegar for at least 5 minutes, then drain and pat dry with paper towels. This trick is also ideal for onion slices you'll be eating on salad or burgers—it removes the harsh burn and brings up the sweetness.

TOP SECRET

Here's the easiest way to remove an avocado pit without damaging the tasty fruit: Slice all the way around the long way with a sharp knife and gently pry the two halves apart. One will still have the large pit in it. Holding that half in your palm, hit the pit with the sharp edge of a chef's knife. The knife will stick lightly into the skin. Turn the knife and pit one-quarter turn, and the pit will lift directly out. Scoop the flesh out with a spoon, or slice the avocado halves and peel off the skin.

Black Bean and Cheese Quesadillas

Long gone are the days when quesadillas were an ethnic dish—now they show up in restaurants across the country. But there's no reason they can't be made at home with ease. Best of all, they're made to order and ready in minutes. Serve with salsa and sour cream.

8 flour tortillas

2 cups grated cheese (try cheddar, Monterey Jack, or queso blanco)

1 1/2 cups canned black beans, drained

2 scallions, including green parts, chopped

PREP TIME: 10 minutes • **COOK TIME:** 12 minutes • **SERVES:** 4

1 Heat a very lightly greased nonstick skillet over medium heat.

2 Lay one tortilla in the pan and cover with a scant 1/2 cup cheese, a few tablespoons of beans, and a sprinkle of scallions, being careful to keep the toppings on the tortilla.

3 Top with a second tortilla and cook for about 3 minutes on each side, turning once and pressing down with the spatula.

4 Remove to a clean cutting board, cool briefly, and cut into 6 pieces with a sharp knife. Repeat with remaining tortillas and ingredients and serve warm.

VARIATION
Chicken Quesadillas
Substitute cooked shredded chicken for the beans. Divide the 1/2 cup of cheese for each tortilla this way: put 1/4 of cheese on the bottom layer, then top with a few tablespoons of chicken and scallions, and then the remaining 1/4 cup of cheese. Putting cheese on either side of the chicken helps the whole quesadilla stick together better, since chicken won't mash down as easily as beans.

TOP SECRET

Homemade quesadillas are addictive, but if you wonder why yours aren't as good as a restaurant version, it's because that chef is likely flattening them. The result is unmatched crispness and even cooking. To press the quesadilla, when you top with the second tortilla, lower the heat, and lay a dry cast-iron pan directly on top of the quesadilla. Cook for 3 minutes, flip, and repeat.

THE RIGHT STUFF

15 Things to Turn into a Quesadilla

There are some dishes that are absolutely perfect vehicles for leftovers. Quesadillas are a great example, because so long as you can get the tortillas to stick to the stuffing, you can pretty much fill it with any leftovers, including:

1 Roast beef and blue cheese dressing

2 Salmon drizzled with teriyaki sauce

3 Tuna and Swiss cheese

4 Sliced sausage and provolone cheese

5 Scrambled, spiced tofu and potatoes

6 Chicken pulled off the bone, with sprouts, guacamole, and cheddar cheese

7 Smoked salmon and cream cheese

8 Bacon, lettuce, tomato, and cheddar cheese

9 Mashed black beans, guacamole, and cheddar cheese

10 Jack cheese with bacon and salsa

11 Ham, eggs, and Swiss cheese

12 Goat cheese and roasted red peppers

13 Turkey with stuffing and Swiss cheese

14 Salami, eggs, and chopped scallions with cheddar cheese

15 Hummus, grilled vegetables, and Monterey Jack cheese

Not-Greasy Buffalo Wings

In a restaurant, there's a good chance that your order of wings have been deep-fried, which makes for crisp skin, yes, but seriously greasy eating. The problem is that the speed of deep-frying cooks the meat and crisps the skin, but it's too fast to melt out all the fat from the interior of each wing piece. This technique results in perfectly crisp wings without extra fat inside.

3 pounds chicken wings

Salt

1/4 cup (1/2 stick) butter

1/2 cup bottled hot sauce, such as Durkee's

Blue cheese dressing (optional)

Celery sticks (optional)

PREP TIME: 5 minutes • **COOK TIME:** 45 minutes • **SERVES:** 4–6

1 Preheat the oven to 350°F. Fully line a rimmed baking sheet with foil, folding it around the edges for an even seal.

2 Trim each wing at the joint to make it into two pieces, discarding the wing tip (often this has already been done when you buy wings). Lay the wings on the foil-lined sheet in one layer and sprinkle with salt.

3 Bake for 45 to 50 minutes, or until the wings are crisp and well-browned. You may need to pour fat off the baking sheet, but the foil will prevent the crust from creating a "shellac" on the baking sheet (and make for super-easy cleanup).

4 In a large bowl, melt the butter and whisk together with the hot sauce (add more if you like hotter wings). Lift the wings directly into the sauce and toss to coat. Serve immediately, with blue cheese dressing and celery sticks, if using.

VARIATION

Apricot-Soy Wings

Bake the wings as described, but for 35 minutes. While the wings are in the oven, combine 1/2 cup apricot jam with 3 tablespoons soy sauce and 1 minced clove garlic in a large bowl. Lift the wings into the bowl and toss to coat. Pour off and discard the fat on the baking sheet before returning the wings to the pan. Bake an additional 10 to 15 minutes, or until the wings are crisply golden brown.

TOP SECRET

Ever wonder how restaurants get their traditional wings to be finger-licking sticky and good? They add a tablespoon of sugar to the hot sauce before applying it to the wings. The result is a mess (to be precise) of caramelized goodness. Just make sure you have plenty of napkins around.

Deviled Eggs with Chives

In the summer, picnic tables seem empty without deviled eggs, especially down South, where many cooks put softened butter into the yolks instead of the mayonnaise favored elsewhere. This version goes gentle on the mayo but gets the sharp tang of mustard and vinegar just right—the "devil" in the name.

8 large hard-boiled eggs

3 tablespoons mayonnaise

3 tablespoons white-wine vinegar

2 teaspoons Dijon mustard

2 tablespoons snipped fresh chives

Salt and pepper, to taste

PREP TIME: 20 minutes • **COOK TIME:** 10 minutes • **MAKES** 16 halves

1 Peel and split the eggs. Put the yolks in a shallow bowl and the whites on a serving platter.

2 Mash the yolks with a fork and combine with the mayonnaise, vinegar, mustard, and chives. Using the fork, whip until fluffy and well-combined. Season with salt and pepper. If the mixture is too thick, add up to 2 teaspoons more vinegar.

3 Use a teaspoon to mound the filling into each egg. Chill 1 hour to let flavors develop.

VARIATIONS

Bacon-Deviled Eggs

Leave the chives out of the recipe and replace them with 3 slices of thick-cut bacon, cooked crisp and crumbled. Stir in the bacon before adding any salt to the yolk mixture, because it may be all the salt you need. Top each egg with a sprinkle of paprika.

Curried-Deviled Eggs

Leave out the chives and add 1 teaspoon curry powder (spicy or not, your choice) to the yolk. Top each egg with a pinch of fresh, chopped cilantro.

TOP SECRET

Tired of eggs that explode during boiling? Chefs have a secret to keeping eggs whole, and it couldn't be easier. Take a straight pin or a needle and prick a tiny hole on the fat end of the egg shell (nothing will leak out; the egg has a protective membrane). This will provide an escape hatch for the heating egg, thus preventing an explosion. Works every time.

Rosemary-Spiced Walnuts

The perfect appetizer to bring to a party or to just have on hand when you have guests over, spiced nuts are delicious and addictive, and a real treat—why else would airlines serve them in first class? It's something simple and easily prepared, but people rarely make them for themselves. Well, now you can.

2 cups unsalted walnuts or walnut halves

2 tablespoons chopped fresh rosemary

1 teaspoon light brown sugar

1/2 teaspoon Kosher salt

1/2 teaspoon cayenne

1 tablespoon extra-virgin olive oil

PREP TIME: 2 minutes • **COOK TIME:** 10 minutes • **MAKES** 2 cups

1 Preheat the oven to 350°F. Toss all the ingredients in a bowl.

2 Spread the nuts on a baking sheet in one layer and bake for 8 to 10 minutes, or until they're golden and fragrant.

3 Serve warm or cool and store up to a week in an airtight jar. (You can rewarm a serving by placing it in the microwave for 30 seconds.)

VARIATION

Sweet and Spicy Pepitas

Replace the nuts with *pepitas*, which are hulled pumpkin seeds (available at gourmet and health-food stores, and also at Mexican markets), increase the sugar to 2 teaspoons, and replace the rosemary with 2 tablespoons Worcestershire sauce and 1/2 teaspoon chili powder.

TOP SECRET

Ten minutes of roasting nuts will make a terrific snack but also a terrific mess on a baking sheet. Chefs avoid the mess and keep their pans ready to use with sheets of parchment paper. Parchment paper is coated with silicone, which is heatproof and nonstick, making it ideal for baking. Even if the exposed paper scorches, it won't burn. One sheet can be used several times—if you're baking cookies, say—or thrown away with any sticking mess remaining. Wax paper is *not* a substitute.

APPETIZERS AND SNACKS

Everyone's Favorite Cheeseball

Remember when a party wasn't a party without a cheeseball? People still love them. Cheeseballs used to come from gourmet stores like a heavy softball packed into a square box. It's amazingly easy to whip one up—and much tastier than the boxed kind when you make it yourself.

1/3 cup unsalted pecans

1 package (8 ounces) cream cheese, softened

8 ounces sharp cheddar cheese, grated

2 tablespoons prepared horseradish

2 scallions, including green parts, finely chopped

PREP TIME: 10 minutes • **COOK TIME:** 0 minutes • **SERVES:** 10–12

1 Pulse the pecans in a food processor until finely chopped. Set aside on a dinner plate.

2 Without washing the bowl of the food processor, pulse the cream cheese, cheddar cheese, horseradish, and scallions until completely combined. Shape the cheese mixture into a ball, cover with plastic wrap, and chill for 20 minutes.

3 Unwrap the cheeseball and roll it in the chopped nuts to coat completely. Rewrap in clean plastic wrap and chill for at least 2 hours, preferably overnight, before serving.

VARIATIONS

Smoked Cheeseball

Replace the pecans with smoked almonds. Replace the cheddar with 1 cup of smoked cheddar and 1 cup of smoked Gouda. Add 1 tablespoon of smoky barbecue sauce.

Wine and Blue Cheese Ball

Pulse 8 ounces of mild blue cheese (Roquefort, Stilton, Maytag Blue) in a food processor until almost smooth. Drizzle in 1/4 cup round-bodied red wine (Bordeaux or Cabernet Sauvignon is ideal), pulse until smooth, turn out onto plastic wrap, shape into a ball, and refrigerate overnight before serving.

TOP SECRET

Chefs use plastic wrap all the time, not merely to store food but also to shape and manipulate it. To mold the cheese mixture with ease, scrape the mixture out of the food processor bowl directly onto a large square of plastic wrap. Draw the edges together and smooth the cheese mixture into a ball. Use plastic wrap for shaping raw pie crust into disks for chilling, and for shaping chilled cookie dough into logs or blocks.

Herby Olives

Forget about those big black olives you used to be able to buy in cans. Nowadays, nearly every supermarket carries good-quality pitted olives of all varieties, and you should take advantage of them. This inexpensive treat is a spiffy way to serve an old favorite to your guests; they'll never know it took you just a few minutes to whip up!

2 cloves garlic, peeled and smashed with the flat side of a knife

1 cup pitted olives, preferably a mix of black and green

1/8 teaspoon red pepper flakes

1/2 tablespoon dried rosemary sprigs

1/2 tablespoon dried thyme

1-inch strip of lemon rind

Extra-virgin olive oil

PREP TIME: 3 minutes • **COOK TIME:** 5 minutes • **SERVES:** 10–12

1 Place the garlic, olives, pepper flakes, rosemary, thyme, and lemon rind in a bowl, and combine well.

2 Put the olive mixture in a sealable glass jar, and pour in olive oil, to cover. Seal the jar tightly, shake, and refrigerate for 2 days to combine flavors.

3 Bring to room temperature before serving.

LEFTOVER LUXURIES

It happens all the time: Sometimes we just buy too much of a good thing. If you find yourself with leftover pitted olives on your hands, you're in luck: Place them in a food processor along with 2 peeled cloves of garlic and pulse until pureed, thinning out with olive oil, if it's too thick. This is called a tapenade—a delicious olive paste that's served all over the Mediterranean. It will keep in a sealed jar in your fridge for up to 2 weeks.

TOP SECRET

Have you ever been served restaurant olives so packed with flavor that you could swear they've been marinating for weeks? Well, they haven't. Here's the secret: Olives—marinated or not—benefit from a few minutes of gentle heat. Before you serve the olives, place them in a small, heavy skillet and set over low heat until they are warm. Stir well, and serve immediately.

SAVE THAT LIQUID GOLD!

13 Things to Do with Leftover Herby Olive Marinade

When you're done with the Herby Olives (opposite page), do not throw out the oil they've been packed in—it's liquid gold! Sealed, it will keep in your refrigerator for at least a week. Here's what to do with it:

1
Drizzle it on cooked pasta instead of tomato sauce.

2
Toast slices of French or Italian bread, and use it instead of butter.

3
Drizzle it on broiled fish, after cooking.

4
Drizzle it on leftover sliced roast beef.

5
Use it as a dip for cold, boiled vegetables.

6
Brush vegetables with it before grilling.

7
Sauté fish in it instead of using plain oil.

8
Drizzle it on roasting baby potatoes.

9
Blend it with soft goat cheese to make an herby sandwich spread.

10
Drizzle it on just-cooked hamburgers for a hit of flavor.

11
Blend it with vinegar and a drop of mustard for home made salad dressing.

12
Drizzle it on cold boiled shrimp.

13
Drizzle it on a steak that's just come off the grill.

Quick Beef and Scallion Roll Ups

Called *negamaki* in Japanese restaurants, this yummy and quick appetizer is a tasty melding of textures and flavor. Chopped fresh cilantro and toasted sesame seeds add intoxicating aromas and crunch.

8 asparagus stalks, trimmed and cut into 3-inch lengths

8 thin slices (about 1/4 pound) sirloin steak

4 scallions, trimmed and cut into 3-inch lengths

2 teaspoons canola oil

3 tablespoons bottled teriyaki sauce

1 tablespoon toasted sesame seeds

1 tablespoon chopped fresh cilantro

PREP TIME: 15 minutes • **COOK TIME:** 20 minutes • **SERVES:** 4

1 Bring a small saucepan of water to a boil. Blanch the asparagus in the water for 1 minute, then drain. Meanwhile, pound the steak slices to 1/8-inch thickness.

2 Place 2 pieces of asparagus and 1 piece of scallion near one end of a beef strip. Roll the beef around the vegetables. Repeat to form 8 bundles.

3 In a large nonstick skillet over medium-high heat, heat the oil. Add the beef rolls. Brown for 2 minutes, turning frequently. Add the teriyaki sauce, lower the heat to medium, and simmer for 3 minutes.

4 Transfer the rolls to a serving platter. Sprinkle with the sesame seeds and cilantro.

VARIATION

Pork Negamaki

Instead of beef, use boneless pork loin (not tenderloin).

TOP SECRET

Sometimes the best way to prepare a quick dish is by using jarred, premade sauce. But don't feel like you need to use it as is; if you like a bit of spice, add a teaspoon of hot sauce to it. If you like it more succulent, add a teaspoon of ketchup to it. Or, add both!

APPETIZERS
AND SNACKS

Simple Jalapeño Poppers

This favorite snack food can be time consuming to make, not to mention unhealthy. Instead of battering and deep frying, we use a secret ingredient that not only crisps up but also gives a lot of smoky flavor. Be careful...they're addictive!

10 jalapeño peppers, seeded, deveined, and halved lengthwise (wear gloves when handling)

4 ounces cream cheese, softened

10 uncooked bacon strips, halved

PREP TIME: 10 minutes • **COOK TIME:** 25 minutes • **MAKES** 20

1 Preheat the oven to 350°F.

2 Stuff each jalapeño half with about 2 teaspoons of the cream cheese. Wrap with bacon and secure with a toothpick.

3 Place on a broiler rack that has been coated with cooking spray. Bake for 20 to 25 minutes, until the bacon is crisp. Remove the toothpicks and serve immediately.

VARIATIONS

Cilantro and Lime Poppers

Mix some chopped fresh cilantro and lime zest into the cream cheese before stuffing the peppers.

Super Creamy Chili Poppers

Melt 3 ounces Monterey Jack cheese, let cool, and fold into the cream cheese before stuffing the peppers.

LEFTOVER LUXURIES

It's likely that there won't be any leftovers when you make this dish. But in case there are, simply chop up what's left and fold them into a quesadilla (see page 52). Drizzle with salsa, and enjoy!

TOP SECRET

Instead of deep-frying poppers, wrap them in bacon! The bacon is succulent, flavor-packed, and adds a textural crunch to these yummy snacks.

Pacific Chicken Pizza Tarts

Everyone loves pizza, and you'll be astonished at how quickly this one becomes a family favorite. Here, tortillas are the flatbread, peanut sauce stands in for traditional tomato sauce, the cheese is Monterey Jack, and the topping is ginger-spiked sautéed chicken. It's a fun combination that you won't soon forget!

1/2 cup rice-wine vinegar

2 1/2 tablespoons light brown sugar

2 tablespoons peanut butter

1 tablespoon soy sauce

5 teaspoons canola oil

1 1/2 teaspoons peeled grated fresh ginger

1 clove garlic, minced

1 tablespoon chopped fresh cilantro

2 boneless, skinless chicken breast halves, cut crosswise into 1/4-inch-thick strips

2 flour tortillas

1 cup shredded Monterey Jack cheese

PREP TIME: 15 minutes • **COOK TIME:** 20 minutes • **SERVES:** 2

1 Preheat the oven to 425°F. Coat a baking sheet with cooking spray. Combine the vinegar, brown sugar, peanut butter, and soy sauce in a small bowl.

2 Heat 2 teaspoons of the oil in a large saucepan over medium-high heat, then add the ginger and garlic and cook for about 15 seconds, just until fragrant. Add the vinegar mixture and bring to a boil. Cook for 5 to 6 minutes, or until the mixture is thick. Remove from the heat and stir in the cilantro.

3 Heat the remaining 1 tablespoon oil in a large nonstick skillet over medium-high heat. Add the chicken and cook for about 1 1/2 minutes, per side, until lightly browned. Transfer to the saucepan with the vinegar mixture.

4 Place the tortillas on the baking sheet and bake for about 5 minutes, until lightly toasted. Remove from the oven and sprinkle each with 1/2 cup of the cheese. Top each with half of the chicken mixture. Bake for about 7 minutes, until hot and the tortillas are crisp. Cut into wedges and serve immediately.

VARIATION

Tofu-Scrumptious Pizza Tart
Replace the chicken with 1 block of drained and sliced extra-firm tofu.

TOP SECRET

It's the peanut butter in this delectable dish that provides the silky smooth "base"—replacing tomato sauce in traditional pizza. For extra zip, use chunky peanut butter and drizzle it with hot sauce.

Nachos Grande

Put out a plate of nachos and they'll disappear in no time. Here's a plate of nachos that's anything but ordinary. Fresh pineapple complements the creamy avocado and creates a spicy-sweet flavor to contrast the jalapeño peppers.

1 can (16 ounces) refried beans

1 bag (10 ounces) restaurant-style tortilla chips

1/4 cup drained sliced pickled jalapeño peppers

3 cups shredded Monterey Jack cheese

1 1/2 cups diced fresh pineapple

1 Hass avocado, peeled, pitted, and diced into 1/4-inch pieces

1/2 cup sour cream

PREP TIME: 10 minutes • **COOK TIME:** 10 minutes • **SERVES:** 6

1 Preheat the oven to 425°F. Coat a large baking sheet with cooking spray.

2 Heat the beans in a small saucepan over medium heat.

3 Arrange the tortilla chips on the prepared baking sheet and top with the beans, jalapeños, cheese, and pineapple. Bake for 4 to 5 minutes, until the cheese melts.

4 Remove from the oven and slide the nachos onto a large serving platter. Top with the avocado and sour cream. Serve immediately.

VARIATION
Chili-Mango Nachos
Instead of refried beans, substitute 1 1/2 cups drained chili, and top with mango instead of pineapple.

DID YOU KNOW?
If you have a jar of pickled jalapeños in your fridge, they'll keep for approximately a year, mellowing as they age.

TOP SECRET
Whenever you cook with salt or spice, a wonderful way to offset the heat is with fruit. The best fruit for dishes like nachos are citrus fruits, like tangerines, papayas, mangos, oranges, and even kiwifruits.

3 SOUP SMARTS
SIMPLE BROTHS TO HEARTY STEWS

Soup secrets are some of the culinary world's most potent ones; did you know that if you add leftover, stale bread to one Italian soup, you'll wind up with a dish fit for Roman gods? Or that if you add a touch of cornstarch to chicken broth, you have the makings of a Chinese soup that's a regular on menus everywhere? The fact is that professional chefs can make great soups out of anything, and now you can, too! That free-floating ability often leads to some seriously good food. Soup cooks often say that their best results were sheer serendipity—you just have to look at the ingredients in your fridge in a new light. And in this delicious chapter, that's what you'll learn to do!

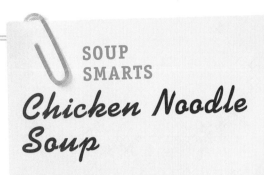

SOUP SMARTS

Chicken Noodle Soup

A great shortcut to classic chicken soup, with rich, flavorful broth. Normally, chicken soup is even better the next day, but this one is great right out of the pot.

4 quarts chicken stock

4 chicken breasts, bone in, skin removed

1 onion, diced

2 carrots, diced

2 stalks celery, thinly sliced

8 ounces egg noodles

Salt and Pepper, to taste

PREP TIME: 10 minutes • **COOK TIME:** 45 minutes • **SERVES:** 8

1 In a large, heavy soup pot, bring the stock to a simmer and add the chicken. Simmer for about 25 minutes, until the chicken is cooked through, skimming off any foam that rises. Remove the breasts to a platter to cool slightly.

2 Meanwhile, add the onions, carrots, and celery and cook for 10 minutes, or until the vegetables are tender.

3 While the vegetables cook, strip the meat off the bones and cut into cubes, discarding the bones.

4 Place the meat back into the soup with the noodles and simmer for 6 to 7 minutes, or until the noodles are tender. Taste and add salt, if needed, and a generous grinding of pepper.

VARIATION
Matzo Ball Soup

While the chicken breasts are simmering, in a medium bowl, combine 1 cup matzo meal with 4 beaten eggs, 1/2 cup seltzer, 2 tablespoons vegetable oil, and a sprinkle of salt and pepper. Cover the bowl and refrigerate the mixture while you finish preparing the soup. When the vegetables are tender, instead of adding the noodles and chicken, drop rounded tablespoonfuls of the matzo mixture into the simmering pot of soup. Clap on the lid and cook for 30 minutes. Add the diced chicken meat and heat through.

TOP SECRET

Classic chicken soup is made by simmering a whole chicken with aromatic vegetables, then discarding the solids after they have rendered all their flavor into the stock. But when chefs don't have the time, they use the best stock they can buy, prepackaged. Go ahead and do it; making chicken soup from water and chicken is valiant and traditional, but not always necessary.

SOUP SMARTS

Egg Drop Soup

This classic of Chinese home cooking is a simple soup of chicken broth and egg, seasoned with nothing more than a little sesame oil and some chopped scallions, so that the flavor of the egg shines through. Try it this simple way at least once—it's a warming standby for nights when you need some supper fast.

4 cups
chicken stock

2 eggs

1/2 teaspoon
toasted sesame oil

Salt

2 scallions,
including green
parts, thinly sliced

PREP TIME: 1 minute • **COOK TIME:** 5 minutes • **SERVES:** 2

1 Bring the stock to a boil in a saucepan over medium-high heat. While the stock heats, beat the eggs in a small bowl with the sesame oil.

2 With the stock at a rolling boil, slowly drizzle in the egg mixture, which will "bloom" in the boiling soup. Drag a fork (or a pair of chopsticks) through the soup to pull the egg into shreds.

3 Taste and add salt, if needed, and serve with a generous sprinkle of scallions on top.

VARIATION

Egg Drop Soup with Tomato and Wontons

For a much richer soup, stir 1 finely diced tomato and 1/4 cup frozen green peas into the boiling stock before adding the egg. If you have frozen dumplings on hand, stir in a handful and allow the soup to simmer for 6 to 8 minutes, to cook the dumplings through. Thicken the broth slightly with 1 tablespoon cornstarch whisked into 1/4 cup water and simmer gently for 2 minutes, then drizzle in the beaten egg. Season with salt or soy sauce, and serve with scallions and chili-garlic sauce on the side, if desired.

LEFTOVER LUXURIES

When you're cutting up a chicken, put the wing tips (and wings, too), backbone, and neck into a small saucepan with 3 cups water, a pinch of salt, and an unpeeled onion, cut in half. Add a few peppercorns, if you like, and simmer very gently for 1 to 2 hours. Strain and keep the resulting stock in the freezer. This flavorful brew will make any vegetable soup far more delicious.

TOP SECRET

The restaurant version of egg drop soup is nearly always served in a thickened, almost glossy broth, a look that you can only achieve with cornstarch. You can do this by whisking 2 tablespoons cornstarch into 1/3 cup water, then drizzling this into the boiling stock before adding the egg. Cook for 2 to 3 minutes, until the stock thickens, then add the egg.

SOUP SMARTS

Thai Coconut Soup

The fragrant, steaming bowl of eye-poppingly zesty soup that often shows up as the first course at a Thai restaurant is surprisingly easy to make at home. Lemongrass and exotic ingredients such as kaffir lime leaves and galangal make up the classic version, but you can make a mean facsimile with ingredients easier to find in your pantry.

6 cups
chicken stock

2 boneless, skinless
chicken breasts,
cut into
1/4-inch slices

1 can (14 ounces)
coconut milk

2 cloves garlic,
minced

1 tablespoon
freshly grated
ginger

2 chilies, such
as tiny Thai bird
chilies or jalapeños,
seeded and chopped

1 lemon,
zest and juice

1 lime,
zest and juice

1/4 cup fish sauce
(*nam pla*)

2 cups white
mushrooms,
thinly sliced

Salt and pepper,
to taste

1/4 cup fresh
cilantro leaves,
coarsely chopped

PREP TIME: 15 minutes • **COOK TIME:** 20 minutes • **SERVES:** 6

1 Bring the stock to a boil in a large, heavy soup pot. Add the chicken and poach lightly for 3 to 4 minutes.

2 Add the coconut milk, garlic, ginger, chilies, lemon zest and juice, lime zest and juice, fish sauce, and mushrooms and return to a boil. Reduce the heat and simmer for about 10 minutes, or until the mushrooms are cooked through.

3 Taste and adjust seasoning. You may need a bit of salt, and also additional lime juice to balance the creamy and sour flavors.

4 Serve sprinkled with the cilantro.

VARIATIONS

Thai Coconut Soup with Noodles
Add 4 ounces thin rice noodles with the other ingredients. The noodles will thicken on standing, so if you're reheating the soup the next day, you may need to add a little water.

Thai Coconut Soup with Shrimp
Leave out the chicken. Bring the stock to a boil, adding and simmering the ingredients for 10 minutes. Add 1 pound shelled medium shrimp and cook for 2 to 3 minutes, or until the shrimp is bright pink.

TOP SECRET
You can replace high-calorie coconut milk with light or reduced-fat coconut milk, and the taste will still be delicious. And if you have an aversion to cilantro (50% of the population does), replace it with an extra squeeze of lime.

SOUP SMARTS

Oyster Stew

Oyster stew is a milky soup that showcases the flavor of fresh oysters with aplomb, but it is also delicious made with canned oysters. Use real butter and whole milk. Oyster stew is ethereal and yet a solidly satisfying food, best eaten simply accompanied by crackers or bread.

4 tablespoons (1/2 stick) butter

3 scallions, including green parts, thinly sliced

4 cups whole milk

1 pint shucked fresh oysters (with their liquor) or 2 cans (8 ounces each)

Salt and pepper, to taste

Dash of cayenne

PREP TIME: 2 minutes • **COOK TIME:** 10 minutes • **SERVES:** 4

1 Heat the butter in a large saucepan and cook the scallions briefly, 2 to 3 minutes, or until just tender but not browned.

2 Add the milk and oysters (with juice). Heat through, 6 to 8 minutes. Season with salt and pepper and the cayenne. Serve immediately.

VARIATION

Thick and Creamy Oyster Stew

After the scallions have cooked 2 minutes, stir in 2 tablespoons flour, cooking and stirring until smooth and thick but not browned. Very slowly stir in 2 cups milk, whisking until no lumps remain. Blend in 2 cups light cream or half-and-half and the oysters. This heavier, richer version makes an excellent appetizer in smaller portions.

TOP SECRET

To gild the lily, add dry sherry to the soup just before eating—don't boil the sherry, which cooks off the delicate flavor, but stir a tablespoonful into each soup bowl after pouring.

SOUP SMARTS

Clam Chowder

Chowder is welcoming to lots of guest stars such as corn or fish. Don't leave out the bacon, which provides the agreeable smoky undertone to the creamy soup. The traditional accompaniment is crackers—try small crispy oyster crackers.

6 strips bacon, chopped

1 large onion, diced

3 large potatoes, peeled and diced

3 cups whole milk

2 cups chicken stock

1 bottle (8 ounces) clam juice

1 can (6 1/2 ounces) clams, with juice

Salt and pepper, to taste

PREP TIME: 10 minutes • **COOK TIME:** 25 minutes • **SERVES:** 6

1 Place the bacon in a stew pot over medium heat and cook until it starts to crisp.

2 Add the onions and potatoes to the bacon and its fat and lower the heat. Cover and sweat for 5 to 7 minutes, or until the vegetables are softened.

3 Add the milk, stock, and bottled clam juice and bring to a boil. Reduce heat and simmer gently for about 15 minutes, until the potatoes are tender and the soup starts to reduce and thicken.

4 Stir in the clams and their juice, and heat through. Season with salt and pepper. Serve piping hot.

VARIATION

Bacon and Corn Chowder

Remove the bacon from the pan and set aside, leaving the fat in the pan. Cut the kernels off of 3 ears of corn, reserving any milky juices as well. Stir in the corn and its juice, along with the corncobs, and 2 teaspoons fresh chopped thyme leaves. Simmer for 10 minutes, then remove the corncobs and stir in the crumbled crisp bacon. Serve hot.

TOP SECRET

If you can get fresh clams with ease, use 1 1/2 pounds of them, shucked, with their juices reserved, in place of a can of clams. To ensure that you get every drop of the tasty liquor into your chowder, you can also cook the clams in the chowder. Scrub them well, discard any open ones, and drop them into the boiling soup. After 3 to 4 minutes, the clams will open (discard any that don't). Either lift out the shells, scraping the clams into the soup, or ladle the whole clam shells with soup into the serving bowls.

SOUP SMARTS

Cream of Broccoli Soup

This is truly a template recipe, designed to help you make soup out of any fresh vegetable you might have, in about 20 minutes or less. It works well for hard root vegetables such as potatoes, carrots, fennel, parsnips, or turnips, as well as for green vegetables such as broccoli, spinach, cabbage, chard, or kale.

3 tablespoons butter

1 medium onion, chopped

2 tablespoons flour

4 cups chicken stock

1 bunch broccoli, trimmed and chopped

1/2 cup milk or cream

Salt and pepper, to taste

1/8 teaspoon red pepper flakes

PREP TIME: 4 minutes • **COOK TIME:** 20 minutes • **SERVES:** 4

1 Melt the butter in a saucepan over medium heat and add the onions. Stir to combine, then cover, and sweat the onions over low heat for 5 to 10 minutes, until softened.

2 Stir in the flour and cook for 2 to 3 minutes. Slowly blend in the stock and bring to a boil. Add the broccoli, reduce the heat, and simmer for another 10 minutes, or until the broccoli is tender.

3 Add the milk or cream, and puree the soup directly in the pan with a hand blender (or carefully, in batches, in the blender).

4 Season with salt and pepper and the red pepper flakes.

VARIATION

Cream of Roasted Vegetables

To intensify the flavor, roast the vegetables first. Thinly slice the vegetables you want—carrots and fennel make a lovely soup—and toss with the onions and a clove of minced garlic. Drizzle with olive oil and sprinkle lightly with salt. Roast at 450°F degrees on a baking sheet for 15 to 20 minutes, or until browned and tender, shaking the pan and tossing the vegetables once or twice. Add the vegetables to the simmering stock with the milk or cream.

DID YOU KNOW?

For the best flavor in a cream soup, don't combine more than two vegetables (besides onions and garlic). Potatoes work well with nearly anything, as do carrots, but strong-flavored vegetables such as turnips or fennel don't pair up as easily.

TOP SECRET

If you don't live in an area that has lengthy growing seasons (like California) and you still want that fresh veggie taste in your soup, do what the pros do: Find the best quality frozen vegetables available in your area. Most frozen vegetables are flash frozen shortly after they've been picked, making them a healthy alternative to fresh.

SOUP SMARTS
Hearty Chili

Huge pots of chili simmer all day at chili cook-offs, but crushed tomatoes and canned beans are the key to speeding up chili at home. There's room within this basic recipe to improvise. Doll up the finished product with grated cheddar cheese, chopped scallions, and a dollop of sour cream.

1 medium onion, diced

2 cloves garlic, minced

1 pound ground beef

1 can (16 ounces) kidney beans, drained and rinsed

1 can (28 ounces) crushed tomatoes

2 tablespoons tomato paste

1 tablespoon chili powder

1 teaspoon salt

PREP TIME: 10 minutes • **COOK TIME:** 1 hour plus • **SERVES:** 4

1 Heat a saucepan over medium heat and add the onions, garlic, and beef. Cook until the meat is starting to brown and the onion is softened.

2 Add the beans to the pan with the tomatoes, tomato paste, and chili powder. Bring to a boil, reduce the heat, and simmer, loosely covered, for at least 1 hour, until sauce is thickened. If you have time, add a bit of water and let it cook longer, to let the flavors mingle.

3 Taste and season with more salt and black pepper, if desired.

VARIATION
Green Chili
Replace the ground beef with 2 pounds cubed pork. Leave out the beans. Replace the beans with 2 cans (4 ounces each) diced green chilies and 2 cups chicken broth.

TOP SECRET
Try adding a splash of red wine or 1/2 cup of that morning's coffee (black only) along with the tomatoes and beans to deepen and enrich the flavor.

SOUP SMARTS

Homemade Cream of Tomato Soup

The fresh taste of this soup, made of canned tomatoes and milk, cannot be equaled by canned cream of tomato, where the flavor is often masked by thickeners and too much salt. The tiny pinch of baking soda in the soup keeps the acidic tomato from curdling the milk. Be sure to use a gentle touch in adding the baking soda—too little, and the milk will curdle; too much, and you'll taste it in the finished product.

1 can
(16 ounces)
whole plum
tomatoes,
with juice

Pinch of
baking soda

2 1/2–3 cups milk

Salt and pepper,
to taste

Dash of cayenne
(optional)

PREP TIME: 3 minutes • **COOK TIME:** 10 minutes • **SERVES:** 4

1 Place the tomatoes (with juice) in a large saucepan over medium heat and break up the tomatoes into small bits with a knife and fork or a potato masher.

2 When the tomatoes have come to a boil, reduce the heat and add the baking soda, no more than 1/4 teaspoon. The tomatoes will foam up; stir until the foam subsides.

3 Slowly stir in the milk and heat until just simmering. Do not boil the milk. Season with salt and pepper, and a dusting of cayenne, if using, and serve immediately.

VARIATION

Spicy Tomato Soup with Pasta

Add up to 1 teaspoon of hot sauce to the soup along with 1 cup of cooked pasta—macaroni is nice, as are egg noodles or cooked spaghetti. Serve with a generous sprinkle of freshly grated Parmesan for a quick meal that's still immensely satisfying.

TOP SECRET

If you add milk directly to tomatoes, it curdles and splits into lumps. Baking soda tames the acid in canned tomatoes and prevents the soup from curdling. But too much baking soda will rob the soup of flavor, leaving the tomatoes bland and boring. To give the soup the best flavor, try to use the bare minimum of baking soda possible to make the tomatoes foam, starting with a dash, and using no more than 1/4 teaspoon altogether.

THE SECRET WAY TO STORE SOUPS

The beauty of making soups and stews is that it's almost impossible to make them in small quantities, which means that, with a little planning and the right tools, you'll always have a quick, delicious meal just waiting for you, tucked into your freezer. Most people think that all that's needed is a plastic freezer container (or several) for that delicious beef stew that they slaved over...but nothing could be further from the truth.

Most chefs stick to the tried and true heavy-duty freezer bag because they're able to remove air from it easily, which is key for keeping soups fresh (depending upon its contents, it will keep for 3 to 6 months). Here's what chefs advise:

 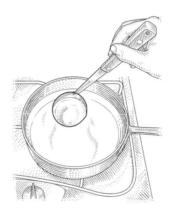 

1 Place a gallon-size, heavy-duty ziplock bag on a large, rimmed cookie sheet, and open it up.

2 Ladle in 2 to 3 cups of stew or soup, enough to steady the bag as it sits on the sheet.

3 Pick up the soup pot and carefully pour the balance into the bag. Starting from one side of the bag, zip it closed, pressing out the air as you close it.

4 When you get to an inch before the opposite end of the bag, press down on the empty portion of the bag, to expel the rest of the air. Zip it closed, and label and date the bag.

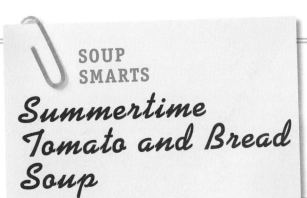

SOUP SMARTS

Summertime Tomato and Bread Soup

Like oyster stew, this is another dish where the result is far more than the sum of its parts. This is Italian home cooking, substantial enough to serve as a meal, but light and very fresh. Use good bakery bread such as a crusty sourdough. This soup can only be made in the summer, when the basil is fresh and the tomatoes are flavorful and perfectly ripe. Serve with Parmesan for dusting on top.

2 tablespoons extra-virgin olive oil

3 large ripe tomatoes, cut into chunks

2 cloves garlic, 1 minced, 1 sliced in half

4 cups chicken stock

Pinch of red pepper flakes

Salt and pepper, to taste

4 slices sourdough bread

2 or 3 leaves, fresh basil, sliced

PREP TIME: 6 minutes • **COOK TIME:** 14 minutes • **SERVES:** 4

1 Heat the oil in a large saucepan over medium heat. Add the tomatoes and garlic and cook 3 to 4 minutes, until the tomatoes soften and the garlic smells pungent.

2 Add the stock and season with salt and pepper and the pepper flakes. Bring to a gentle simmer, mashing the tomato chunks against the side of the pan with the back of a spoon, and cook for about 10 minutes.

3 While the soup is simmering, toast the bread and brush it with some olive oil. Rub the remaining clove of garlic over the surface and lay each slice of bread in the bottom of a serving bowl.

4 Stir the basil into the soup and pour the soup over the bread. Serve immediately.

VARIATION

Italian Tomato Soup with Eggs

Break 4 eggs onto the surface of the simmering soup, cover the pot, and leave for 3 to 4 minutes to poach. Lift each egg gently into a serving bowl on top of the toasted bread. Stir the basil into the soup and spoon over the bread and eggs. Serve with Parmesan on the side.

TOP SECRET

If you use real parmigiana reggiano cheese (not the stuff that comes in the tin, but the whole hunk of imported cheese from Parma), save the rind! As you simmer any tomato-based soup, toss in this bit of "garbage," and the flavors will astound you!

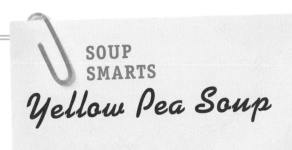

SOUP SMARTS

Yellow Pea Soup

In Sweden, dense, meaty yellow pea soup is the traditional supper served on Thursday nights, from school cafeterias and army mess tables to prisons, not to mention in many, many homes. It is traditionally accompanied by an anise-scented rye bread and followed up by dessert of thin, delicate Swedish pancakes with a dollop of lingonberry preserves and a splash of cream.

1 pound (2 cups) dried yellow peas

2 quarts water

2 small yellow onions, diced

1 small yellow onion, peeled, with 3 cloves stuck in it

2 smoked ham hocks

1/2 pound lean pork, cut into chunks (optional)

Salt and pepper, to taste

Spicy brown mustard (for serving)

PREP TIME: 12 hours (including soaking) • **COOK TIME:** 2 hours • **SERVES:** 6

1 Soak the peas overnight in cold water to cover. Drain and place in a large, heavy soup pot with the water, onions, and ham hocks and pork, if using.

2 Simmer for 2 hours, or until the peas have cooked down to a tender mush. Remove onion and cloves. Taste and season with salt and pepper. Serve with the mustard.

VARIATION

Split Pea Soup

Replace the yellow peas with green split peas. Add 2 large peeled and diced carrots and 2 thinly sliced celery stalks. Omit the optional pork chunks. For the last 10 minutes of cooking, stir in 1 teaspoon chopped fresh thyme leaves.

DID YOU KNOW?

Whole dried yellow peas are a particularly Swedish ingredient, but you'll often find them among the dried beans in the supermarket. If not, you can replace them with the ubiquitous yellow *split* peas, also known in Indian cooking as *dal*. Soup made with yellow split peas will have a finer, mealier texture, and it benefits from the addition of 1 teaspoon mild curry powder.

TOP SECRET

Savvy cooks have long known that smoked ham hocks are an inexpensive and easy way to add body to soups. They add meaty undertones and also a lot of salt. Never salt a soup containing ham hocks until you taste it just before serving. There's a good chance it won't need any at all.

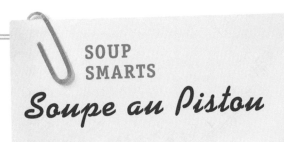

SOUP SMARTS

Soupe au Pistou

This French summertime soup is bursting with garden vegetables, and it gets a huge splash of flavor just before serving when you stir in a spoonful of *pistou*, a bright herby condiment.

SOUP

2 tablespoons extra-virgin olive oil

1 large leek, well-washed and sliced

2 cloves garlic, minced

1 stalk celery, sliced

1 large carrot, diced

2 quarts water

3 medium potatoes, diced

2 medium zucchini, diced

2 cups fresh green beans, cut into 1-inch pieces

1 can (15 ounces) cannellini beans, drained and rinsed

3/4 cup pasta shells or macaroni

1 teaspoon chopped fresh thyme leaves

PISTOU

1 cup packed fresh basil leaves

2 cloves garlic

1/2 cup extra-virgin olive oil

1/2 cup freshly grated Parmesan cheese

Salt, to taste

PREP TIME: 15 minutes • **COOK TIME:** 35 minutes • **SERVES:** 6

1 *For the soup:* Heat the oil in a large, heavy soup pot and cook the leek, garlic, celery, and carrot, for about 10 minutes, until lightly browned.

2 Stir in the water, potatoes, zucchini, green beans, cannellini beans, pasta, and thyme. Cook for about 25 minutes, until the potatoes and pasta are tender.

3 *For the pistou:* Put the basil leaves in a food processor with the garlic and pulse to chop. With the machine running, drizzle in the olive oil until you have a fine puree. Add the cheese and pulse to combine. Taste and add salt, if needed.

4 Serve the soup with pistou on the side so each diner can add a spoonful to his or her bowl.

VARIATION

Minestrone

You'll see how close French and Italian cooking can be if you turn this same recipe into a classic Italian minestrone: Double the amount of garlic and add a 15-ounce can of diced tomatoes (with juice). Leave out the potatoes and increase the pasta to 1 cup. Stir in 1 teaspoon dried oregano leaves instead of the thyme. Don't make the pistou, but do serve your minestrone with lots of freshly grated Parmesan to sprinkle on top.

TOP SECRET

If you don't have the time to make pistou, simply buy store bought pesto sauce, and use it as a replacement. They're virtually the same thing.

SOUP SMARTS
Meaty Borscht

There are as many recipes for borscht as there are Eastern European grandmothers, but this is a hearty and satisfying wintry version that's full of beefy flavor.

2 pounds beef short ribs

3 quarts water

2 teaspoons salt

3 large beets, peeled and chopped

1/2 pound red cabbage, chopped (about 3 cups)

1 large onion, diced

1 carrot, diced

Salt and pepper, to taste

Sour cream (for serving)

PREP TIME: 30 minutes • **COOK TIME:** 2 1/2 hours • **SERVES:** 6

1 Put the ribs in a large, heavy soup pot and add the water and salt. Bring to a boil, reduce the heat, and simmer gently for 1 hour, skimming off any foam that rises.

2 After an hour, add the beets, cabbage, onions, and carrots and continue to simmer for 1 1/2 hours longer, until the vegetables are tender, the soup is thick, and the meat is falling off the bones.

3 Remove and discard the bones. Taste and add salt and pepper, if needed. Serve in bowls with a hefty dollop of sour cream on top.

VARIATION
Vegetable Borscht

Leave out the beef ribs altogether and use chicken or beef stock instead of the water, if you like. Add 2 tablespoons tomato paste with the chopped vegetables. Add 2 tablespoons chopped fresh dill before serving. Serve hot or chilled with sour cream and an additional sprinkle of fresh dill. Puree for a suave and velvety silky red soup.

TOP SECRET

Make borscht even richer by roasting the beets first, which greatly intensifies their sweetness and earthy flavor. Scrub the beets well and wrap them tightly in foil. Roast on a baking sheet at 350°F for 1 hour, until tender when pierced with a knife tip. When cool enough to handle, unwrap and strip off the skin, which will come away easily.

SOUP SMARTS
Chicken Tortilla Soup

A good tortilla soup, based on a simple tomato and chicken broth or stock base, is really all about the toppings—an extravagant spread of ripe avocado, cheese, onions, cilantro, sour cream, scallions, lime, and, most especially, homemade tortilla strips.

1 can (15 ounces) whole tomatoes (with juice)

2 tablespoons chipotle chilies in adobo

1 medium white onion, chopped

2 cloves garlic

2 quarts chicken stock

2 boneless, skinless chicken breasts

1 1/2 teaspoons cumin

6 corn tortillas (6-inch)

Vegetable oil for frying

Salt, to taste

Diced avocadoes (for serving)

Chopped fresh cilantro leaves (for serving)

Chopped scallions (for serving)

Shredded Jack cheese (for serving)

Sour cream (for serving)

Lime wedges

PREP TIME: 10 minutes • **COOK TIME:** 35 minutes • **SERVES:** 6

1 In a blender or food processor, puree the tomatoes (with juice), chilies (strained from the adobo sauce), onions, and garlic.

2 Pour into a large heavy soup pot over medium heat and add the stock. Bring to a boil, reduce the heat, and add the chicken and cumin. Simmer for 15 minutes, or until the chicken is cooked and soup is lightly thickened.

3 Meanwhile, cut the tortillas into 1/2-inch strips. Bring 1 inch of cooking oil to 350°F in the bottom of a heavy saucepan over medium heat. Fry the tortilla strips in batches for about 2 minutes, or until golden brown. Lift onto a paper towel–lined plate with a slotted spoon. Sprinkle the hot tortilla strips with salt.

4 To serve, ladle the soup into bowls and top each with a generous tangle of hot tortilla strips. Serve the accompaniments in bowls on the side.

VARIATION
Shrimp and Hominy Tortilla Soup
Leave out the chicken and add 1 can (15 ounces) hominy, drained. Simmer the soup for 20 minutes instead of 15 and then add 1 pound peeled medium shrimp. Cook for 5 minutes, until the shrimp is bright pink. Serve at once with the tortilla strips and toppings.

TOP SECRET

Chipotles packed in adobo are really smoked jalapeños, and the adobo sauce that they come in is worth its weight in gold. Add just a teaspoon of the sauce to hot soups, stews, or gravies to ratchet up the flavor tremendously.

SOUP SMARTS

Beef Stew

Homemade beef stew never goes out of style, and we all yearn for the kind our mothers made (or the kind we wish they had). Rich brown gravy, tender chunks of vegetables, and a finish of bright green peas are the hallmark. This recipe produces that to perfection.

2 pounds beef chuck, cut into 2-inch cubes

1/4 cup flour

1 teaspoon salt

1/4 teaspoon pepper

2 tablespoons cooking oil

2 yellow onions, diced

2 cloves garlic, minced

4 cups beef stock (or water)

1 cup red wine

4 medium potatoes, cubed

2 large carrots, cut into chunks

1 teaspoon chopped fresh thyme leaves

1/2 cup frozen green peas

PREP TIME: 20 minutes • **COOK TIME:** 2 hours • **SERVES:** 6

1 In a shallow bowl, toss the beef chunks with the flour and salt and pepper until the meat is lightly coated. Heat the oil in a large heavy stew pot over medium-high heat and brown the meat in two batches (adding a bit more oil, if needed), until lightly browned, about 10 minutes altogether for each batch. Remove the meat to a platter.

2 In the oil remaining in the pan, cook the onions and garlic until the onions are lightly browned and tender. Add the stock or water and wine; stir, scraping up any browned bits from the bottom.

3 Return the meat to the pan and add the potatoes and carrots. Cover the pan and simmer gently over low heat for 1 1/2 to 2 hours, until the meat is tender and the sauce is thick.

4 Stir in the thyme leaves and peas and cook for an additional 5 minutes, until the peas are cooked. Season with salt and pepper, if needed, and serve.

VARIATION

Provençal Beef Stew

For an unusual take on beef stew, add the sunny flavors of Southern France with orange zest and black olives. Leave out the potatoes and add an additional carrot and the grated zest of 1 orange. Instead of green peas, stir in oil-cured pitted, coarsely chopped olives. Serve with mashed potatoes and sprinkle each serving with coarsely chopped fresh parsley leaves.

TOP SECRET

What is the number one chef secret for succulent beef stew? It's easy, and it's probably right there in your cupboard: a package of dried onion soup mix. If salt is not a concern, add one package of this mix to the stew as it's cooking. The result will be packed with delicious onion flavor and leave your guests scratching their heads.

SOUP SMARTS

Irish Stew

Real Irish stew is made with lamb, as anyone from Ireland can tell you. Turnips are optional, carrots are a sometimes thing, but potatoes are absolutely vital—and in Ireland, it's often served with more potatoes—boiled or mashed—on the side.

2 1/2 pounds lamb stew meat, cut into 1 1/2-inch cubes

1/4 cup flour

2 teaspoons salt

1/4 teaspoon pepper

2 tablespoons cooking oil

3 quarts water

4 large carrots, cut into 2-inch pieces

2 medium turnips, cut into 1-inch chunks

1 large onion, sliced

3 large potatoes, sliced 1/4-inch thick

Salt and pepper, to taste

PREP TIME: 10 minutes • **COOK TIME:** 2 hours • **SERVES:** 6

1 In a shallow bowl, toss the meat with the flour, 1 teaspoon salt, and pepper until the meat is lightly coated. Heat the oil in a large heavy stew pot over high heat and brown the meat in two batches, removing the first to a platter. Return all the browned meat to the pot and add the water and 1 teaspoon salt. Simmer for 1 hour, partially covered.

2 Add the carrots, turnips, onions and potato, and simmer for 1 more hour, partially covered. Taste and season with additional salt and pepper, if needed. If the stew is too thin, remove the cover and simmer for an additional 5 to 10 minutes to thicken.

3 Serve in bowls, with or without more potatoes.

VARIATION
Irish Stew with Dumplings
Whisk together 1 1/2 cups flour, 2 teaspoons baking powder, and 1 teaspoon salt. In a small saucepan, melt 2 tablespoons butter in 3/4 cup whole milk and stir in 1/4 cup chopped fresh parsley and 1/3 cup raisins. Add to the flour mixture and stir just until combined. Drop by rounded tablespoons onto the simmering stew near the end of the cooking time, cover tightly, and cook for 12 minutes without lifting the lid.

TOP SECRET

Buy the best lamb you can find—it really should be made with lamb, and not lamb's older cousin, mutton. The potatoes should be cooked slow enough to have time to fall apart, thickening the sauce naturally. The one fussy thing you can do to improve Irish stew is add dumplings. Some of them even include raisins, which may sound odd until you come across these delectable pockets of chewy sweetness in your savory stew.

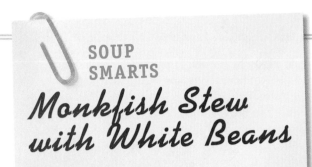

SOUP SMARTS

Monkfish Stew with White Beans

This sunny, French-inspired stew provides a lot of return for little effort. The unusual flavors go together in minutes, and the flaky monkfish chunks are succulent against the bright tomato and fennel base of the stew. Serve alone in bowls, over rice, or with creamy, buttery mashed potatoes.

2 tablespoons extra-virgin olive oil

2 medium fennel bulbs, sliced, feathery tops finely chopped and reserved for garnish

1 small onion, thinly sliced

2 cloves garlic, minced

2 tablespoons chopped fresh rosemary leaves

1 cup white wine

1 cup water

1 can (28 ounces) diced tomatoes (with juice)

2 cans (14 ounces each) cannellini beans, drained and rinsed

1 pound monkfish, boned, skinned, and trimmed into 1 1/2-inch cubes

1/3 cup sour cream

Salt and pepper, to taste

PREP TIME: 10 minutes • **COOK TIME:** 35 minutes • **SERVES:** 6

1 Heat the oil over medium heat in a large heavy stew pot. Cook the fennel bulbs and onions for 7 to 8 minutes, or until translucent and tender but not browned. Add the garlic and rosemary and cook for another minute, just until you smell the garlic.

2 Add the wine, water, tomatoes (with juice), and beans and bring to a boil. Reduce the heat and simmer gently for 15 minutes, until the vegetables are tender.

3 Stir the fish into the simmering stew and cook for 10 minutes longer, until the fish is cooked through.

4 Blend in the sour cream (See "Top Secret" below) and taste. Add salt and pepper, if needed. Garnish with a handful of fennel fronds.

VARIATION

Rosemary and White Bean Stew

Make this into a completely vegetarian dish—vegan, even—by leaving out the monkfish. Omit the water and add 1/2 teaspoon grated orange zest and 1 tablespoon pastis, the anise-flavored liquor that is the drink of choice in the South of France. The subtle anise flavor of the fennel is highlighted by the pastis, and both blend beautifully with the orange and tomato flavor.

TOP SECRET

To keep sour cream from curdling when adding it to a hot soup, blend a small amount of it together with an equal amount of soup, in a separate bowl. Whisk, and then add back to the pot.

Hungarian Goulash

Somewhere midway between a soup and a stew, goulash is wonderful served over buttered egg noodles. If you want to eat it as a soup, add another cup of chicken broth and spoon it into bowls. Be sure to use fresh paprika for the best flavor.

2 tablespoons vegetable oil

2 pounds beef chuck, cut into 2-inch pieces

2 medium yellow onions, chopped

2 cloves garlic, minced

1 tablespoon paprika

1 teaspoon caraway seeds

1 tablespoon tomato paste

2 cups chicken broth

1 red bell pepper, cored, seeded, and chopped

Salt and pepper, to taste

Sour cream (for serving)

PREP TIME: 10 minutes • **COOK TIME:** 1 1/2 hours • **SERVES:** 6

1 Heat the oil in a large heavy stew pot over medium-high heat. Add the beef and cook for 5 to 7 minutes, turning often, until browned on all sides.

2 Add the onions and cook, stirring, for 3 to 5 minutes, or until softened. Add the garlic and cook 1 minute longer. Stir in the paprika, caraway seeds, tomato paste, and broth. Bring to a boil, stirring to pick up any browned bits on the bottom. Lower the heat, add the bell peppers, then cover and simmer for 1 1/2 hours.

3 Season with salt and pepper, if needed. Serve the goulash with a spoonful of sour cream.

VARIATION

Mushroom Goulash

Add 1 pound sliced cremini mushrooms while softening the onions. Add an extra 1/2 cup chicken broth for a fuller-bodied goulash. You can also substitute veal for the beef chunks for a lighter-flavored stew.

TOP SECRET

If the only paprika you have is an old bottle of red powder that you used to sprinkle on deviled eggs last summer, it's time to throw it away and start fresh. Real Hungarian paprika, available at many supermarkets and also at gourmet and spice markets, is a pungent, fragrant spice made of ground sweet red peppers. It imparts a depth and smokiness to a dish and adds real flavor, not just its brilliant orange-red color. There is also a smoky-hot version available, but classic goulash is usually made with the sweet kind.

Spicy Sausage Gumbo

Making a big pot of gumbo may sound like whipping up a tricky gourmet dish, but the only trick to gumbo is browning the roux—the mixture of flour and oil that underpins the stew.

1/4 cup vegetable oil

1/2 cup all-purpose flour

1/2 pound spicy pork sausage

2 onions, chopped

2 stalks celery, chopped

1 large green bell pepper, chopped

1 large red bell pepper, chopped

2 quarts chicken stock

1 teaspoon salt

1/2 teaspoon cayenne

1 box (10 ounces) frozen okra

2 pounds large shrimp, peeled

Cooked white rice (for serving)

4 scallions, including green parts, sliced

PREP TIME: 10 minutes • **COOK TIME:** 40 minutes • **SERVES:** 6

1 In a large heavy stew pot, cook the oil and flour together over low heat, stirring very frequently, for about 30 minutes, until a deep, rich dark brown. Keep the heat low to prevent the roux from turning black—it should be the color of a milk chocolate bar.

2 Stir in the sausage, onions, celery, and peppers. Cook for about 6 minutes, stirring often, until the vegetables are tender.

3 Add the stock, salt, and cayenne and bring to a boil. Reduce the heat and simmer, uncovered, for 30 minutes. Stir in the okra and cook 8 minutes, until tender. Just before serving, add the shrimp and heat for about 3 minutes, or just until cooked through. Taste and adjust salt. Serve hot over the rice, sprinkled with the scallions, and with hot sauce on the side.

VARIATION

Gumbo Z'Herbes

Leave out the shrimp and the okra. Instead, stir in at least three different varieties of greens: 1 box (10 ounces) frozen spinach, 1 box (10 ounces) frozen chopped turnip greens, and 1 box (10 ounces) collard greens. Simmer the frozen greens at least 20 minutes, until tender.

TOP SECRET

If your roux turns from milk chocolate brown to dark chocolate brown, throw it out and start over—that way, you're only wasting a few tablespoons of flour and oil rather than a whole pot of stew ingredients. A few tablespoons of a well-made roux will permeate an entire stewpot with a nutty flavor, but a few tablespoons of a too-dark roux will add an undeniable burnt flavor. Stir the roux continually while cooking so you can monitor the color. As long as there is a golden undertone, you're still in the "nutty" flavor range.

THE FINE ART OF BROWNING MEAT

Sounds Simple, Doesn't It?

The truth is, if you don't brown stew meat correctly, any number of things can go wrong. You can overcrowd the pan and wind up steaming the meat in its own juices; if the meat has been dusted with flour, you can steam the flour as well and wind up with paste. If you use the wrong kind of oil, you can burn it, and the meat, and the pan. If you use all butter, you can burn it, and the meat, and the pan.

Browning meat correctly is the key to making a delicious, flavor-packed stew, and here are three easy steps to make sure you'll never steam your meat again.

1 Use a heavyweight stew or soup pot. A lighter one might be easier to lift, but it will conduct heat poorly, and you'll wind up with hot spots (and cool spots).

2 Go easy on the flour. If the recipe instructions tell you to dredge the meat in flour, do so, but do so lightly. Too much, and you'll wind up with paste.

3 Heat the oil you use until it shimmers; if it smokes, it's too hot and you'll scorch it. When it shimmers, add a few pieces of meat at a time to the pan—no more than five or six of average stew meat.

4 Wait, and be patient. Do not stir for 5 minutes, and then, using tongs, rotate the chunks of meat so that all sides are browned. Repeat.

5 If you're making a large portion, remove the browned meat to a plate, cover loosely, and then add back to the pan (with all of the yummy accumulated juices), when the meat has browned completely.

SOUP SMARTS
Cheese Soup

Like the soldier in the story who taught the villagers to make soup out of a stone, cheese soup is what to make when there seems to be nothing to eat. Warm and comforting, it's delicious with hot buttered toast or crackers—much better for supper than simply cold cheese on bread.

1 clove garlic

2 tablespoons butter or oil

1 onion, chopped

1 stalk celery, chopped

2 tablespoons all-purpose flour

3 cups chicken or beef stock

2 cups milk

8 ounces cheddar cheese

1 teaspoon Worcestershire sauce

Hot sauce, to taste

Salt and pepper, to taste

PREP TIME: 4 minutes • **COOK TIME:** 15 minutes • **SERVES:** 4

1 Mince the garlic in a garlic press. Heat the butter or oil in a large saucepan over medium heat. Add the garlic, onions, and celery and sauté for 4 to 6 minutes, or until the vegetables are softened.

2 Stir in the flour and cook for 2 minutes. Stir in the stock and milk and bring to a simmer.

3 Meanwhile, grate the cheddar cheese and drop it into the soup while stirring. Stir until the cheese is melted. Lower the heat and simmer gently, without boiling, for 4 to 5 minutes longer, until the soup is thickened.

4 Add the Worcestershire sauce, and season with hot sauce and salt and pepper.

VARIATION
Cheese and Potato Soup with Bacon
When you cook the onions and celery, add one large peeled and finely diced potato, and simmer until tender. While the soup simmers, cook 4 slices of bacon until crisp, then crumble on top of the soup when serving.

TOP SECRET
For the finest essence of garlic, use a press instead of a knife to mince. This technique is ideal specifically for silky soups and stews, when you want the flavor of the garlic, but not pieces of it.

SOUP SMARTS

Turkey Noodle Soup

After Thanksgiving is over and the guests have departed, the inevitable question is, "What shall we do with all that turkey?" Here's (at least) one answer! Comforting, delicious, and packed with flavor, it freezes well, but not until next Thanksgiving.

9 cups chicken or turkey stock

4 carrots, peeled and shredded

3 stalks celery, sliced

1 small onion, chopped

1 teaspoon rubbed sage

1/2 teaspoon freshly ground black pepper

3 whole cloves

1 bay leaf

2 cups diced cooked turkey

1 cup macaroni

1/4 cup chopped fresh parsley

PREP TIME: 15 minutes • **COOK TIME:** 1 hour, 20 minutes • **SERVES:** 6

1 In a large Dutch oven or soup pot over medium-high heat, combine the stock, carrots, celery, onion, sage, and pepper.

2 Make a spice bag by placing the cloves and bay leaf in the center of a small piece of cheesecloth or a clean coffee filter. Bring up the edges and tie securely with cotton string. Add the spice bag to the pot. Bring to a boil, reduce the heat, and simmer, covered, for about an hour, or until the carrots are tender.

3 Add the turkey, macaroni, and parsley and simmer, covered, for about 15 minutes, until the macaroni is tender and the soup is heated through. Remove the spice bag before serving.

VARIATION

Turkey Corn Soup

Omit the cloves and the macaroni, and add 1 cup frozen corn kernels to the soup with the celery and onion.

TOP SECRET

To avoid the unpleasantness the comes along with accidentally chewing on a whole clove, try this trick, instead: Place them in a square of gauze, tie up the corners with some long, heavy thread, and then tie the end of the thread to one of the pot handles. When the soup is done, extract the gauze, and the cloves!

Harvest Squash Soup

This satisfying and savory autumn soup is warming on cool nights. Serve it with chunks of crusty bread as the first course in a meal featuring roast pork.

1 1/2 cups chopped onions

1 tablespoon vegetable oil

4 cups mashed cooked butternut squash

3 cups chicken broth

2 cups unsweetened applesauce

1 1/2 cups milk

1 bay leaf

1 tablespoon fresh lime juice

1 tablespoon sugar

1 teaspoon curry powder

1/2 teaspoon ground cinnamon

1/2 teaspoon salt (optional)

1/4 teaspoon freshly ground black pepper

1/4 teaspoon ground nutmeg

PREP TIME: 15 minutes • **COOK TIME:** 35 minutes • **SERVES:** 10

1 In a large saucepan or Dutch oven, sauté the onion in the oil for about 4 minutes, until tender.

2 Add the squash, broth, applesauce, milk, bay leaf, lime juice, sugar, curry powder, cinnamon, salt, if using, pepper, and nutmeg. Simmer, uncovered, for about 30 minutes, until the flavors have blended.

3 Remove the bay leaf before serving.

VARIATION

White Bean and Squash Soup

Add 2 drained 15-ounce cans white beans to the pot along with the squash.

FIX IT FAST

To save time, look for frozen butternut squash in the freezer section of well-stocked supermarkets. If you can't find it, peel 2 butternut squash, discarding the seeds. Chop and steam over simmering water for about 20 minutes, or until tender. Mash.

TOP SECRET

The key to the divine flavor in this soup is the applesauce, which adds a fruity edge without overt sweetness.

Cheddar Cheese and Broccoli Soup

If you love cheese but are watching calories, don't despair. Here's a comforting soup recipe with all the creamy richness of real cheddar cheese and plenty of health-boosting broccoli.

1 pound broccoli

1 tablespoon extra-virgin olive oil

1 small onion, chopped

1 stalk celery, chopped

2 tablespoons all-purpose flour

1 can (15 ounces) reduced-sodium chicken broth

1 can (12 ounces) evaporated fat-free milk

1 1/2 cups shredded reduced-fat cheddar cheese

1/2 teaspoon freshly ground black pepper

1/4 teaspoon ground nutmeg

Salt, to taste

PREP TIME: 15 minutes • **COOK TIME:** 20 minutes • **SERVES:** 6

1 Trim and peel the broccoli stems. Cut off 12 small florets. Coarsely chop enough remaining broccoli to equal 2 cups. Blanch the chopped broccoli and florets in boiling water for about 2 minutes, or just until bright green. Drain and set aside.

2 Heat the oil in a medium saucepan over medium heat. Sauté the onions and celery for about 5 minutes, until soft.

3 Whisk in the flour and cook for 1 minute. Add the broth and evaporated milk. Cook, stirring constantly, for about 5 minutes, or until the mixture simmers and thickens.

4 Add the chopped broccoli, cheese, pepper, nutmeg, and salt. Stir about 3 minutes, or until the cheese melts and the soup is heated through. Serve 1 cup per person, topped with the broccoli florets.

VARIATION

Cheddar Cheese and Asparagus Soup
Make the soup with asparagus, trimmed and coarsely chopped, instead of the broccoli.

TOP SECRET

This is a dish that almost everyone loves, and traditionally, it would be thickened with pure cream. The trick here is to replace that cream with evaporated fat-free milk. The results will be astonishing!

Cock-a-Leekie Soup

This chicken and leek soup is a staple comfort food in Scottish households.

8 cups water

1 stewing chicken (3-4 pounds), giblets removed

6 large leeks with tops, washed and sliced

1 bay leaf

1/2 teaspoon salt

1/2 teaspoon black pepper

1/2 cup long-grain white rice

1/4 cup chopped parsley

PREP TIME: 5 minutes • **COOK TIME:** 2 hours, 20 minutes • **SERVES:** 6

1 In a 6-quart Dutch oven or soup pot, bring the water, chicken, half of the leeks, the bay leaf, salt, and pepper to a boil over high heat, skimming off any foam. Reduce the heat, cover, and simmer, skimming the surface occasionally, for 2 hours, or until the chicken is very tender and falls away from bone.

2 Using a slotted spoon, transfer the chicken to a plate. When it's cool enough to handle, remove the skin and bones and tear the meat into shreds, then return it to the pot.

3 Add the rice and the remaining leeks and bring to boil. Reduce the heat and simmer, covered, for 20 minutes, or until the rice is tender. Remove the bay leaf and stir in the parsley.

VARIATION
Cock-a-Leekie Stew
Instead of the rice, use 3/4 cup pearled barley for a more traditional dish.

TOP SECRET

When you're making a long-cooking chicken-based soup or stew, it pays to use an old hen, a capon, or a pullet. The stronger taste is absolutely ideal in this case, but you won't want to turn leftovers into sandwiches: On its own, the flavor of the meat is too strong.

Quick-and-Easy Lemony Turkey Rice Soup

Lemon and cilantro add a deliciously different twist to turkey soup.

6 cups chicken broth

1 can (10 ounces) condensed cream of chicken soup

2 cups cooked rice

2 cups diced cooked turkey

1/4 teaspoon black pepper

2 tablespoons cornstarch

1/4 cup fresh lemon juice

1/4 cup minced fresh cilantro

PREP TIME: 5 minutes • **COOK TIME:** 5 minutes • **SERVES:** 6

1 In a large saucepan, combine 5 1/2 cups of the broth, the soup, rice, turkey, and pepper. Bring to a boil and boil for 3 minutes.

2 In a small bowl, combine the cornstarch and the remaining 1/2 cup broth until smooth. Gradually stir into the hot soup. Cook and stir for 1 to 2 minutes, or until thickened and heated through.

3 Remove from heat. Stir in the lemon juice and cilantro.

VARIATION

Quick Avgolemono Soup

Start with all the broth but omit the condensed soup and cornstarch. Instead of the cornstarch mixture, whisk 2 eggs in a small bowl, lower the heat on the soup, and carefully whisk them in, beating the whole time. Do not add cilantro. Serve immediately.

TOP SECRET

The condensed cream of chicken soup is a lifesaver here! Not only does it pack a punch of chicken flavor; it adds silky texture and helps pave the way for the inclusion of cornstarch, which can sometimes get lumpy.

4 HERE'S THE BEEF (AND PORK)!

There's far more to life—and to beef!—than hamburgers.
And while a good hamburger isn't as easy to make as it looks, producing a succulent steak that's perfectly pink in the middle is the hallmark of a real pro. Like everything, there are prized secrets to handling meat; cooking it to perfection; tenderizing tough, inexpensive cuts; and making the most of prime pieces...and these tricks are worth their weight in gold! But the real trick to meat cooking is extracting the best possible flavor and the maximum tenderness from the cheaper cuts of meat—which are often the ones that have the meatiest flavor, anyway.

Sirloin Steaks with Wine and Mushroom Sauce

Thinner steaks (less than 1 inch thick) are perfect when you're dealing with slightly tougher cuts of meat, like sirloin. Overcook any steak and you'll have a tough, flavorless meal, but a quick fry in a very hot pan will leave them succulent and tender.

Salt and pepper, to taste

2 sirloin steaks (10 ounces each), no more than 3/4 inch thick, at room temperature

1 tablespoon vegetable oil

1 tablespoon unsalted butter

1 clove garlic, minced

8 ounces fresh white mushrooms (about 2 cups), sliced

1/4 cup white wine

1/4 cup cream

1/2 tablespoon minced fresh Italian parsley

PREP TIME: 8 minutes • **COOK TIME:** 15 minutes • **SERVES:** 2

1 Place a dry cast-iron skillet over medium-high heat for 1 to 2 minutes. Salt and pepper the steaks generously on both sides, pour in the oil, and when it begins to shimmer, carefully lay the steaks in the pan.

2 Cook 3 to 4 minutes, then turn and cook another 3 minutes for a medium steak. Remove the steak from the pan to a plate and loosely drape with foil.

3 Reduce the heat to medium and add the butter to the pan. Add the garlic and cook for about 30 seconds. Add the mushrooms and cook for 7 to 8 minutes, stirring occasionally, until the mushrooms are softened and browned around the edges.

4 Pour in the wine, whisk lightly, and cook for 1 to 2 minutes, then stir in the cream. Return the steaks to the pan to coat with the sauce, and serve immediately, topped with the parsley.

VARIATION

Flank Steaks with Blue Cheese–Mushroom Sauce

Substitute 8-ounce pieces of flank steak for the sirloin. Add 4 ounces of crumbled blue cheese to the sauce along with the cream. Slice the steaks into 3/4-inch-thick slices on the diagonal and fan each over a serving plate. Top with the sauce and serve immediately.

TOP SECRET

Cooking cold beef (or chicken, pork, or lamb) results in tough meat, so let meat come to room temperature *before* you cook it. If you don't, you'll have to overcook the meat to get the cold interior cooked, and you'll inevitably burn the exterior.

HERE'S THE BEEF

Perfect Roast Beef

Here's a foolproof technique for making lip-smacking good roast beef no matter what size roast you're working with. You can use this technique for any cut from the loin or rib sections, the chuck eye, and top round roast, which can often be quite inexpensive. The roast should cook for 15 minutes per pound.

1 beef roast (rump roast, sirloin tip, top round roast, chuck eye)

Salt and pepper, to taste

PREP TIME: 10 minutes • **COOK TIME:** Varies according to weight
SERVES: Varies according to weight

1 Preheat the oven to 400°F. Place a large dry cast-iron pan over medium-high heat.

2 Sprinkle salt and pepper all over the outside of the roast and sear it in the pan on all sides, until brown.

3 Place the roast on a rack in a low-sided roasting pan and cook for 15 minutes per pound, reducing the heat to 275°F after 30 minutes.

4 Test the internal temperature at the center of the roast with a digital instant-read thermometer. Remove the roast when the internal temperature reaches your preferred doneness (140° to 145°F for medium), keeping in mind that the roast will heat up about 5° degrees more as it rests. Allow the meat to rest for 15 minutes on a platter, before carving.

VARIATION
Perfect Prime Rib
Use prime rib instead of other cuts of meat, but don't cook it past medium-rare (internal temperature of 130° to 135°F), or the rich beefy flavor will start to dissipate into dry chewiness. Ask the butcher to "French" the bones, stripping them of any skin and fat so they brown decoratively as the meat roasts.

TOP SECRET
For the best roast beef, plan ahead: The night before roasting, season the meat on all sides with freshly ground black pepper; 3 hours before roasting, season with salt.

Old Time Oven-Roasted Pot Roast with Brown Gravy

There are few things more comforting on a dark winter's night than taking the lid off a potful of steaming hot, thick brown gravy, succulent meat, and tender root vegetables. This is the perfect way to cook cuts that aren't suitable for roasting or frying. The slow, moist cooking will break down all the connective tissues in tougher cuts from the chuck or rump sections.

1 boneless shoulder
pot roast or chuck
or rump roast
(5 pounds)

Salt and freshly
ground black
pepper, to taste

4 tablespoons
all-purpose flour

2 tablespoons
vegetable oil

2 large onions,
coarsely chopped

4 cups beef stock

2 large carrots,
peeled and cut
diagonally into
1-inch rounds

2 large potatoes,
peeled and cubed

2 teaspoons salt

PREP TIME: 15 minutes • **COOK TIME:** 2 1/2 hours • **SERVES:** 6

1 Preheat the oven to 350°F. Salt and pepper the roast, and pat half of the flour over the outside. Place a large, ovenproof Dutch oven over medium heat, and heat the oil until it shimmers. Add the beef, and sear it all over until golden brown. (If you don't have a covered pot that can go from stovetop to oven, sear the beef in a frying pan then place it in a deep, covered casserole dish.)

2 Remove the beef from the pot and cook the onions in the oil for about 5 minutes, until lightly browned and softened. Add the remaining flour to the pan and stir to cook for 2 minutes, then slowly blend in the stock, scraping up any browned bits from the bottom of the pan.

3 Return the beef to the pan and add the carrots, potatoes, and the 2 teaspoons salt, and a liberal amount of pepper, to taste. Cover with a tight-fitting lid and place in the oven for 2 to 2 1/2 hours, stirring every hour or so, until the meat is tender and the vegetables are falling apart. Add more stock or water if needed to keep it from getting dry. The flour and potato will make the brown gravy become thick. Add more salt and pepper, if needed, and serve.

VARIATION

To stretch this dish, either buy a larger piece of meat to start—or increase the vegetables. Add an additional carrot and potato, 2 chopped celery stalks, 4 small peeled and diced turnips, 8 ounces of sliced mushrooms, and a can of whole tomatoes (with juice), using kitchen shears to halve the tomatoes in the pot.

TOP SECRET

When you brown the meat, take your time, and don't move the beef around. Place it on one side and sear for 3 to 5 minutes, then turn and repeat for maximum flavor.

Beef Stroganoff

It's an oldie but a goodie, this mixture of beef strips in a mushroom and sour cream sauce. Serve with hot egg noodles tossed with butter, and a green vegetable such as peas or spinach.

2 tablespoons vegetable oil

1 1/2 pounds beef tenderloin, trimmed into strips

1 large yellow onion, thinly sliced

1 clove garlic, minced

2 tablespoons unsalted butter

8 ounces mushrooms (about 2 cups), thinly sliced

1 tablespoon tomato paste

1 tablespoon all-purpose flour

1 cup beef stock

Salt and pepper, to taste

1/2 cup sour cream

PREP TIME: 10 minutes • **COOK TIME:** 20 minutes • **SERVES:** 6

1 In a heavy cast-iron skillet over medium-high heat, heat the oil until it shimmers, then cook the beef in two batches until browned, about 1 minute per side. Remove the beef to a bowl and add the onions and garlic to the pan. Cook until softened and lightly browned and remove to the bowl with the beef. Do not wipe the pan out.

2 Melt the butter in the hot pan and cook the mushrooms for about 10 minutes, or until golden brown. Blend in the tomato paste and sprinkle the flour over all. Stir to combine, then slowly blend in the stock, stirring constantly to prevent lumps from forming.

3 Return the beef and onions to the pan and cook for about 5 minutes (add a bit more stock if you like a saucier dish). Taste and season with salt and pepper, if needed. Blend in the sour cream, heat through for 1 to 2 minutes, and serve.

VARIATION

Hamburger Stroganoff

Replace the beef tenderloin with lean ground sirloin. Just spoon off any excess fat that collects, push the meat to one side, and add the onions and garlic to the pan. Cook until softened, then push over the onions and cook the mushrooms until lightly browned.

TOP SECRET

Why cook with oil *and* butter when both are fats? Cooking oil can withstand higher temperatures while butter cooks at a lower temperature but adds much more flavor to a dish and helps aromatics such as mushrooms and onions cook to a golden brown finish. If you want to get the benefits of both, combine 1 tablespoon cooking oil with 1 tablespoon butter.

Simply Succulent Steak

Sometimes, a simple, perfectly seasoned steak is all you want. And there are as many ways to cook it as there are cuts of steak. The grill is great, but if the weather is bad or you just don't have a grill, the next best thing is a cast-iron pan. Make sure the steak is at room temperature when you cook it, and if you're cooking this without benefit of a stove hood, open your windows because it will smoke.

2 boneless ribeye steaks, approximately 1 inch thick

Salt and pepper, to taste

Lemon wedges (optional)

PREP TIME: 3 minutes • **COOK TIME:** 9 minutes • **SERVES:** 4

1 Place a large dry cast-iron skillet over medium-high heat. Lightly sprinkle the steaks on both sides with salt and pepper.

2 Carefully put the steaks in the pan, and do not move them: Don't flip them, touch them, or poke them. After 5 minutes, the steaks should release from the bottom of the pan. Carefully turn them, and continue to cook for another 4 minutes, for medium-rare. Remove to a platter, loosely tent with foil, and let rest for 8 minutes.

3 To serve, slice against the grain and drizzle with a squeeze of fresh lemon juice.

TOP SECRET

When cooking at a high heat, it is always preferable to use an oil that has a high "smoking point." Why? The lower the smoking point, the more quickly the oil will blacken and burn (and you'll have to start the recipe all over again, assuming you haven't thrown out the pot). The top two high-smoking-point oils commonly used are vegetable oil and canola oil, although peanut and grapeseed oil also work well. Olive oil, while it's great for quick sautéing and medium-heat searing, doesn't hold up to high heat well at all.

Beef Fajitas

Fajitas are super-speedy if you have store-bought salsa and ready-grated cheese. All the busy cook has to do is sear the meat and vegetables while someone else preps the toppings. Then plunk everything on the table and let everyone assemble their own fajitas.

2 tablespoons vegetable oil

1 pound round steak, sliced into thin strips

1 large yellow onion, sliced into thin strips

1 large green bell pepper, cored, seeded, and sliced into thin strips

1 large red bell pepper, cored, seeded, and sliced into thin strips

1 1/2 teaspoons ground cumin

2 limes

Salt and pepper, to taste

Soft corn tortillas (for serving)

Grated cheddar cheese (for serving)

Chopped lettuce (for serving)

Salsa (for serving)

Sour cream (for serving)

PREP TIME: 10 minutes • **COOK TIME:** 10 minutes • **SERVES:** 4

1 Heat the oil in a skillet over medium-high heat until shimmering. Add the meat to the skillet, and cook for 6 to 8 minutes, or until it is well-browned and cooked through. Remove to a plate, and cook the onions and peppers with the cumin for 6 to 8 minutes, or until the vegetables are softened and lightly browned in spots.

2 Return the beef to the pan to heat through and pour the juice of 1 lime over all, tossing to combine. Sprinkle with salt and pepper, if needed.

3 Serve immediately with tortillas and toppings.

VARIATION
Chicken Fajitas
Replace the beef with 3 boneless, skinless chicken breasts and add 1 diced tomato when you return the browned chicken to the pan with the peppers and onions.

TOP SECRET
Are your tortillas stiff as a board? Completely wet a clean dish towel under the kitchen tap and squeeze out any excess water. Wrap the damp towel around a stack of about 12 tortillas. Place directly on the turntable of the microwave and heat on high for 2 to 3 minutes, until the package is steaming.

Pork Schnitzel

This less-expensive play on traditional Weiner schnitzel (made with veal) is quick and easy, and once you master it, it will become a regular in your recipe repertoire. Apply the same technique to fish or chicken, and dinner is just a cutlet or fillet away. Fresh breadcrumbs are best here, but use prepackaged if you're in a rush.

4 boneless, center-cut pork chops, pounded to 1/4-inch thickness

Salt and pepper, to taste

2 eggs

2/3 cup unbleached flour

2 cups unseasoned breadcrumbs

2 tablespoons extra-virgin olive oil

3 tablespoons butter

Lemon wedges

Fresh parsley

PREP TIME: 15 minutes • **COOK TIME:** 20 minutes • **SERVES:** 4

1 Sprinkle each pork chop liberally with salt and pepper. Beat the eggs in a shallow bowl. Spread the flour on one plate and the breadcrumbs on another.

2 Lightly dredge each chop in the flour, then dip it in the egg and lay it in the breadcrumbs, turning so that the crumbs adhere to both sides.

3 Heat the oil and the butter together in a large skillet over medium heat, and cook the breaded chops a few at a time, without crowding the pan. Cook for about 3 minutes on each side, until lightly browned. Remove the finished schnitzel to a platter in a warm oven while you cook the rest of the chops. Serve garnished with the lemons and parsley.

VARIATIONS

Chicken Cutlets
Replace the pork with thin-sliced skinless, boneless chicken breasts, or even chicken tenders (kids love them).

Parmigiana Cutlets
Add 2 tablespoons freshly grated Parmesan cheese to the breadcrumbs.

TOP SECRET

Using the bottom of an 8-inch cast-iron skillet to pound pork, beef, or even chicken is preferable to a mallet, which can tear the meat. Place each piece of meat between 2 sheets of plastic wrap to further avoid tearing.

GOING AGAINST THE GRAIN

It doesn't matter if you're cooking up a pricey steak, a Sunday roast, or a cheaper cut. It doesn't even matter how perfectly you cook it. If you slice meat with the grain, it will either crumble, or it will shred. The key is to slice meat against the grain, every time, and the result will be delicious and hot-knife-through-butter tender. Here's how to do it:

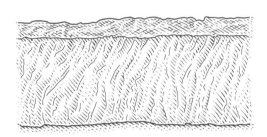

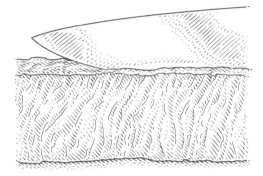

1 When the meat comes out of the pan, look at it closely. The surface grain won't be consistent, but it will have a general direction to it.

2 With a very sharp slicing knife, slice literally across the grain. Arrange the slices on a platter, and let the juices continue to settle before serving.

Spectacular Saltimbocca

The name of this famous Italian recipe literally translates to "jump in the mouth," and it does sort of make you want to hop around with joy at its happy melding of veal, ham, sage, and butter cooked in lightly sweet wine. Use prosciutto or Parma ham, if you can, or thin slices of plain cooked ham. If you don't have Marsala or dry sherry, use a white wine.

4 veal cutlets, pounded thin

Salt and pepper, to taste

4 slices of prosciutto or Parma ham, or plain cooked ham, sliced thin

4 whole fresh sage leaves

2 tablespoons extra-virgin olive oil

1 tablespoon unsalted butter

3/4 cup dry Marsala or dry sherry

Juice of 1/2 a lemon

PREP TIME: 15 minutes • **COOK TIME:** 30 minutes • **SERVES:** 4

1 Sprinkle each veal cutlet with salt and pepper. Lay a slice of ham on each piece of veal and lay 1 sage leaf on the ham. Roll each piece up and secure with a wooden toothpick.

2 Heat the oil and butter in a skillet over medium-high heat and fry the rolls of meat for about 5 minutes altogether, turning regularly, until the outsides are well-browned. Pour in the wine or sherry, bring to a simmer, then lower the heat and cover the pan.

3 Cook for 6 to 8 minutes, until the meat is cooked through. Squeeze the lemon juice over it and serve immediately.

VARIATION

Chicken Saltimbocca

Replace the veal with chicken. Instead of stuffing with ham and sage, try topping each cutlet with a slice of mozzarella and a strip of roasted red pepper and a basil leaf, or a slice of salami and a few fresh rosemary leaves.

LEFTOVER LUXURIES

If you have any rolls of saltimbocca left over, refrigerate overnight. The next day, slice them thinly on the diagonal and use to layer on a sandwich with sliced provolone, fresh tomatoes, lettuce, roasted red pepper, and a little sliced onion. Drizzle with a tangy vinaigrette for the best "Italian" sub you've ever had!

TOP SECRET

In the case of saltimbocca, the only reason for the toothpick is to hold the roll together. If you don't want to roll the veal (or chicken), place the seasoned meat in the pan, top with the sage leaf and then the ham, and don't move the cutlet around; in 1 to 2 minutes, the ham will "melt" into place on cutlet! Magic!

HERE'S THE BEEF

Roast Beef on the Grill

Cooking a whole roast beef on the grill can be a delicate proposition: It can be tough to get the inside moist and perfectly cooked without burning the exterior. An oil-based marinade here adds an extra layer of protection as well as a hint of garlic to the finished roast. For best results when roasting on the grill, make sure the coals aren't too hot, and use a digital instant-read thermometer.

1/2 cup extra-virgin olive oil

3 tablespoons fresh lemon juice

2 cloves garlic, minced

1 teaspoon salt

1/2 teaspoon black pepper

1 top sirloin roast (5 pounds)

PREP TIME: 10 minutes (plus 3 hours marinating) • **COOK TIME:** 40 minutes
SERVES: 6–8

1 Mix the oil, lemon juice, garlic, salt, and pepper in a 1-gallon ziplock plastic bag. Place the roast in the bag, seal it, and turn to coat evenly. Refrigerate and marinate for at least 3 hours, or overnight.

2 Remove the roast from the refrigerator and let it come to room temperature while you prepare a medium-hot fire on a gas or charcoal grill. Take the roast out of the marinade and pat it dry with paper towels.

3 Place the roast on the grill over direct heat and cook, turning frequently, for 10 minutes, or until the outside is crisped and browned (don't leave it unattended at this point). Move the roast over indirect heat, and continue to cook with the lid down for about 30 minutes. The interior should register 130° to 135°F, when tested with a digital instant-read thermometer, for medium-rare, which will make the roast perfectly tender and juicy.

VARIATION
Barbecued Chuck Roast
Substitute a 5-pound piece of chuck roast for the sirloin. Marinate overnight in 2/3 of a bottle of your favorite spicy barbecue sauce, then pat the meat dry and discard any remaining marinade. During the last 10 minutes of grilling, brush the roast with the remaining 1/3 bottle of sauce.

TOP SECRET
If the roast appears to be cooking slowly, resist the urge to crank up the fire. Always use a digital instant-read thermometer, and for the best flavor, remove the roast 5°F below where you want it to be. Let it stand on a platter for 15 minutes, loosely draped with foil, and the internal temperature will continue to rise.

Spicy Asian-Style Grilled Beef Ribs

Sometimes called Texas ribs, beef back ribs are a 7-boned slab that comes from the same area as prime rib. In dealing with such a big slab, it helps to precook the ribs, then finish them up by grilling for 20 minutes, mopping with sauce for the last 10 minutes. Your main concern is a long slow precooking to get the meat tender.

2 slabs back ribs or Texas ribs, 7 ribs each

2 cups water

1/4 cup soy sauce

1/4 cup olive oil

1 1/2 tablespoons sesame oil

1 tablespoon sherry

1 tablespoon honey

3 teaspoons minced fresh ginger

3 cloves garlic, minced

1 teaspoon red pepper flakes or Chinese red chili sauce

PREP TIME: 10 minutes • **COOK TIME:** 1 hour • **SERVES:** 4–6

1 Preheat the oven to 325°F. With the tip of a sharp paring knife, remove any membrane on the back of the ribs. Put the ribs in a roasting pan and add the water to the bottom of the pan. Seal the pan tightly with foil, then roast for 1 hour.

2 Mix the soy sauce, olive oil, sesame oil, sherry, honey, ginger, garlic, and pepper flakes or chili sauce in a small bowl.

3 When ready to grill, prepare a medium-hot fire on a gas or charcoal grill. Grill for 35 minutes, turning every 10 minutes or so, and mopping frequently with the sauce. To serve, cut the ribs into individual pieces.

VARIATION

Beef Ribs with Redeye Mopping Sauce

This eye-opening mopping sauce doesn't have added sugar so it's far less likely to char on the outside of the beef ribs. Omit all the sauce ingredients and combine, in a small bowl, 1/2 cup strong black coffee with 1/2 cup ketchup, 2 tablespoons Worcestershire sauce, 2 tablespoons apple-cider vinegar, 1 tablespoon molasses, 1 teaspoon Tabasco, 1 teaspoon salt, and 1 teaspoon black pepper. Use this to mop the ribs for the last 20 minutes of cooking.

TOP SECRET

If you prefer to do all the cooking on the grill, it's crucial to keep the meat from burning while you slow-cook to tenderize. The easiest way is to wrap the ribs in foil, ideally after first rubbing them with a spice rub (try 1 tablespoon paprika, 1 tablespoon dried oregano, 1 tablespoon sugar, 2 teaspoons salt, and 1 teaspoon cayenne). Place them over medium coals for about 1 hour, turning the foil package now and then, until the ribs are tender. Unwrap the meat and cook directly over the coals for another 20 minutes, mopping with a sauce for the last 10 minutes, until the outside is browned and crisped.

Super Stuffed Cheeseburgers

A piece of cheese melted on top of a burger is good, but a piece of cheese melted *inside* is something else entirely. It's a little bit of effort for a lot of return, resulting in a super moist burger that's permeated with flavor. For the best burgers, buy ground round, which is relatively lean and very tasty.

2 pounds
ground round

1 small onion,
minced

1 tablespoon
Worcestershire
sauce

1 tablespoon
Dijon mustard

1 tablespoon fresh
parsley, minced

6 thin slices
cheddar cheese
(about 6 ounces)

PREP TIME: 15 minutes • **COOK TIME:** 15 minutes • **SERVES:** 6

1 Place the meat in a large bowl and use your hands to mix in the onions, Worcestershire sauce, mustard, and parsley. Mix just until combined.

2 Form 12 thin patties from the meat mixture. Top 6 of them with a slice of cheese, then cover each with another patty. Pinch the edges all around to make sure they are well-sealed.

3 Prepare a medium fire on a gas or charcoal grill.

4 Lay the burgers on the grill and cook for 5 to 7 minutes on each side, or until browned. These will take a little longer to grill than normal burgers, and you need to give them time to cook through, so watch carefully to make sure they don't burn. You want them to be hot all the way through; if the cheese is oozing out and the burgers are brown, remove and serve.

VARIATIONS

British Burger

Start with ground round and mix with 1 small minced onion and 2 tablespoons A-1 Steak Sauce. Stuff each with 1 1/2 tablespoons of crumbled Stilton blue cheese.

Greek Burger

Start with the ground round and mix with 2 teaspoons dried oregano. Stuff each burger with 1 1/2 tablespoons crumbled feta cheese mixed with pitted, chopped Kalamata olives.

TOP SECRET

Contrary to popular belief, the best way to make a tasty, tender, juicy burger is to *not* pack it firm, and to *not* flatten it out once it's on the grill or in the pan. When you form burgers, make sure your hands are cold; form them so that they just hold together. Any tighter, and you'll have a hockey puck.

Beer-Basted London Broil

London broil is a relatively cheap cut, cooks quickly, and is sublime when cooked properly. It needs to be medium-rare for the best flavor—overcooked, it's almost inedibly chewy.

1 teaspoon salt

1 teaspoon freshly ground black pepper

3- to 4-pound slab of London broil

2 cloves garlic, minced

3 tablespoons olive oil

Juice of 1 lemon

1 bottle of malty beer (try Samuel Adams Boston Ale or Newcastle Brown Ale)

PREP TIME: 5 minutes • **COOK TIME:** 16 minutes • **SERVES:** 6

1 Sprinkle the salt and pepper over the meat and pat it in. In a large ziplock plastic bag, combine the garlic, oil, lemon, and beer. Put in the meat, seal the bag, and turn to coat the meat evenly. Refrigerate for about 1/2 hour.

2 Prepare a medium-hot fire on a gas or charcoal grill. When you're ready to grill, remove the steak from the bag and discard the remaining marinade. Lay the steak on the grill and cook for 6 to 8 minutes on each side. Remove to a warmed serving platter, loosely drape it with foil, and allow the meat to rest for 10 minutes.

3 Using a carving knife, slice diagonally across the shorter end. Serve immediately.

VARIATION

London Broil with Curry Mayonnaise

Skip the marinade and simply rub the London broil with oil and salt. Serve with a sauce made of 1 cup mayonnaise blended with 2 tablespoons fresh lemon juice, 1 minced clove garlic, and 1 1/2 teaspoons curry powder or paste.

DID YOU KNOW?

It's vital to cut London broil against the grain because the meat is quite fibrous otherwise. Slice diagonally, at a sharp angle, across the shorter end, which will give you tender slices that are also wider than if you just cut straight through.

TOP SECRET

For the best result, uncover the meat the night before you cook it and let it air-dry overnight in the fridge. Then rub with a little cooking oil and season well with salt. The result will be a caramelized crisp outer crust and a meltingly juicy interior.

Roast Pork with Crackling

Crackling is what pork skin is called when it has been roasted into delectable crispness. It's a celebratory kind of dish native both to the American South and to Italy—made all the more special because you have to work to find pork with the skin on at most American supermarkets. If you can't find pork with the skin on, just use a roast well-padded in fat.

1 pork loin roast (5 pounds), with a good layer of fat and the skin on

Salt and freshly ground black pepper

1 bunch fresh sage leaves, minced

PREP TIME: 5 minutes • **COOK TIME:** 2 hours • **SERVES:** 6

1 Preheat the oven to 400°F. With a very sharp knife, score the skin all the way around, to make carving easier and to let the fat run. Season the pork well with salt and pepper and rub the sage all over the outside. Lay it on a rack in a roasting pan, skin-side up.

2 Place in the oven and roast for 30 minutes, then reduce the heat to 350°F and roast for another 1 1/2 hours. Pork loin should be cooked for about 25 minutes per pound, give or take a few minutes, depending on whether the roast is long and thin or short and fat. After the first 30 minutes, open the oven and baste the roast with the pan juices. Repeat every 15 to 20 minutes during the cooking time.

3 The internal temperature should be about 145°F on an instant-read thermometer. The juices should run clear and not be rosy. When the roast is finished, let it rest, loosely covered in foil, for about 15 minutes before serving.

4 Slice about 1/4 inch thick, and serve some crackling with each portion.

VARIATION
Pork Roast with Rosemary and Garlic

Make several slits in the pork with a sharp knife, and insert slivers of garlic in the slits. Lay branches of rosemary in the bottom of the roasting pan and put the roast directly on top of them. Drizzle the whole roast with olive oil and sprinkle with salt and pepper before roasting.

TOP SECRET

Gone are the days when pork had to be cooked to gun-metal gray in order to kill *Trichinosis*. Remove the roast from the grill or oven when it registers 145°F, and let it rest, undisturbed. Its internal temperature will continue to rise, its juices will settle, and the result will be scrumptious and not, well, *gray*.

Pork Chops with Apples and White Wine

Pork that's not overcooked is delicate and moist. Add some apples and white wine, and you have quite a gourmet dinner. You can use a tart apple such as Granny Smith or a sweeter one such as Golden Delicious—whatever is in your fruit bowl will work.

4 pork chops, 3/4 inch thick

Salt and pepper, to taste

2 tablespoons butter

3 apples, peeled, cored, and thinly sliced

1/2 cup white wine

PREP TIME: 5 minutes • **COOK TIME:** 15 minutes • **SERVES:** 4

1 Season the chops with salt and pepper. Melt the butter in a skillet over medium-high heat. Add the chops and cook for 3 to 4 minutes, without turning, until browned on one side.

2 Turn the chops and add the apples to the pan. Cover and cook for 7 to 8 minutes, or until the chops are cooked through and the apples are softened. Remove the meat to a serving platter, leaving the apples.

3 Turn the heat to high and pour the wine over the apples and deglaze the pan. Bring to a boil over high heat and cook several minutes until the liquid is slightly reduced. Season with salt and pepper, if needed. Pour over the chops and serve immediately.

VARIATION

Breaded Pork Chops with Applesauce

Dip each pork chop in 1 egg beaten in a shallow bowl with 2 tablespoons milk. Mix 2 cups fine breadcrumbs with 1/3 cup Parmesan cheese and a sprinkle of salt and pepper in another shallow bowl. Dip the pork chops in the breadcrumbs, then cook in several tablespoons of oil in a skillet over medium heat, for about 6 minutes per side, or until cooked through. Cook 3 thinly sliced apples in 2 tablespoons butter until tender, and season with 1 tablespoon honey and 1 teaspoon cinnamon. Add to the pork chops and serve.

TOP SECRET

Fresh out of white wine for cooking? No matter—this recipe just needs a bit of tartness to complement the flavor and bring out the natural sweetness of the pork. In place of wine, substitute 1/2 cup apple juice plus 3 tablespoons apple-cider vinegar.

Pork Medallions in Beer and Mustard

The tangy mustard and beer sauce enriched with cream make this dish substantial and hearty for something that cooks so quickly. If you make mashed potatoes, you'll have a warming dish indeed for a cold night, but it's just as good served with noodles or rice.

1 1/2 pounds pork tenderloin

Flour

Salt and pepper, to taste

2–3 tablespoons olive oil

1 cup full-bodied beer

2 tablespoons Dijon mustard

1/2 teaspoon dried thyme

1/4 cup light cream

PREP TIME: 8 minutes • **COOK TIME:** 22 minutes • **SERVES:** 6

1 Slice the tenderloin on the diagonal into 1/2-inch rounds (these are called medallions). Dust generously with flour and sprinkle with salt and pepper.

2 Heat the oil in a large nonstick skillet over high heat and quickly sauté all the medallions for 6 to 8 minutes, turning, until well-browned.

3 Pour in the beer, then blend in the mustard and add the thyme. Reduce the heat and simmer for 8 to 10 minutes.

4 Add the cream and generously season with salt and lots of black pepper. Simmer another 5 minutes and serve.

VARIATION

Pork Medallions with Dried Cherries and Port

After browning the pork medallions, lift them onto a plate. Pour into the hot pan 1/2 cup port wine, 1/2 cup chicken stock, 1/2 cup dried cherries, and 1 teaspoon chopped fresh thyme leaves. Bring to a boil and simmer gently for 2 to 3 minutes, scraping up any browned bits from the bottom of the pan. Add 1/4 cup heavy cream and heat until bubbling. Return the pork to the pan to heat through and serve at once.

TOP SECRET

Mustard is the secret weapon of many a chef's sauce. In large quantities, it provides the familiar zing and bite of mustard—but in small quantities, it adds lift and zing without an overt mustard flavor, serving more as the wine or vinegar or lemon juice of a sauce, a sharp counterpoint that brings the other flavors into sharp relief. It also helps emulsify a sauce or dressing, bringing the ingredients together in a creamy richness. That's why a teaspoon of Dijon mustard is a chef's standard issue when making vinaigrette.

GIVE IT A POKE TO SEE IF IT'S COOKED

There's a lot of fancy-schmancy cookware and gadgetry out there meant to streamline the cooking process, and one of the best—and most useful—tools to own is a digital instant-read thermometer. Insert this doohickey into cooking chicken or meat, and you have a foolproof way to determine whether or not you should remove dinner from the oven *before* it's overcooked. But what if you don't have a thermometer? Try the next best thing: your index finger.

The poke test is not just for professional chefs; in fact, it's a very easy way to see whether or not meat is cooked, and it's easier than it sounds. Just make sure your hands are clean, and neither cold nor hot.

1 Remove the cooked steak to a platter.

2 Wait 1 minute.

3 Poke it gently with the soft part of your index finger.

- If the meat feels "loose" and soft, and you can poke deeply into it, it's very rare.

- If there is some resistance and the depression you make remains when you remove your finger, it's rare to medium-rare.

- If there is less resistance and no depression remains, it's medium-rare to medium.

- If there is no resistance, it's well done (or you've probably overcooked it!)

4 Once you've determined that the steak is cooked to your liking, drape the platter with foil and let the meat rest for another 8 minutes before slicing.

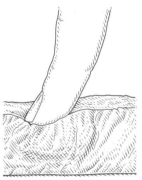

Asian Grilled Pork Chops

You could call this flavor teriyaki, but this marinade has so much more going on: sweet, spicy, gingery, garlicky. People lick their fingers and fight for the scraps. The marinade is based on a classic Chinese recipe and works beautifully on the grill. Be sure to use thin-cut pork chops and be careful not to overcook or burn them.

3 cloves garlic, minced

1/4 cup dark soy sauce

1/4 cup Worcestershire sauce

3 tablespoons ketchup

3 tablespoons apple-cider vinegar

1 tablespoon grated fresh ginger

1 tablespoon honey

2 teaspoons cornstarch

2 teaspoons sugar

1/2 teaspoon red pepper flakes

8 pork chops, cut 1/2 inch thick

Fresh cilantro (for serving)

PREP TIME: 5 minutes (plus 30 minutes marinating) • **COOK TIME:** 8 minutes
SERVES: 4

1 Add the garlic, soy sauce, Worcestershire sauce, ketchup, vinegar, ginger, honey, cornstarch, sugar, and pepper flakes in a ziplock bag. Add the pork chops to the bag, turning to coat them evenly. Marinate for 1/2 hour.

2 Prepare a medium-hot fire on a gas or charcoal grill. Lift the chops from the marinade and let any excess drip off (reserving the marinade), then lay them on the grill over direct heat. Grill for 3 to 4 minutes on each side. Remove the meat to a platter and cover with foil to keep warm.

3 Pour the reserved marinade into a small saucepan and heat to boiling. Pour it over the cooked chops and sprinkle the platter generously with chopped cilantro. Serve immediately.

VARIATION

Asian Grilled Shrimp

Instead of pork, marinate 1 1/2 pounds large shrimp in their shells for 30 minutes, then grill for 2 to 3 minutes per side until pink and opaque. As soon as they have lost all translucency, whisk them off the heat. When grilling shrimp over direct heat, either gas or charcoal, it helps to put them on skewers for easier handling.

DID YOU KNOW?

It's not just because your better half is being difficult: Recent studies show that a full 50% of the American population cannot tolerate cilantro because they don't have a key enzyme. If you're missing that enzyme, cilantro will taste like soap. What to do? Replace the cilantro with minced basil.

TOP SECRET

Light and dark soy sauce don't actually refer to their respective sodium counts. Dark soy sauce contains molasses, which gives it a richer, more full-bodied flavor, and light soy sauce is literally thinner, making it perfect for use as a condiment. If you want to turn your light soy sauce dark, add 1 teaspoon blackstrap molasses to 1/2 cup soy sauce in a cup and whisk well. Store in the refrigerator.

Pork Souvlaki with Tzatziki

Meaty cubes of pork are marinated in a potent sauce, then threaded onto skewers and quickly sizzled over a hot fire to leave the edges browned and crispy. Serve these cubes in a split pita with the yogurt-cucumber garlic sauce known as tzatziki. The finished dish leaves you in a happy haze of garlic.

SOUVLAKI
1/2 cup extra-virgin olive oil

1/4 cup fresh lemon juice

4 cloves garlic, finely chopped

1 1/2 teaspoons dried whole oregano

1 teaspoon salt

1/2 teaspoon pepper

2 1/2 pounds boneless pork shoulder, cut into 1-inch cubes

6 pita breads

TZATZIKI
2 cups plain Greek yogurt

Juice of 1 lemon

1 large cucumber, peeled, seeded and chopped

1 clove garlic, minced

1 teaspoon salt

Freshly ground black pepper

1/4 cup extra-virgin olive oil

PREP TIME: 5 minutes (plus 30 minutes marinating) • **COOK TIME:** 12 minutes
SERVES: 6

1 *For the souvlaki:* Mix the oil, lemon juice, garlic, oregano, salt, and pepper in a ziplock bag, then add the pork pieces. Seal the bag and turn to coat the pork evenly. Leave in the refrigerator for at least an hour, or overnight.

2 Prepare a medium-hot fire on a gas or charcoal grill. Thread the pork pieces onto 6 metal skewers and lay the skewers on the grill directly over the flame. Cook about 5 minutes per side, turning once, until browned with crisp edges.

3 Brush the pitas lightly with olive oil on each side and lay them on the hot grill over direct heat for about a minute on each side, taking care that they do not burn. Remove and cut each in half (there are 2 halves for each skewer).

4 *For the tzatziki:* Combine the yogurt, lemon juice, cucumbers, garlic, salt, and pepper in a blender. Process at a low speed, slowly pouring in the olive oil. Don't process into a smooth puree, but leave it a little chunky. Serve immediately with the souvlaki.

VARIATION
Chicken Souvlaki
Replace the pork with 6 boneless, skinless chicken breasts cut into 1 1/2-inch chunks. Do not marinate longer than about an hour.

TOP SECRET
If you can't find Greek yogurt where you live, make your own, using this trick: Line a small colander with a layer of cheesecloth. Add plain yogurt and let it drip through for at least 1 hour. What's left will be thick, rich, and perfect to turn into tzatziki.

Braised Lamb Shanks

Lamb shanks, usually sold from the front legs, were once "throw-away" cuts. They are packed with flavor and they're an especially delicious part of the lamb, but they always require long and slow cooking to make them tender and succulent. Don't scrimp on browning the shanks well first at a high heat.

3 tablespoons extra-virgin olive oil

6 lamb shanks

Salt and freshly ground black pepper, to taste

Flour

3 medium onions, chopped

6 cloves garlic, minced

2 cups dry red wine

3 cups water

1 can (6 ounces) tomato paste

1 teaspoon red pepper flakes

1 teaspoon ground cumin

1 teaspoon ground paprika

1 teaspoon ground ginger

1/4 teaspoon ground cinnamon

1 teaspoon salt

1/2 teaspoon pepper

Juice of 1 lemon

Rice or pilaf (for serving)

PREP TIME: 10 minutes • **COOK TIME:** 2 hours • **SERVES:** 6

1 Heat the oil in a large stew pot or Dutch oven over medium-high heat. Season the shanks well with salt and pepper, then dust them with flour and brown them on all sides in the hot oil, turning frequently, 5 to 7 minutes.

2 Lower the heat to medium, add the onions and garlic, and cook for 5 to 8 minutes, or until the onions are softened and lightly browned.

3 Add the wine, water, tomato paste, pepper flakes, cumin, paprika, ginger, cinnamon, the 1 teaspoon salt, and the 1/2 teaspoon pepper. Stir well to combine. Increase the heat and bring to a boil, then reduce to medium-low, cover loosely, and simmer for 1 1/2 to 2 hours, until the meat is falling off the bone. Add more water or wine during cooking if the liquid boils off too quickly.

4 Stir in lemon juice, adjust seasonings, if needed, and serve with rice or pilaf.

VARIATION

Braised Beef Short Ribs

Swap in meaty beef short ribs for the lamb shanks and omit the cumin, cinnamon, and ginger, adding in 1 teaspoon grated orange zest instead.

TOP SECRET

Chefs often recommend cooking stews the day before to let the flavors meld, but short ribs and shanks are often cooked the day before for another, more pressing reason—it cooks out the copious fat that can be found in these cuts, and then you can skim it off the top the next day before serving. Put the whole pot in the refrigerator, if you have room, then scrape off and discard the congealed fat before reheating the next day.

Hearty Stuffed Meat Loaf

Hard to believe, but this delicious stuffed meat loaf takes only 15 minutes to put together. It's meat and potatoes—all in one dish!

1 cup soft breadcrumbs

1/2 cup beef broth

1 egg, beaten

4 teaspoons dried minced onion

1 teaspoon salt

1/4 teaspoon Italian seasoning

1/4 teaspoon freshly ground black pepper

1 1/2 pounds ground beef

4 cups frozen shredded hash browns, thawed

1/3 cup grated Parmesan cheese

1/4 cup minced fresh parsley

1 teaspoon onion salt

PREP TIME: 15 minutes • **COOK TIME:** 50 minutes • **SERVES:** 8

1 Preheat the oven to 375°F.

2 Combine the breadcrumbs, broth, egg, minced onion, salt, Italian seasoning, and pepper in a large bowl. Let stand for 2 minutes.

3 Add the beef and mix well. On a piece of wax paper, pat the meat mixture into a 10-inch square.

4 Combine the hash browns, Parmesan, parsley, and onion salt in a large bowl. Spoon over the meat. Roll up, jelly roll–style, removing the wax paper as you roll. Pinch the edges and ends to seal. Place, seam-side down, in an ungreased shallow baking pan. Bake about 40 minutes, or until the meat is no longer pink.

VARIATION

Meat Loaf Tuscana

Give the meat loaf more flavor by using a mixture of ground beef, ground pork, and ground veal. Some markets sell this ready-made combination as "meat loaf mix".

TOP SECRET

It doesn't matter if you're making meatballs or meat loaf...a sure way to add not only flavor but also moisture (very important) is by including thawed frozen hash browns. You'll get an instant savory, well-rounded flavor and a supermoist and light texture.

Asian Marinated Pork Strips

This easy-to-make, lip-smackingly delicious dish comes together in less than 1/2 hour, making it ideal for weeknight suppers. Better still, the finished product freezes brilliantly for up to 3 months.

5 tablespoons soy sauce

1/4 cup ketchup

3 tablespoons vinegar

3 tablespoons chili sauce

3 tablespoons sugar

2 teaspoons salt

1/8 teaspoon freshly ground black pepper

3 cloves garlic, minced

2 cans (12 ounces each) lemon-lime soda

2 pork tenderloins (about 2 pounds), cut lengthwise into 1/2-inch strips

PREP TIME: 10 minutes • **COOK TIME:** 15 minutes • **SERVES:** 6

1 In a large ziplock bag or shallow glass container, combine the soy sauce, ketchup, vinegar, chili sauce, sugar, salt, pepper, garlic, and soda.

2 Add the pork and turn to coat. Seal the bag or cover the container and refrigerate for at least 4 hours, or overnight.

3 Preheat a grill to medium-high. Drain and discard the marinade. Thread the pork onto metal or soaked bamboo skewers. Grill for about 12 minutes, until browned and the juices run clear.

VARIATION

Spicy Peanut Pork Kebabs

Serve these pork skewers with a spicy peanut dip made by whisking together 3/4 cup chicken broth, 1/2 cup peanut butter, 2 tablespoons teriyaki sauce or soy sauce, 1 teaspoon toasted sesame oil, and 1 1/2 teaspoons hot-pepper sauce.

LEFTOVER LUXURIES

Sauté 1 cup leftover white rice in 1 tablespoon vegetable oil, add 1/2 cup diced leftover pork, 2 diced green onions, and 2 tablespoons soy sauce. Serve immediately.

TOP SECRET

Top chefs know the secret to succulent flavor when it comes to pork, some beef dishes, and ham: soda! In this case, lemon-lime soda creates a flavorful marinade with just the right touch of citrus, plus sugar for caramelization. Cola does the exact same thing when brushed onto ham.

HERE'S THE BEEF

Short-Rib Soup

This soup has it all—aromatic broth, tender beef, and flavorful barley and vegetables.

2 cups frozen lima beans, thawed

2 cups cut green beans, thawed

4 cups water

2 pounds beef short ribs

1 can (14 ounces) diced tomatoes (with juice)

1 cup coarsely chopped carrots

3/4 cup chopped onion

1/3 cup medium pearled barley

1 tablespoon salt

1 tablespoon sugar

1/2 teaspoon dried basil

1 bay leaf

PREP TIME: 10 minutes • **COOK TIME:** 2 1/2 hours • **SERVES:** 6–8

1 Drain the lima beans and green beans, catching the drained liquid in a Dutch oven or soup pot, and set aside.

2 Add the water, beef, tomatoes (with juice), carrots, onions, barley, salt, sugar, basil, and bay leaf to the pot. Bring to a boil, then reduce the heat and simmer, covered, for about 2 hours, or until the beef is tender.

3 Remove the beef from the pot. When it's cool enough to handle, remove the meat from the bones, cut into bite-size pieces, and return it to the pot. Add the beans and cook for about 10 minutes, until heated through. Remove the bay leaf before serving.

VARIATION

Garden Fresh Short-Rib Stew

Replace the canned beans with fresh ones, and the tomatoes with 1 fresh large tomato, chopped.

LEFTOVER LUXURIES

Press a store-bought pie crust into the bottom of a casserole or baking dish (depending on how much soup you have left over), also pressing the dough up the sides of the dish. Ladle in the soup three-quarters of the way full, and cover with a second pie crust. Trim, place on a cookie sheet, and bake at 350°F until golden.

TOP SECRET

In the dead of winter (when you'd likely make this dish), don't fret about not having good-quality vegetables: In fact, frozen veggies can be some of the best quality you'll find, anywhere. It's always better to use fresh, but every chef knows that the secret to delicious fresh vegetables out of season is to use frozen ones, which are preferable to canned.

Burgundy Beef Stew

This slow-cooked stew is a tantalizing amalgam of rich, warming flavors—perfect for a midwinter dinner party.

1 tablespoon canola oil

12 ounces eye round of beef, trimmed and cut into 1/2-inch chunks

3 bacon slices, coarsely chopped

1 1/2 cups frozen pearl onions, thawed

3 carrots, thinly sliced

4 cloves garlic, slivered

1 tablespoon sugar

12 ounces mushrooms, quartered

2 tablespoons all-purpose flour

1/2 cup dry red wine or chicken stock

3/4 cup water

3/4 teaspoon dried thyme

3/4 teaspoon salt

1/2 teaspoon black pepper

PREP TIME: 20 minutes • **COOK TIME:** 1 1/2 hours • **SERVES:** 4

1 Preheat the oven to 350°F. Heat the oil in a medium ovenproof Dutch oven over medium high heat until shimmering. Add the beef and cook for about 5 minutes, until browned. Using a slotted spoon, transfer the meat to a plate.

2 Add the bacon, onions, carrots, and garlic to the pot. Sprinkle with the sugar and cook for about 7 minutes, until the onions are golden. Add the mushrooms and cook for about 4 minutes, until tender.

3 Return the beef and any juices to the pot. Sprinkle with the flour and cook, stirring, for about 3 minutes, until the flour is absorbed.

4 Add the wine or stock and bring to boil. Add the water, thyme, salt, and pepper and return to a boil. Cover and bake for about 1 hour, until the meat is tender.

VARIATION

Coq au Vin Rouge

Replace the beef with a chicken cut up into 6 pieces and proceed with the recipe, omitting the water.

LEFTOVER LUXURIES

This recipe freezes well, so store whatever you have left over in a heavy-duty ziplock bag, and freeze for up to 4 months. Reheat slowly, over low heat (and not in the microwave, which will just toughen the meat).

TOP SECRET

The trick to getting perfectly brown, gooey, caramelized onions every time is a simple one: Add sugar. The one caveat is that you can not leave the stove after you've added it because sugar burns quickly. Sprinkle it in, keep an eye on it, and the minute the onions turn the color of perfectly toasted bread, continue with the recipe.

Pot-au-Feu

This classic French country dish is not only mouthwatering and delicious but it's also relatively low in fat.

4 medium leeks

6 flat-leaf parsley sprigs

6 thyme sprigs

1 bay leaf

3 pounds bone-in chicken pieces

1 garlic head, separated into cloves and peeled

1 teaspoon salt

1 teaspoon pepper

5 cans (14 ounces each) low-sodium chicken broth

1 medium head green cabbage (about 2 pounds), cut into 8 wedges

1 pound carrots, peeled and cut into 2-inch pieces

1 pound small red potatoes, scrubbed and halved

1 pound beef tenderloin

PREP TIME: 20 minutes • **COOK TIME:** 1 1/2 hours • **SERVES:** 6–8

1 Cut the roots and dark green tops from the leeks. Cut the white parts in half lengthwise and rinse well, swishing to remove sand. Tie the leek tops, parsley sprigs, thyme, and bay leaf together with cotton kitchen string.

2 In a large soup pot, combine the chicken, tied leeks, the white parts of the leeks, the garlic, 1/2 teaspoon of the salt, and 1/2 teaspoon of the pepper. Pour in the broth and add enough water to cover. Bring to a boil, then reduce the heat and simmer, uncovered, for 30 minutes.

3 Submerge the cabbage, carrots, potatoes, and beef in the broth. Simmer for 30 minutes, or until the beef is done to taste (135° to 140°F for medium-rare).

4 Add the remaining 1/2 teaspoon of salt and the remaining 1/2 teaspoon of pepper. Slice beef thinly and serve in shallow soup bowls with the vegetables.

VARIATION
Chicken-in-the-Pot
Omit the beef and instead, add another pound of skinned bone-in chicken breasts.

DID YOU KNOW?
Pot-au-feu is traditionally served as a multi-course dish; when it's done, the vegetables are removed whole, as are the meats. The soup is then strained, eaten as the first course, and the vegetables and meats are sliced and eaten as the second. Yum!

TOP SECRET
The key to rich taste in this soup is the combination of leek tops, parsley, thyme sprigs, and bay leaf; traditionally, this is called a bouquet garni. Next time you cook leeks, save those woody tops exactly for this purpose! Freeze them, and you'll always have some available.

Baked Beef Stew

Put this stew together, pop it into the oven, and go about your business. It practically cooks itself!

1 cup water

2 pounds lean beef stew meat, cut into 1-inch cubes

1 cup canned tomatoes, cut up

6 carrots, cut into strips

3 medium all-purpose potatoes, peeled and quartered

1/2 cup thickly sliced celery

1 medium onion, sliced and separated into rings

3 tablespoons quick-cooking tapioca

1 slice bread, crumbled

PREP TIME: 10 minutes • **COOK TIME:** 3 1/2 hours • **SERVES:** 6–8

1 Preheat the oven to 325°F. Grease a 3-quart baking dish.

2 In a large bowl, combine the water, beef, tomatoes, carrots, potatoes, celery, onions, tapioca, and bread. Spoon into the baking dish, cover, and bake for 3 1/2 hours.

VARIATION

Brazilian Pork Stew

Replace the beef with pork loin. Add 1 cup chicken stock, 1 can hominy, and the juice from 1 lime.

TOP SECRET

How to thicken a delicious stew? The combination of tapioca and bread does the trick without the addition of flour.

5 LOVE THAT CHICKEN!

Chicken is like a blank palette that the clever cook can paint with any kind of seasoning. There's hardly a meat-eating culture in the world that doesn't eat chicken, so poultry's passport is well-stamped when it comes to yummy flavors. From Chinese stir-fries and simple Indian curries to French coq au vin and the most perfectly scrumptious roasted bird you've ever tasted, if you think you're bored with chicken, you're about to be surprised. Of course, good chicken does take some attention, not to mention a few secret tricks that will put the "wow" back in dinner, every time.

LOVE THAT CHICKEN!

Sublime Herb-Stuffed Roast Chicken

If you think roast chicken needs to be seasoned and basted, tended and fussed over in order to be moist, forget everything you've ever learned, and read on. This roast chicken is cooked fast, hot, and partially upside down, and it may well be the best you've ever tasted. Cast iron is key to getting the heat high enough, and it works for any bird up to 4 1/2 pounds.

Salt and pepper, to taste

1 whole chicken (3–4 1/2 pounds), at room temperature

2 cloves garlic, peeled and thickly sliced

1–2 bunches of fresh tarragon, thyme, or rosemary

1 tablespoon vegetable oil

PREP TIME: 6 minutes • **COOK TIME:** 35 minutes • **SERVES:** 4

1 Preheat the oven to 425°F. Liberally salt and pepper the chicken on top and bottom, and inside the cavity. Insert the garlic between the skin and the breast, distributing it as evenly as you can. Push fresh herbs under the breast skin and in the cavity (the more herbs, the more flavorful the chicken will be).

2 Wipe the inside of a large cast-iron pan with the oil, and set the bird in it, breast-side up. Roast for 20 minutes. Remove the pan from the oven and, using sturdy kitchen tongs, flip the bird over onto its breast. Roast for another 20 minutes. Remove and rotate the chicken so that it is breast-side up again. Roast for 20 minutes longer.

3 Remove the chicken to a serving platter, tent with foil, and let rest for 15 minutes before carving.

VARIATIONS

Asian-Scented Roast Chicken
Instead of herbs, place a small knob of peeled ginger and one star anise in the cavity. Drizzle the bird lightly with sesame oil and a teaspoon of soy sauce.

Lemon-Roasted Chicken
Rub half a cut lemon over the entire chicken, top and bottom. Give the lemon a gentle squeeze and stuff it into the cavity along with the herbs.

TOP SECRET

Ask any French grandmother or any French chef, and they'll tell you that the best way to make a roast chicken is to rotate it so that all parts cook evenly. Using this technique, there's no need to massage the bird with butter (which admittedly makes the bird taste good, but also makes it greasy). All you need is a sturdy pair of spring-action tongs and a thick kitchen glove.

LOVE THAT CHICKEN!

Crispy Ritzy Chicken Breasts

This method for quick-cooking deliciously crispy chicken breasts will become a standby. Eat them alone, with a squeeze of lemon juice or any sauce, or with the fresh tomato sauce in this recipe. But these cutlets don't need a sauce to be an excellent meal. The addition of crushed crackers gives the cooked chicken breasts a crispy bite, but you can use flour alone. It helps them brown and to look more appetizing.

CHICKEN
12 crushed Ritz crackers

2 tablespoons all-purpose flour

Salt and pepper, to taste

Pinch of paprika

4 skinless, boneless chicken breasts

2–3 tablespoons vegetable oil or olive oil

SAUCE
2 medium ripe tomatoes, halved and cored

2 tablespoons fresh lemon juice

1 clove garlic

Salt and pepper, to taste

2–3 tablespoons extra-virgin olive oil

PREP TIME: 10 minutes • **COOK TIME:** 14 minutes • **SERVES:** 4

1 *For the chicken:* Combine the cracker crumbs, flour, salt, pepper, and paprika on a plate, and roll the chicken in it, pressing to coat evenly.

2 Heat the oil in a skillet over medium-high heat. Put the breasts in the pan and cook for 5 to 7 minutes on each side, or until golden brown and cooked through. Remove to a serving plate.

3 *For the sauce:* While the chicken is cooking, squeeze the tomato halves, discarding the excess juice and seeds. Cut the tomatoes into chunks straight into a blender or food processor. Add the lemon juice along with the garlic and a dash of salt and pepper. With the machine running, drizzle in the oil and blend until the sauce is smooth and creamy. Serve on the side with the hot chicken.

VARIATION
Crispy Chicken Breast Salad with Basil Dressing
Whiz a handful of fresh basil leaves into the tomato sauce, along with 2 tablespoons Parmesan cheese and 2 tablespoons plain yogurt. Slice the cooked chicken breasts, hot or cold, on the diagonal and serve on a bed of mixed greens with the dressing drizzled over the top. Top with a sprinkle of chopped toasted walnuts.

LEFTOVER LUXURIES
When you're making chicken breasts for dinner, cook a couple of extra ones and store them in the refrigerator. Slice them on the diagonal during the week to top a salad for dinner or use them on sandwiches.

TOP SECRET
Using Ritz crackers as a chicken coating is an old, favorite Southern standby; the flavor is buttery and incomparably crispy. Place the crackers in a ziplock bag, close it, and roll over it with a rolling pin until the crackers are crushed. You might not ever use breadcrumbs again!

LOVE THAT CHICKEN!

Cashew Chicken

If you think cashew chicken is something you only get in a Chinese restaurant, you'll be surprised at the speed, ease, and wonderful freshness of this fast and elegant stir-fry. Be sure to prepare all the ingredients before cooking; it's a necessity to keep up with the speed of the stir-frying process. Be sure to put the rice on before starting the chicken, or you may find you've gotten too far ahead of yourself.

1 cup chicken stock

2 tablespoons soy sauce

2 teaspoons cornstarch

2 tablespoons vegetable oil

3 boneless, skinless chicken breasts, cut into strips

1 large yellow onion, coarsely chopped

1 small green bell pepper, cored, seeded, and diced

3 cloves garlic, minced

2 tablespoons minced fresh ginger

1/4 teaspoon red pepper flakes

1/2 cup roasted unsalted cashews

White rice, for serving

PREP TIME: 20 minutes • **COOK TIME:** 10 minutes • **SERVES:** 4

1 In a small bowl, stir together the stock, soy sauce, and cornstarch; set aside.

2 Heat a wok over high heat and then add the oil. Stir-fry the chicken for about 5 minutes, until just cooked. Lift into a medium bowl and set aside.

3 In the hot wok, stir-fry the onions, peppers, garlic, ginger, and pepper flakes for 5 minutes, until the peppers are cooked through and the onion is golden brown in spots.

4 Pour the soy sauce mixture over the peppers and onions and simmer for 2 minutes, until thickened and glossy. Return the chicken to the pan with any juices in the bowl and stir in the cashews. Serve immediately over white rice.

VARIATION
Chicken and Broccoli
Leave out the chicken stock when you blend the soy sauce and cornstarch. Omit the bell pepper and cashews and substitute with 1 small head of broccoli trimmed into florets (thick stems peeled and sliced thin). Stir-fry the onions, garlic, and ginger without the broccoli, then add the broccoli and 1 1/2 cups chicken stock and cook for about 4 minutes, or until the broccoli is tender-crisp.

TOP SECRET

Whether you're using a wok or a heavy-duty skillet, first heat the pan dry over high heat for several minutes *before* adding the oil. On a hot surface, the microscopic pores of the metal open. The oil coats them, making the whole pan less inclined to stick. Do *not* try this with a nonstick pan, which can give off dangerous chemical vapors if heated without anything in it.

LOVE THAT CHICKEN!

Old-Fashioned Fried Chicken

Southern fried chicken is shallow-fried. The trick is to cook the meat through to the bone while getting the crust to a rich mahogany color at the same time. The buttermilk marinade is a classic Southern trick to draw blood away from the bones and also to impart a pleasant tangy flavor. You can use milk if you prefer.

1 whole chicken (3 1/2 pounds), cut up into 8 pieces

2 cups buttermilk

2 cups flour

1 tablespoon sweet paprika

1 1/2 teaspoons salt

1 teaspoon ground ginger

1 teaspoon pepper

4 cups vegetable, canola, or peanut oil

PREP TIME: 10 minutes (plus 20 minutes marinating) • **COOK TIME:** 30 minutes
SERVES: 6

1 Put the chicken in a large bowl or ziplock bag and pour the buttermilk over it. Marinate for at least 20 minutes, or up to 2 hours.

2 In another ziplock bag, combine the flour, paprika, salt, ginger, and pepper. Heat the oil over medium-high heat in a large, deep-sided skillet, preferably cast iron.

3 While the oil is heating, lift the chicken pieces from the buttermilk and toss them in the flour until well-coated. Using tongs, carefully place the pieces into the hot oil, crowding them slightly to make them fit (any that don't must wait for the next round of cooking, or you can start a second pan).

4 Cook, turning occasionally, until browned, tender, and cooked through. Larger pieces such as breasts will take up to 30 minutes; smaller pieces such as wings may be done after 20 minutes. The chicken should be a dark brown, not burned, and a digital instant-read thermometer in the breast should read 165°F. Drain on paper towels and serve hot or at room temperature.

VARIATION

Oven-Fried Chicken

Preheat the oven to 375°F. Dry the chicken pieces well with paper towels. Dip in beaten egg, then in 1 1/2 cups breadcrumbs mixed with 1 tablespoon Italian seasoning. Let the breaded chicken rest for 5 minutes while you preheat 3 tablespoons oil in a 9 x 13-inch baking dish in the oven. Lay the chicken in the hot pan and bake for 30 minutes. Turn the pieces and bake an additional 20 to 30 minutes, until crisp, browned, and tender.

> **TOP SECRET**
>
> Never cover frying chicken. The crust will get moist instead of crispy.

Basque-Style Chicken

The sunny-flavored sauce of bell peppers, tomatoes, and garlic simmers while you brown the chicken, which gets a bath in the peppers to finish cooking through to the bone. Serve over white rice.

2 tablespoons extra-virgin olive oil

2 large red bell peppers, cored, seeded, and sliced

2 large green bell peppers, cored, seeded, and sliced

3 medium yellow onions, chopped

3 cloves garlic, thinly sliced

3/4 cup dry white wine

1 can (28 ounces) whole tomatoes (with juice)

1 whole chicken (3 pounds), cut into 10 pieces (breasts halved)

Salt and pepper, to taste

Cayenne or hot paprika, to taste

PREP TIME: 10 minutes • **COOK TIME:** 40 minutes • **SERVES:** 6

1 In a large skillet, heat 1 tablespoon of the oil over medium heat and fry the peppers and onions for 6 to 8 minutes, or until just softened. Add the garlic and cook for 1 minute.

2 Stir in the wine and the tomatoes (with juice), breaking them up into pieces as you go. Cover the pan and simmer on low heat for 20 minutes, or until the vegetables are tender and the sauce thickens.

3 Meanwhile, heat the remaining 1 tablespoon of oil in another skillet over medium-high heat. Season the chicken with salt and pepper and brown in the oil on all sides, turning several times.

4 Season the vegetables with salt and pepper and cayenne or paprika. Add the chicken to the vegetables and simmer over medium heat for another 15 minutes, or until the chicken is cooked through and the sauce is thickened.

VARIATION

Chicken Cacciatore

Leave out the green bell pepper. Dice the red bell peppers instead of slicing them, and substitute red wine for the white. Add 1 1/2 teaspoons whole dried oregano in place of the cayenne or paprika.

TOP SECRET

Here's a secret trick that every chef knows, which will save you the expense of buying crushed tomatoes: Open a can of whole tomatoes, and then use your kitchen shears to scissor them to pieces, while they're still in the can. Voilá! Instant crushed tomatoes, and no mess.

LOVE THAT CHICKEN!

Coq au Vin

The name of this French classic refers to a rooster cooked in wine—the oldest, toughest bird in the coop and one that required long stewing to be tender. Nowadays, a chicken takes center stage, and consequently the dish doesn't have to simmer all day. This Burgundian dish is always made with red wine, despite that long-held injunction "red with meat, white with chicken." Serve with mashed or boiled potatoes.

1 tablespoon vegetable oil

6 slices thick-cut bacon, diced

1 medium yellow onion, diced

1 large carrot, peeled and diced

2 cloves garlic, minced

1 whole chicken (3 1/2 pounds), cut up into 8 pieces

Salt and pepper, to taste

1 bottle dry red wine (about 3 cups)

2 cups water

4 sprigs fresh thyme

2 bay leaves

2 tablespoons unsalted butter

8 ounces button mushrooms, halved (about 2 cups)

12–15 pearl onions (1 pound), peeled

PREP TIME: 15 minutes • **COOK TIME:** 1 1/2 hours • **SERVES:** 6

1. Heat the oil in a large, heavy stew pot until shimmering, and add the bacon. Add the onions, carrots, and garlic and cook for 8 to 10 minutes, until translucent and starting to brown. Remove to a medium bowl, and gently wipe out most of the bacon fat with a paper towel.

2. Season the chicken with salt and pepper and brown on all sides in the stew pot, about 8 minutes altogether.

3. Pour in the wine and water. Add the thyme, bay leaves, and onion mixture. Bring to a boil, then reduce the heat to medium-low. Cover and simmer gently for an hour.

4. Meanwhile, melt the butter in a large skillet over medium heat and cook the mushrooms until the edges brown lightly, about 4 minutes. Add the mushrooms and pearl onions to the stew and cook for another 20 minutes with the lid off, until the sauce is thickened and the vegetables are tender. Remove the thyme stems and bay leaves before serving.

VARIATION

Coq au Vin Blanc

You *can* make a coq au vin with a full-bodied white wine. Try a French Chardonnay, which doesn't have the heavy oaky flavor of most California chardonnays, and use a mixture of wild mushrooms in place of the button mushrooms.

TOP SECRET

The depth of flavor from a good coq au vin comes from the careful browning of the component parts, from the onions and carrots to the chicken pieces. These caramelized natural sugars blended with the wine are what have made the dish a classic, so don't rush that part, or you'll just wind up making boiled chicken. Take your time!

LOVE THAT CHICKEN!

Curried Chicken Thighs with Cucumber Raita

Chicken thighs are dark meat, so they're much moister and more flavorful than breasts, but they typically take longer to cook properly in order for the layers of fat in them to melt. This easy weeknight chicken dish isn't a classic curry, but instead a pleasing curry braise with a light cucumber and yogurt sauce, requiring nothing more than a green salad and some rice.

CHICKEN

6 large boneless, skinless chicken thighs

1/3 cup hot or mild curry paste

2 tablespoons vegetable oil

1 clove garlic, minced

1 teaspoon minced fresh ginger

1 cup chicken stock

RAITA

1 medium cucumber, peeled

1 small red onion

1 fresh jalapeño pepper, seeded

1/2 teaspoon salt

1/4 teaspoon cumin

1/2 cup plain yogurt

1 tablespoon fresh lemon juice

PREP TIME: 8 minutes • **COOK TIME:** 25 minutes • **MAKES:** 6 servings

1 *For the chicken:* Smear the chicken with the curry paste on both sides. Heat the oil in a nonstick skillet over medium-high heat and sauté the chicken for about 5 minutes on each side, until browned.

2 Add the garlic and ginger and cook for 2 minutes, until just pungent, then pour in the stock. Bring to a boil, lower the heat, cover tightly, and simmer gently for 20 minutes, until the chicken is cooked through.

3 *For the raita:* Cut the cucumber and onion into 3 to 4 coarse chunks as you drop them into the food processor. Add the pepper to the processor bowl along with the salt, cumin, yogurt, and lemon juice. Pulse briefly until it becomes coarse and chunky. Do not puree into a mush.

4 Serve the chicken with the raita on the side.

VARIATION

Creamy Curried Chicken Thighs

Cut the chicken thighs into 1 1/2-inch pieces and brown them well along with the garlic and ginger and 1 large thinly sliced onion. When the chicken is browned and the onion soft and golden, about 10 minutes, stir in 1/4 cup curry paste and 2 cups chicken stock. Simmer for 10 minutes to thicken. Instead of making the raita, stir in 1/2 cup plain yogurt and simmer for 1 to 2 minutes longer, or until heated through. Season with salt and pepper and serve over rice.

TOP SECRET

Hot enough for you? If you accidentally bite into a jalapeño, or your curry sauce winds up being too spicy, don't attempt to douse the flame in your mouth with water, because all it will do is make it feel hotter. The best way to extinguish the "fire" is with beer, or anything carbonated, from sparkling cider to soda.

THE CHEATING CHEF AT HOME

CHICKEN CARVING MADE EASY

Simple Steps to Save Time, Money, and Stress

Chefs know the truth: Buying and roasting a whole chicken and then carving it is far less expensive then buying precut parts and roasting them separately. They also know that most birds are constructed the same way, so if you master this simple technique, future Thanksgivings will be far less worrisome when it comes time to carve Tom Turkey. If your recipe requires cut-up chicken parts, buy a whole uncooked one, and follow these steps.

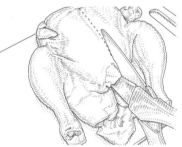

1 Using a sharp carving knife or kitchen shears, cut along the breastbone.

2 Turn the bird over, and cut along the backbone. You now have two halves. Slice the leg and thigh away from one breast half. Repeat on the other side. Then slice the thigh away from the leg, and repeat on the other side. You now have six pieces. Set the legs and thighs aside.

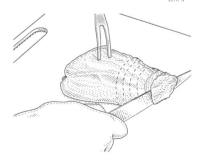

3 Slice each breast half across the grain, widthwise, rather than lengthwise. Trick: If the breast bone gets in the way, use a teaspoon to help nudge the meat off the bone once you've made the slices.

LOVE THAT CHICKEN!

Chicken with Mustard and Cream

The fragrant sauce is perfect for whatever parts of the chicken happen to be on sale—you can make this with thighs, wings, drumsticks, breast pieces (cut each breast in half width-wise for more even cooking) or even a whole cut-up chicken.

8 pieces of chicken, skinned

Salt and pepper, to taste

1 tablespoon unsalted butter

2 tablespoons extra-virgin olive oil

8 ounces white mushrooms (about 2 cups), thinly sliced

1 cup dry white wine

1 teaspoon dried thyme or Herbs de Provence

2 tablespoons Dijon mustard

1/2 cup light cream or half-and-half

PREP TIME: 6 minutes • **COOK TIME:** 35 minutes • **SERVES:** 6

1 Sprinkle the chicken with salt and pepper. Heat the butter and oil together in a heavy skillet over medium-high heat and add the chicken, cooking for 8 to 10 minutes, browning it well on all sides. Remove the chicken to a plate.

2 Add the mushrooms to the pan. Cook for about 5 minutes, or until lightly browned and softened.

3 Put the chicken back in the pan and pour in the wine. Add the thyme or herbs and cover tightly. Simmer over low heat for 25 minutes, until the chicken is cooked through and tender.

4 Remove the chicken to a clean serving plate, leaving the cooking liquids in the pan. Stir the mustard and cream into the pan and simmer for 2 to 3 minutes, until thickened. Season with salt and pepper, then pour over the chicken to serve.

VARIATION

Paprika Chicken with Caraway Dumplings

Replace the thyme or herbs with sweet paprika and add 1/2 cup sour cream instead of the mustard and cream. In a medium bowl, blend 2 cups Bisquick with 1/2 cup water, then add 2 teaspoons caraway seeds and combine. Add dollops onto the simmering chicken during the last 10 minutes of cooking time. Cover and cook until the dumplings are cooked through.

TOP SECRET

Cooking in mustard is a time-honored way for chefs to add a big hit of flavor without many additional ingredients or time-consuming reductions. But for even *more* flavor impact, they make an herbal infusion. If the recipe calls for thyme, for instance, whisk it into the mustard the day before you cook the dish, then cover tightly and refrigerate. The result? Magnificent.

LOVE THAT CHICKEN!

Devilish Chicken Breasts

The "devil" in the mix, as with deviled eggs, refers to the sharp prickle of mustard that needles your tongue—temptingly—and this dish is potent with it. Don't be tempted to lower the amount of mustard or you'll miss out on the charm. Cooking softens the intense flavor of the Dijon, so it's not a burning experience, and as good as the chicken is right out of the pan, it's that much better the next day.

6 chicken breast halves

1/2 cup Dijon mustard

1 cup bread crumbs

1/2 teaspoon cayenne

1 tablespoon unsalted butter, softened

PREP TIME: 10 minutes • **COOK TIME:** 30 minutes • **SERVES:** 6

1 Preheat the oven to 450°F. In a large bowl, toss the chicken together with the mustard to coat well.

2 On a large plate, stir together the bread crumbs and cayenne. Press the chicken breasts into the crumbs, coating well.

3 Place the chicken on a large, rimmed metal baking sheet. Dot each piece with butter. Bake, turning once, for 35 to 40 minutes, until the chicken is golden brown and cooked through. Remove to a platter and let the chicken rest for 5 minutes before serving.

VARIATION
Deviled Chicken Wings
Substitute spicy brown deli mustard for the Dijon and 3 pounds of cut chicken wings (tips discarded) for the breasts. Reduce the cooking time by about 5 minutes to prevent burning the crumb crust on the smaller pieces of chicken. Serve warm or at room temperature.

DID YOU KNOW?
Although mustard seems to last forever in the fridge, it does lose potency. The volatile oils of the tiny mustard seed are what give the condiment its bite, and after some months, Dijon mustard, in particular, is noticeably less spicy than when you bought it, making a huge difference when you add it to sauces and dressings. If you're a mustard-lover, buy mustard in small quantities, not huge jars, and get a fresh one every few months. Yellow ballpark mustard gets a lot of bite from white vinegar, so it doesn't lose flavor as recognizably as Dijon, but even so, the freshness is obvious when you taste an old and new bottle side by side.

TOP SECRET
Mustard's claim to fame is as a condiment, usually on hot dogs, hamburgers, and sandwiches. But many chefs, when preparing lower-cholesterol breaded cutlets, replace egg with mustard, since bread crumbs adhere to mustard even better than they do to beaten egg. Plus, mustard's fat and cholesterol counts are virtually nil. Use this technique anytime you make cutlets, stronger-flavored fish, and even fried eggplant.

LOVE THAT CHICKEN!

Asian-Style Sesame Chicken Wings

America is such a nation of Buffalo wing-eaters, always trimmed into two little "wingettes," that you rarely see whole-wing preparations. But whole wings are more like dinner and less like cocktail snacks. Serve these sticky, finger-licking wings with steamed broccoli and noodles tossed with soy sauce and sesame oil, and you'll develop a new appreciation for whole wings.

2 tablespoons vegetable oil

2 cloves garlic, minced

1 tablespoon grated fresh ginger

1/2 teaspoon red pepper flakes

1/4 cup soy sauce

1/4 cup honey

2 tablespoons brown sugar

1 teaspoon toasted sesame oil

12 whole chicken wings (about 4 pounds), tips removed

1/4 cup sesame seeds

1 scallion, finely sliced

PREP TIME: 15 minutes • **COOK TIME:** 35 minutes • **SERVES:** 6

1 Preheat the oven to 425°F and line a rimmed baking sheet with foil. Grease it lightly.

2 In a small saucepan, gently heat the oil and sauté the garlic, ginger, and pepper flakes for 1 to 2 minutes. Stir in the soy sauce, honey, and brown sugar and bring to a boil. Remove from the heat and stir in the sesame oil.

3 In a large bowl, toss the wings together with the sauce. Arrange on the foil, avoiding crowding, and bake for about 35 minutes, until browned and tender.

4 Sprinkle with sesame seeds and return to the oven for 3 to 4 minutes to toast the seeds. Remove to a serving plate and sprinkle with the scallions. Serve warm or at room temperature.

VARIATIONS

Sesame Chicken Drumsticks

Substitute an equal amount of drumsticks for the wings. Sesame Drumsticks are great picnic food, with a higher proportion of meat to sticky sauce simply by nature of how they're built.

Grilled Herb-and-Garlic Wings

In a food processor, puree a handful of fresh parsley and basil, a few sprigs of thyme, 3 cloves garlic, 1 cup bread crumbs, 1/2 cup olive oil, and salt and pepper. Toss whole chicken wings (or drumsticks) in this mixture, which will cling in loose clumps. Don't worry—all will come out well. Lay on a hot grill and cook, moving and turning frequently to avoid charring, until wings are tender and the clumps of crumbs are golden, about 25 minutes.

TOP SECRET

When covering a baking sheet with foil, be sure to always put the shiny side up. The shiny surface reflects heat to the underside of the chicken and helps it to cook evenly.

LOVE THAT CHICKEN!

Orange-Glazed Roast Duck

Used to be that this old standard, *duck à l'orange*, was a time-consuming dish to make, often greasy and fatty, and best relegated to the professional restaurant kitchen. Not anymore! Here is a simple and ingenious way to get that delicious flavor you love with a standard kitchen ingredient, and to keep it yummy and crisp with a very basic trick. It's just ducky!

1 whole duck (4–5 pounds)

Salt and pepper, to taste

3/4 cup fresh orange juice

2 tablespoons soy sauce

PREP TIME: 15 minutes • **COOK TIME:** 1 hour • **SERVES:** 4–6

1 Preheat the oven to 375°F. While the oven is preheating, bring a stockpot of salted water to a fast boil on top of the stove. Gently poke a fork into the breast meat ten times. Place the entire duck in the stockpot and boil for 10 minutes. Remove, drain, and pat dry with paper towels.

2 Salt and pepper the duck inside and out. Place on a rack in a roasting pan, add a cup of water to the pan, and place it in the oven for 30 minutes. Meanwhile, in a cup, mix together the orange juice and soy sauce. Remove the duck from the oven and baste it with the sauce. Repeat every 10 minutes, for another 30 minutes

3 Remove the glazed duck from the oven and let it rest on a platter, loosely tented with foil, for 10 minutes. Carve as you would a chicken.

VARIATION

Plum-Glazed Roast Duck

Replace the orange juice and soy sauce with 3 tablespoons plum preserves and 1 tablespoon water.

FIX IT FAST

If the duck is getting dark too quickly, remove it from the oven, pour off the fat that's gathered in the bottom of the pan, and loosely cover it with foil until the last 30 minutes of the cooking process.

TOP SECRET

There are two secrets to a great duck dish: The first—giving the duck a bath in boiling salted water—is an ages-old kitchen trick designed to help draw out some of its fat (ducks are notoriously fatty), helping it to have super-crispy skin. The second trick—using orange juice or preserves—is a no-fail way to add fruit flavor any time of year, with a standard kitchen ingredient.

LOVE THAT CHICKEN!

Middle-Eastern Chicken and Rice Salad

Rotisserie chickens are ideal for any dish that requires cooked chicken. Strip the meat off the bones, coarsely chop very large pieces such as the breasts, and proceed with any recipe calling for cooked chicken, such as this Middle Eastern–inspired salad—a whole meal in a bowl. The turmeric gives the salad its distinctive and lovely yellow color. A full-fat plain yogurt gives a better flavor here than nonfat.

3/4 cup plain yogurt

1/4 cup fresh lemon juice

1 clove garlic, minced

1/2 teaspoon curry powder

1/2 teaspoon ground cumin

1/2 teaspoon turmeric

1/4 teaspoon ground cinnamon

1/2 cup chopped fresh parsley

Salt and pepper, to taste

3 cups cooked chicken meat (from 1 rotisserie chicken), cubed

3 cups cooked white rice, cooled but not cold

2 scallions, thinly sliced

1 jar (8 ounces) artichoke hearts, drained and coarsely chopped

3/4 cup golden raisins or chopped dried apricots

1/2 cup slivered toasted almonds

PREP TIME: 15 minutes • **COOK TIME:** 0 minutes • **SERVES:** 6

1 Blend the yogurt, lemon juice, garlic, curry powder, cumin, turmeric, cinnamon, and parsley in a small bowl and season with salt and pepper.

2 In a large serving bowl, combine the chicken, rice, scallions, artichokes, and raisins or apricots. Pour in the yogurt dressing and toss gently, being careful not to break up the chicken and artichokes.

3 Garnish with almonds and serve.

VARIATION

Lettuce Wraps

Leave out the yogurt and all the spices. Toss the chicken with 1/2 cup chopped fresh cilantro, a little soy sauce, sesame oil, and a splash of rice wine vinegar. Pull the outer leaves off a head of Boston or Bibb lettuce and roll a few tablespoons of the salad in it, perhaps with a small dash of hot sauce or a light sprinkle of red pepper flakes. Roll up and eat like a burrito.

TOP SECRET

Are you working with older dried spices from your cupboard? Enhance their possibly faded flavors and bring the essential oils back to the surface by toasting the spices very lightly before adding them to the dressing. In a small dry skillet over medium-high heat, toss all the spices and cook, shaking the pan frequently, for 1 to 2 minutes, just until you smell the scent of the spices getting pungent. Instantly remove them from the pan and pour them into the dish in which you'll be making the dressing. Leaving them in the hot pan, even off the heat, will result in the spices taking on a burnt flavor.

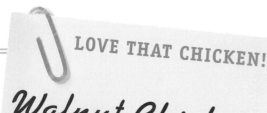

LOVE THAT CHICKEN!

Walnut Chicken Salad with Peaches

So many versions of chicken salad are heavy with mayonnaise and overbearing with big chunks of celery. This version doesn't leave out either the mayo or the celery, but rather than being the primary players, they're only supporting actors to the real stars of fresh summer peaches and toasted walnuts. You can use leftover roasted chicken, obviously, but the slightly smoky flavor of a rotisserie chicken is ideal here.

SALAD

3 cups cooked chicken meat (from 1 rotisserie chicken), cubed

2 ripe peaches, peeled and cubed same size as the chicken

2 scallions, thinly sliced

1 stalk celery, thinly sliced

1 cup toasted walnuts, coarsely chopped

1 head Bibb or Boston lettuce

DRESSING

3/4 cup Greek yogurt (not fat-free)

2 tablespoons sherry vinegar

2 tablespoons chopped fresh tarragon

Salt and pepper, to taste

4 tablespoons chopped fresh chives

PREP TIME: 20 minutes • **COOK TIME:** 0 minutes • **SERVES:** 6

1 *For the salad:* In a large bowl, layer the chicken, peaches, scallions, celery, and walnuts. Do not combine. Arrange 2 or 3 leaves of lettuce on each serving plate, cupped loosely together.

2 *For the dressing:* In a small bowl, whisk together the yogurt, vinegar, and tarragon. Season with salt and pepper.

3 Just before serving, pour the dressing over the salad and toss very gently to combine, avoiding crushing the peaches. Spoon the salad into the lettuce cups and sprinkle with chives. Serve immediately.

VARIATION

Curried Chicken Salad with Mango

Replace the peaches with 1 diced mango and 1/3 cup golden raisins. Make the dressing of half yogurt, half mayonnaise, tossed with 1 to 2 teaspoons mild curry powder and 2 tablespoons fresh lemon juice instead of the vinegar. Leave out the tarragon. Substitute cilantro for the chives. Serve in lettuce cups or make sandwiches on soft buttery rolls or toasted cinnamon-raisin bread.

TOP SECRET

Like people, most foods have perfect soul mates, and in the case of chicken, every chef knows that it's definitely tarragon. If you want to duplicate the supple and well-rounded taste of fancy-pants luncheon chicken salad and all you have is a rotisserie chicken, mince up tarragon and add it...carefully. A little goes a long way!

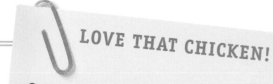

Better Barbecued Chicken

The primary challenge of grilling chicken is to get it cooked through and tender at the bone without charring it on the outside—no mean feat over an open flame. This lip-smacking good recipe offers simple instructions that will forever change the way you think about cooking over fire.

3 quarts cold water

1/3 cup Kosher salt

1 whole chicken (3 1/2 pounds), cut up, or 3 1/2 pounds chicken legs or thighs

2 cups bottled barbecue sauce

PREP TIME: 20 minutes (includes brining) • **COOK TIME:** 35 minutes • **SERVES:** 6

1 Mix the water and salt in a large bowl and soak the chicken pieces for at least 20 minutes, or up to 1 hour. Remove and pat dry.

2 Prepare a medium-hot fire in a gas or charcoal grill. If using charcoal, burn the coals down to a gray color with a red underglow, then heap the coals in the center of the grill. If using gas, preheat one side of the grill on high.

3 Arrange the chicken around the outer edges of the grill rack over the charcoal, or on the turned-off side of the gas grill. Cook, turning frequently for 20 to 25 minutes, until chicken is cooked through and browned.

4 Brush the barbecue sauce on the chicken. Grill for several minutes more, then turn and brush the other side with sauce. Grill and brush for about 7 minutes altogether, watching carefully to ensure that sauce is not charring. Remove the chicken to serving platter.

VARIATION

Egg-and-Vinegar Barbecued Chicken

In a gallon-size ziplock bag, place 1 beaten egg, 1 cup apple-cider vinegar, 1/2 cup olive oil, 1 tablespoon Kosher salt (or 2 teaspoons table salt), 1 teaspoon Italian seasoning or whole dried oregano, and 1 teaspoon pepper. Put the chicken in the bag and seal, turning to coat each piece well. Marinate the chicken for at least 2 hours, and preferably overnight. Grill as above, skipping the additional basting on the grill. Discard the remaining marinade.

TOP SECRET

Here's the way to make a fully cooked, juicy barbecued bird with nary a drop of pink meat. Bring the chicken to room temperature before you put it on the grill. Make absolutely sure that you're cooking it over indirect heat. Slow and steady wins the race; take your time, and you'll be rewarded!

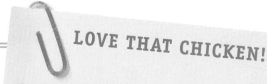

LOVE THAT CHICKEN!

Whole Chicken with Herbs under a Brick

Butterflied, marinated, then pressed flat and sizzled under bricks on the grill, this chicken is fragrant with herbs and incredibly moist. There are versions in many cultures, from the Italian "chicken under a tile" (*al mattone*) to Russian Chicken Tapaka. This one is more Italian, jazzed up with extra herbs. To keep it tidy, wrap the bricks in foil and keep a spray bottle of water handy to spritz flare-ups as the fat drips.

1/4 cup extra-virgin olive oil

Juice and zest of 2 lemons

2 cloves garlic, coarsely chopped

1 tablespoon chopped fresh rosemary

1 tablespoon chopped fresh sage

1 tablespoon chopped fresh tarragon

1 1/2 teaspoons red pepper flakes

1 teaspoon salt

1 teaspoon pepper

1 whole chicken (3 1/2 pounds), butterflied

Several whole sprigs fresh rosemary

2 cloves garlic, slivered

PREP TIME: 12 hours (includes marinating) • **COOK TIME:** 35 minutes • **SERVES:** 6

1 In a small bowl, combine the oil, lemon juice, chopped garlic, chopped rosemary, sage, tarragon, pepper flakes, salt, and pepper. Rub the herb mixture all over the chicken on both sides. Cover with plastic wrap and marinate in the refrigerator for at least 2 hours, or overnight.

2 Cut slits through the skin of the chicken on each side of the breast and on each thigh and push a sprig of rosemary and a few slivers of garlic into each cut, and let come to room temperature.

3 Prepare the grill and let the coals burn down to a medium heat, gray with a red underglow. Place the chicken on the center of the grill, breast-side down, and weight it with two bricks wrapped in foil, flattening the chicken as much as possible. Cook for 20 minutes, spritzing flare-ups, as necessary, with a spray bottle of water. Turn the chicken over. Replace the bricks and cook for another 15 minutes. Remove from the grill and serve.

VARIATION
Butterflied Chicken with Pesto
Instead of the herb mixture, make a loose pesto in the food processor or blender with 2 large handfuls of basil leaves, 1/2 cup olive oil, 3 cloves garlic, salt, pepper, 1/4 cup Parmesan cheese, 1/4 cup walnuts, and 1/4 cup plain yogurt. Smear all over the butterflied chicken, including pushing it under the skin, and marinate overnight in a covered dish in the refrigerator.

TOP SECRET
No bricks around? No problem. Find the heaviest cast-iron pan you can, and use it instead. For truly flat cooking, press down on the chicken with the pan before marinating until it looks like a butterfly.

LETTING IT REST THE RIGHT WAY (AND THE WRONG WAY)

Every piece of meat and poultry, after being cooked, needs to rest. But like everything, there's a right way to rest just-cooked food, and a wrong way. Letting it rest allows the internal juices of whatever you're cooking to settle, making it far juicier than it would be if you just sliced into it right away. Plus, slicing into a just-cooked chicken or duck or a pork or beef roast will spill its internal juices all over your counters, platter, and cutting board; you want that lusciousness *in* your meat, not on your kitchen floor.

1 Remove the poultry or meat roast from the oven and place it on a platter.

2 Loosely tent it with enough foil to keep the foil from touching the top of it. Crimp the edges on the sides of the platter.

3 Do not hermetically seal the platter in foil, or you'll continue to steam-cook whatever you're making and it will wind up tough.

The Right Way

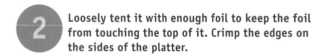

The Wrong Way

LOVE THAT CHICKEN!

Chicken Breasts with Pepper Jack and Bacon

Cheese and bacon are always crowd-pleasers, and these easy chicken breasts on the grill are no exception. The bacon keeps the breasts moist on the grill or on the stovetop. The flavors are hearty and bold, and you can slap it on a bun with some spicy mustard and eat standing up.

6 boneless, skinless chicken breasts halves

6 slices (1/4 inch thick) Pepper Jack cheese

6 slices hickory-smoked bacon

PREP TIME: 15 minutes • **COOK TIME:** 15 minutes • **SERVES:** 6

1 Using a narrow sharp knife, such as a fillet knife, make a wide horizontal slit in the side of each chicken breast half. Put the cheese inside, wrap a slice of bacon around the stuffed breast, and secure it with a toothpick.

2 Prepare the grill and let the coals burn down to medium, gray with a red underglow. Arrange the breasts on the center and cook for about 8 minutes on each side, or until browned and cooked through.

VARIATIONS

Goat Cheese and Arugula-Stuffed Chicken

Replace the Pepper Jack cheese with 1/2-inch slices of goat cheese, and push in on top of it 4 to 6 leaves of rinsed and dried arugula. Omit the bacon. Sprinkle with salt and pepper, to taste.

Spinach and Mozzarella Chicken

In a large skillet, cook a pound of fresh baby spinach leaves in 1 tablespoon butter just until wilted. Season with salt and pepper, to taste, and a splash of fresh lemon juice. Stuff the chicken with the spinach. Add a 1/4-inch-thick slice of creamy fresh mozzarella cheese.

Cheddar and Chipotle Chicken

Insert a hefty slice of sharp cheddar cheese into each breast half and add a generous smear of the orange-red adobo sauce from a can of chipotles in adobo. Wrap with bacon.

> **TOP SECRET**
>
> If you're making food for a crowd, don't wait until the last minute: Stuff the breasts first, wrap them in plastic wrap, and refrigerate them. You're not only keeping them cold but the chicken will actually "grab" the stuffing better after a blast in the fridge. Just remember to bring them to room temperature before you cook them.

LOVE THAT CHICKEN!

Tandoori Chicken

The tandoor is an ancient style of clay oven used in India, which cooks at an extremely high heat, keeping meats moist inside and beautifully crisp outside. Here, the grill replaces the tandoor to good effect, and the marinade will make it taste like Indian restaurant fare. Tandoori chicken is typically served with basmati rice and hot puffy naan bread (but you could lightly grill soft white pitas instead).

1 whole chicken
(3 1/2 pounds),
cut up and skinned

1 teaspoon
ground cumin

1 teaspoon ground
coriander

1 teaspoon
red pepper flakes

1 tablespoon grated
fresh ginger

6 cloves garlic,
minced

1 teaspoon salt

1 cup full-fat
plain yogurt

Chopped
fresh cilantro

Lemon wedges

Sweet onions,
thickly sliced

PREP TIME: 12 hours (includes marinating) • **COOK TIME:** 20 minutes • **SERVES:** 6

1 Using a sharp paring knife, slash each piece of chicken diagonally three times, 1/2 inch deep.

2 In a large bowl, combine the cumin, coriander, pepper flakes, ginger, garlic, salt, and yogurt. Add the chicken pieces, turning to coat evenly, working the yogurt mixture into the slits. Cover the bowl and marinate in the refrigerator for 12 hours, or overnight.

3 Prepare the grill and burn the coals down to a medium fire, gray with a red underglow. Heap the coals in the center. Arrange the chicken pieces around the outer edges of the grill, discarding the remaining marinade. Cook for 7 to 10 minutes on each side, turning and moving frequently to avoid burning.

4 Pile the chicken on a platter and garnish with the cilantro, lemons, and onions. Serve hot or at room temperature.

TOP SECRET

What may seem like a perfectly ordinary marinade in fact holds a culinary secret from the Indian sub-continent: yogurt. The enzymes in yogurt, working over the many hours of marinating, break down the collagen in the meat. Papaya has an enzyme called papain, which is similarly powerful, but the risk with papaya is that the meat will grow mushy. Yogurt has a gentler action, resulting in chicken that is velvety textured and exquisitely tender.

LOVE THAT CHICKEN!

Oven-Baked Barbecue Chicken

Thick, flavorful, and finger-licking good, this barbecued chicken will forever make you rethink firing up that grill (and very happy if you don't have one). Best of all, the recipe only requires 5 minutes of preparation.

1/3 cup apple butter

2 tablespoons salsa

2 tablespoons ketchup

1 tablespoon vegetable oil

1/2 teaspoon salt

1/4 teaspoon garlic powder

2 drops Worcestershire sauce

2 drops liquid smoke (optional)

4 boneless, skinless chicken breast halves (about 1 pound)

PREP TIME: 5 minutes • **COOK TIME:** 25 minutes • **SERVES:** 4

1 Preheat the oven to 375°F. Grease an 8-inch-square baking dish.

2 Combine the apple butter, salsa, ketchup, oil, salt, garlic powder, Worcestershire sauce, and liquid smoke, if using, in a small bowl.

3 Add the chicken to the baking pan. Pour the sauce over the chicken.

4 Bake, uncovered, for about 25 minutes, or until the juices run clear when the chicken is pierced with a fork.

VARIATION
Spicy Barbecue Chicken
Kick it up a notch by flavoring the barbecue sauce even more: Add 2 teaspoons molasses, 1/2 teaspoon ground mustard, and 1/2 teaspoon chili powder.

TOP SECRET
As they said in *Fried Green Tomatoes:* "The secret's in the sauce!" In this case, it's the apple butter that gives the barbecue sauce a fruity kick, while retaining its smooth and luscious texture.

LOVE THAT CHICKEN!

Hunter's Chicken

Also known as chicken cacciatore, this is a classic way of braising chicken in a hearty tomato sauce. Mushrooms are usually added for deeper flavor, but we've eliminated that step and replaced it with a secret ingredient. Dinner will be ready in less than an hour.

2 tablespoons extra-virgin olive oil

3 pounds bone-in chicken parts

3/4 teaspoon salt

1/4 teaspoon freshly ground black pepper

2 cups frozen mixed bell pepper strips

1 onion, sliced

6 cloves garlic, sliced

1 jar (26 ounces) tomato sauce with mushrooms

PREP TIME: 15 minutes • **COOK TIME:** 45 minutes • **SERVES:** 4

1 Heat the oil in a large pot over medium-high heat until shimmering. Sprinkle the chicken with the salt and pepper and add to the pot. Cook, turning occasionally, for about 8 minutes, or until the chicken is browned. Transfer the chicken to a plate.

2 Add the pepper strips, onions, and garlic to the pot and cook, stirring occasionally, for 4 to 5 minutes, or until the vegetables start to soften.

3 Add the chicken and sauce. Reduce the heat to medium-low, cover, and simmer for 30 to 35 minutes, until the chicken is very tender.

VARIATION

Spicy Cacciatore

For more kick, stir in a pinch of crushed red-pepper flakes when you sauté the vegetables. Serve with wide egg noodles to round out the meal.

TOP SECRET

Why make a tomato sauce from scratch and go to the trouble of sautéing mushrooms when you can get both those ingredients in one jar? Feel free to use your favorite brand of tomato sauce with mushrooms in this dish, and you'll have a quick-and-easy meal in a jiffy.

LOVE THAT CHICKEN!

Chicken Sloppy Joes

Biscuits are one of America's greatest gifts to the food world, but they can be challenging to make. Not here! And the best news? Sloppy Joes on buttermilk biscuits definitely one-ups the more ubiquitous hamburger rolls.

1 package (16.3 ounces) refrigerated big buttermilk biscuits, such as Pillsbury Grands

1 cup shredded sharp cheddar cheese

1 tablespoon canola oil

2 cloves garlic, minced

1 cup chopped onions

1 cup cored, seeded, and chopped green bell peppers

1 pound ground chicken

1 teaspoon chili powder

1 cup ketchup

2 tablespoons dark brown sugar

1/4 teaspoon salt

PREP TIME: 10 minutes • **COOK TIME:** 20 minutes • **SERVES:** 4

1 Prepare the biscuits according to the package directions. Remove the biscuits from the oven and allow to cool for 5 minutes.

2 Split the biscuits in half and arrange them, tops down, on a baking sheet. Sprinkle each half with 2 tablespoons of the cheese and bake for 3 to 4 minutes, until melted.

3 Meanwhile, heat the oil in a large nonstick skillet over medium-high heat. Add the garlic, onions, and peppers and cook, stirring occasionally, for 4 to 5 minutes, until they start to soften.

4 Stir in the chicken and chili powder and cook for 3 to 4 minutes, or until no longer pink. Add the ketchup, brown sugar, and salt and cook, stirring occasionally, for 4 to 5 minutes longer, until slightly thickened and the chicken is cooked through. Serve sandwiched between two biscuit halves.

VARIATION
Spicy Ancho Sloppy Joes
For more intense flavor, add 1 teaspoon ground cumin, 2 teaspoons Worcestershire sauce, and a shake of ground ancho chili powder.

TOP SECRET

Open up that pantry door...you'll never guess what top secret ingredient lurks in its depths! Brown sugar, which is made by combining white sugar with molasses, is a key ingredient in full-bodied Sloppy Joes and barbecue sauces. You can even turn a cup of ketchup into a simple barbecue sauce by adding brown sugar and a dash of hot sauce. It's that easy!

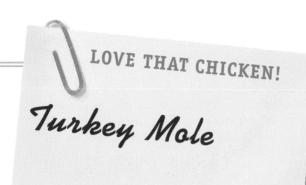

LOVE THAT CHICKEN!

Turkey Mole

When is chocolate sauce not chocolate sauce? When it's mole! This traditional spicy Mexican mélange is a rich combination of onions, garlic, chile peppers, and chocolate, which adds sweetness and a simultaneous yummy sharp edge.

2 teaspoons canola oil

2 large onions, chopped

2 large cloves garlic, minced

1 1/2 tablespoons chili powder

1 tablespoon sesame seeds

1 small red chile pepper, seeded, deveined, and minced (wear gloves when handling)

1 pound turkey breast fillets, cut into 1-inch-wide strips

1/2 teaspoon salt

1 can (14 ounces) whole tomatoes (with juice)

1 cup raisins

1/2 teaspoon ground cloves

1 cup low-fat, chicken broth

3 tablespoons chopped bittersweet chocolate

1/4 cup toasted sliced almonds

2 tablespoons chopped fresh cilantro

PREP TIME: 15 minutes • **COOK TIME:** 30 minutes • **SERVES:** 4

1 Heat the oil in a large nonstick skillet over medium-high heat. Add the onions, garlic, chili powder, sesame seeds, and chile pepper. Sauté for about 10 minutes, until the onions are soft and the sesame seeds are fragrant and toasted.

2 Sprinkle the strips of turkey with the salt. Add the turkey to the skillet and toss with the onion mixture. Stir in the tomatoes (with juice) and raisins. Sprinkle in the cloves.

3 Pour in the broth and bring to a full boil. Reduce the heat to medium-low, cover the skillet, and simmer gently for about 10 minutes, until the turkey is no longer pink.

4 Add the chocolate, almonds, and chopped cilantro, and stir until the chocolate has melted. Spoon into a serving dish and decorate with sprigs of cilantro (optional).

VARIATION
Tacos à la Mole

Dissolve 2 teaspoons cornstarch and 1/4 cup cold water in a measuring cup and whisk the mixture into the pan after the turkey is cooked but before adding the chocolate. Bring to a boil and cook until the sauce thickens, about 2 minutes. Then serve as a filling for tacos, along with lettuce, tomatoes, onions, avocadoes, and cheese.

TOP SECRET

We gave away the secret to this dish—chocolate—above. But chocolate adds a full, round body to any darker sauce! Just add 1 to 2 squares of bittersweet chocolate to beef stew and watch their faces light up!

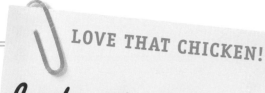

Jerky Turkey with Ginger Barbecue Sauce

Spicy, lip-smacking, and sure to become a favorite, jerk turkey is a Jamaican dish that will have you smiling from ear to ear when you eat it. Make it a day in advance and you'll be in store for some fabulous eats the next day!

5 green onions, chopped

4 cloves garlic

1 onion, quartered

2 jalapeño peppers, seeded and deveined (wear gloves when handling)

1 piece (1/2 inch) fresh ginger, peeled

1/4 cup canola oil

2 tablespoons soy sauce

2 teaspoons allspice

1 teaspoon dried thyme

1 bone-in turkey breast (5–6 pounds)

1 1/2 teaspoons salt

1 cup ginger ale

1 cup jarred barbecue sauce

PREP TIME: 20 minutes • **COOK TIME:** 1 hour, 40 minutes • **SERVES:** 6

1 In a blender, combine the green onions, garlic, onions, jalapeños, ginger, oil, soy sauce, allspice, and thyme. Blend until a thick paste forms, then transfer to a large bowl.

2 With the tip of a sharp knife make several slits all over the turkey breast. Add the turkey to the onion mixture, turning to coat the breast. Refrigerate for at least 4 hours, or overnight, turning occasionally.

3 Preheat a gas grill on high until the thermometer reaches the maximum temperature. Turn off one of the burners and reduce the heat on the other burner(s) to medium. Remove the turkey from the marinade and sprinkle with the salt. On a lightly oiled grill rack, grill the turkey breast over the unlit burner, skin-side down, using indirect heat and turning every 20 minutes for about 1 hour, 40 minutes, until a digital instant-read thermometer inserted into the thickest part of the breast registers 160°F. Remove to a cutting board and let rest for 10 minutes before slicing.

4 Meanwhile, combine the ginger ale and barbecue sauce in a small pot and bring to a boil over medium-high heat. Reduce the heat to medium-low and simmer for 18 to 20 minutes, until thickened and reduced to about 1 3/4 cups.

TOP SECRET

There are some truly delicious jarred sauces on the market these days, but why not take the opportunity to put your own spin on it? One of the best ways to tweak any hot sauce—barbecue or jerk—is to add a bit of ginger ale, which provides a hint of sweetness with a slight edge of ginger. Delicious!

6 SEAFOOD SUPREME

Fish is healthy and, yes, it's marvelously good for you, but it's also just plain delicious. Done right, a dish of seafood really does taste like a briny treasure from the sea. There's no reason that fish at home can't be as good as fish in a restaurant. The next time you're looking for a good dinner, don't automatically buy another package of pork chops—splash out on scallops or take home a pound of jumbo shrimp. And then come here for the tips and recipes to "wow" your friends and family, who may very well change from, "Ew, we're having fish for dinner?" to "Hey, can we have fish for dinner?!"

SEAFOOD SUPREME
Tilapia Fillets with Green Curry Sauce

The bright flavors of coconut, curry, and lime give a yummy Southern Indian flavor to the dish. Make sure you only use unsweetened coconut milk, not thick, sweetened cream of coconut. A green Thai curry paste is excellent here, but even if you only have curry powder, this is very good. If you're trying to get more fish into your diet, this is a recipe you'll turn to again and again.

6 tilapia fillets
(6 ounces each)

2 tablespoons flour

Salt and pepper,
to taste

2 tablespoons
extra-virgin
olive oil

1 medium onion,
finely diced

2 teaspoons
curry paste
(or 1 1/2 teaspoons
curry powder)

1 can (15 ounces)
unsweetened
coconut milk

PREP TIME: 3 minutes • **COOK TIME:** 12 minutes • **SERVES:** 6

1 Pat the fish dry and sprinkle lightly with the flour and salt and pepper. Heat the oil in a large skillet over medium heat. Add the fish and cook for about 6 minutes, turning halfway through, until the edges are lightly browned.

2 Place the fish on a room temperature dish on the back of the stove. Add the onions to the hot pan and cook until they start to brown. Stir in the curry paste and cook for 1 to 2 minutes. Pour in the coconut milk, stirring to blend, and bring to a boil. Simmer for 4 to 5 minutes, until the sauce starts to thicken slightly.

3 Return the fish to the pan and heat through. Serve immediately.

VARIATION
Tilapia with Chile and Lime
Instead of a room temperature plate, remove the fish to a warm plate. Instead of the curry paste and coconut milk, add 1 tablespoon olive oil to the pan along with 1 diced shallot, 1 minced jalapeño pepper, 2 diced plum tomatoes, and a good pinch of cayenne. Cook until tender. Season well with salt and sprinkle with grated lime zest. Spoon this relish over the fish fillets and finish by squeezing fresh lime juice over all.

TOP SECRET

Here's an old French trick that'll be sure to make you smile when you're in a rush and need to use premade sauce with fish: Heat an ovenproof plate or serving platter at 300°F. When the plate is hot, carefully remove it from the oven; grease it lightly with a drop of oil or butter; add delicate fish like tilapia or sole; drizzle with prepared sauce; and let it stand for 5 minutes. Flip the fish carefully, and let it stand for another 5 minutes.

SEAFOOD SUPREME

Seared Salmon with Mustard-Dill Sauce

The marriage between salmon, mustard, and dill is ages old; the piquancy of the mustard cuts through the richness of the fish, and the dill adds a perfectly earthy touch. In this very simple dish, the salmon takes on a gorgeous golden brown crust and finishes in the oven for a perfectly cooked dish every time.

4 salmon fillets (8 ounces each), no more than 3/4 inch thick

1 tablespoon extra-virgin olive oil

Salt and pepper, to taste

1/2 cup light cream

1 1/2 tablespoons Dijon mustard

2 tablespoons chopped fresh dill

PREP TIME: 4 minutes • **COOK TIME:** 20 minutes • **SERVES:** 4

1 Bring the salmon to room temperature, loosely covered. Drizzle it with the oil and sprinkle with salt and pepper.

2 Place a heat-resistant, nonstick skillet over medium-high heat, and add the salmon, skin-side up. Cook without moving for 8 minutes. In a cup or small bowl, mix together the cream, mustard, and dill and pour over the top.

3 Bake for 12 minutes, until the sauce is bubbling lightly and the fish is opaque.

VARIATION

Baked Salmon with Yogurt-Dill Sauce

Skip the cream, mustard, and dill. Instead, drizzle it with olive oil and a bit of fresh lemon juice. Sprinkle with salt and pepper. While the fish cooks, in a small bowl, stir together 1 cup plain yogurt, 2 tablespoons fresh lemon juice, 1/4 cup chopped fresh dill, and salt and pepper. Spoon the sauce over the hot fish before serving.

TOP SECRET

Many salmon recipes instruct you to remove the fish skin *before* cooking to keep things looking neat. Wrong! Roasting fish with the skin on serves two purposes: It actually holds the fish together while you're cooking it, and it helps keep the fish moist. If you must remove the skin, wait until after it comes out of the oven!

GO FISHING IN YOUR TOOL KIT

When you order boneless fish fillets, they are theoretically supposed to be boneless. Unfortunately, though, a few tiny pinbones often remain, especially when dealing with bony fish like salmon or shad. In this case, you can forget about using fancy tools and implements to remove the bones; instead, use needle nose pliers, straight from your tool kit. Here's what to do:

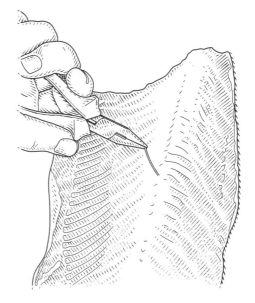

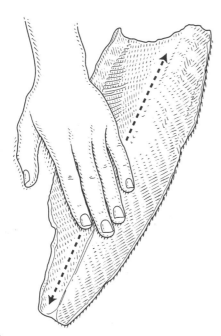

1 Run your hand over the fillet in one direction, and then back again in the other direction. The pinbones will feel like tiny (well) pins.

2 Using needle nose pliers, locate the bones, then grab them and give them a short yank straight out.

SEAFOOD SUPREME

Ginger-Mustard Salmon Burgers

Because it's a relatively "meaty" and oily fish, salmon lends itself well to burgers and won't dry out when cooked.

1/4 cup mayonnaise

1 1/2 tablespoons Dijon mustard

3 teaspoons finely grated fresh ginger

2 teaspoons soy sauce

1 pound skinless salmon fillets

2 scallions, thinly sliced

Salt and pepper, to taste

2 tablespoons oil

4 sandwich buns, split

Mayonnaise, for serving

Tomato slices, for serving

PREP TIME: 10 minutes • **COOK TIME:** 8 minutes • **SERVES:** 4

1 In a small bowl, whisk together the 1/4 cup mayonnaise, 2 1/4 teaspoons of the mustard, 1 1/2 teaspoons of the ginger, and 1 teaspoon of the soy sauce. Set aside.

2 Remove any pinbones from the salmon and cut it into large chunks. Place them in the bowl of a food processor with the scallions, and the remaining 2 1/4 teaspoons mustard, 1 1/2 teaspoons ginger, and 1 teaspoon soy sauce. Sprinkle with salt and pepper. Pulse several times, until coarsely chopped and holding together. Don't overpuree, or the mixture will become a paste.

3 Form the salmon mixture into 4 patties about 3/4 inch thick. Heat the oil in a nonstick skillet over medium-high heat and cook the patties 4 minutes on each side until browned and cooked through.

4 Serve on buns with mayonnaise and tomato.

VARIATION

Ginger-Mustard Tuna Burgers

Replace the salmon with tuna and the Dijon with 2 1/4 teaspoons wasabi paste. Toast a tablespoon of sesame seeds for a minute in a small dry pan over medium heat, and add to the food processor with the tuna mixture.

TOP SECRET

Any kind of burger mixture can stick to your hands when forming patties, but there's a simple solution and it's not oil-based: Water. Put a bowl of water big enough to dip your hands into near your workspace and wet your palms between forming each patty. The burger mixture will pull away cleanly from your hands, leaving a smoother surface for even cooking.

SEAFOOD SUPREME

Zesty Fiesta Shrimp

If you're using frozen shrimp, a little extra butter, chile flakes, and lemon juice will kick up the flavor, as will a quick saltwater brine. Because this dish cooks so quickly, have the rest of your meal ready to serve before you start cooking the shrimp.

2 pounds large fresh or frozen shrimp, peeled and deveined (if wild)

1 teaspoon salt

2 tablespoons extra-virgin olive oil

1 tablespoon unsalted butter

4 cloves garlic, minced

1/2 teaspoon red pepper flakes

3 scallions, thinly sliced

Juice of 1 lemon

PREP TIME: 5 minutes • **COOK TIME:** 5 minutes • **SERVES:** 4

1 Place the shrimp in a large bowl of cool water together with the salt, and let stand for 5 minutes. Drain and rinse.

2 Heat the oil and butter in a large skillet over medium heat. As the foam from the butter subsides, add the garlic and pepper flakes and cook for 1 minute, until the garlic smells pungent.

3 Turn up the heat slightly and add the shrimp and scallions. Cook for 3 minutes, or until the shrimp is opaque and cooked through. Squeeze the lemon juice over the whole dish and serve immediately.

VARIATION

Zesty Asparagus Shrimp

Before adding the garlic, add 1/2 pound 2-inch asparagus pieces (sliced diagonally) and increase the heat to high. Cook for 5 minutes, until the asparagus is becoming tender. Add 1/2 cup white wine to the pan when adding the shrimp.

DID YOU KNOW?

Individually frozen shrimp are excellent to keep in the freezer, not only for a quick dinner but also to add to fried rice or to stir into tomato soup spiced with bit of cumin and lime.

TOP SECRET

To get more juice out of a lemon, try these tricks. Store them in a sealed jar of water in the refrigerator to keep them plump and prevent the essential oils from evaporating. Or, microwave the lemon for 15 seconds before juicing. Thirdly, roll the uncut lemon hard on the countertop under your palm, pressing down with your weight to break the pulp and release all the juice.

SEAFOOD SUPREME
Salmon Cakes with Lime Butter

These tasty little cakes, made from canned salmon, go together in minutes and can be left to chill in the refrigerator all day. When ready to eat, just pat on bread crumbs and fry. Serve on a bed of crisp lettuce with a green vegetable such as peas or asparagus. If you don't have sesame seeds to coat the outsides of the fish cakes, substitute breadcrumbs or crushed cornflakes.

1 small onion, coarsely chopped

3/4 cup breadcrumbs

1 can (15 ounces) salmon, drained

1 egg

2 tablespoons chopped fresh parsley

1 1/2 teaspoons salt

Pepper, to taste

1/4 cup flour

3 tablespoons oil

4 tablespoons (1/2 stick) butter, softened

Zest and juice of 1 lime

PREP TIME: 10 minutes • **COOK TIME:** 10 minutes • **SERVES:** 4

1 Chop the onion in the food processor to dice it. Pulse the diced onion with the breadcrumbs until the onion is finely diced. Add the fish, egg, parsley, salt, and pepper, and pulse just to combine. Don't overprocess into a puree.

2 Form the mixture into 8 small, roundish patties. Dust each lightly with flour. Heat the oil in a large nonstick skillet over medium heat. Add the patties and cook for about 5 minutes on each side, or until golden.

3 Combine the butter with the lime zest and juice. Season with salt and pepper, as desired. Add a dollop on top of each fish cake and serve.

VARIATION
Cod Cakes
Use 2 cups cooked, flaked cod or tilapia (or other white fish) instead of the salmon. Omit the bread crumbs and use only 2 tablespoons finely chopped onions. Also add in 1 cup mashed potatoes. Skip the lime butter and serve with ketchup instead.

TOP SECRET
When you're shallow frying, you're basically using the pan as if it were a griddle, meaning that the heat is transferred directly, not through the oil as with deep-frying. So it's especially important to use a heavy-based pan so that the heat is even, since thin pans tend to create hot spots that burn in places. With something delicate such as fish cakes, a high-quality nonstick pan is helpful, but for most cooking, a well-seasoned cast-iron pan is ideal.

SEAFOOD SUPREME

Scallops with White Wine and Hazelnuts

Buy the biggest, freshest scallops you can find, not those teeny-tiny bay scallops, which look like pencil erasers when cooked and perhaps taste like them, too. The combination of sweet, unctuous scallops and earthy hazelnuts in this dish is a surefire winner and quick enough to prepare on busy weeknights.

1 1/2 pounds large
fresh scallops,
drained

3 tablespoons
unsalted butter

1/4 cup chopped
hazelnuts

1/2 cup white wine

2 tablespoons
chopped
fresh parsley

Salt and pepper,
to taste

PREP TIME: 2 minutes • **COOK TIME:** 8 minutes • **SERVES:** 4

1 Pat the scallops dry with paper towels. Heat the butter in a large nonstick skillet over high heat for just a moment, until sizzling but not browned.

2 Add the scallops and cook for 2 to 3 minutes per side, until the scallops are opaque, white, and just barely cooked through, with a hint of browning at the edges and translucent in the center. Remove the scallops to a warm serving plate.

3 Toss the hazelnuts into the pan and cook for 1 minute, shaking the pan, until toasted and browned. Pour in the wine and bring to a boil for about 2 minutes, or until the liquid is reduced by half. Add the parsley, season with salt and pepper, pour over the scallops, and serve immediately.

VARIATION
Lemon Scallops with Arugula
Sear the scallops in 4 to 5 tablespoons butter. Skip the hazelnuts and white wine and, instead, as soon as you flip the scallops, sprinkle them with a bit of lemon zest and a squeeze of fresh lemon juice. Transfer them to the top of a salad of arugula leaves dressed with olive oil, lemon juice, salt and pepper. Pour the pan juices over the top and serve.

DID YOU KNOW?

The best scallops are sold "dry," which means they haven't been soaked in a bath of phosphate to keep them fresh. This soak not only adds a faint chemical taste to your finished dish, but it loads the scallops up with moisture. "Dry" scallops will sizzle and fry when they hit a hot pan of melted butter. Phosphate scallops will release a lot of milky liquid and end up steaming rather than searing.

TOP SECRET

There is a very fine line between cooked and raw with scallops, and they can be very challenging to not cook to the consistency of rubber. Here's a simple trick: If the scallops are very big, slice them width-wise, straight through the middle, which will give you two, equal-size halves. When you sear the scallops, place them in a hot pan, and don't move them around until they start to become opaque.

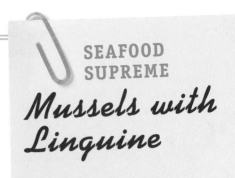

SEAFOOD SUPREME
Mussels with Linguine

If you've never cooked mussels at home, you're in for a treat. They're super-inexpensive compared to other shellfish and they're succulent and sweet—and unlike oysters, you never eat them raw! This out-of-the-ordinary recipe pairs them with linguine for an elegant supper dish.

1 pound dried linguine

2 pounds mussels

1/4 cup extra-virgin olive oil

3 cloves garlic, minced

1 teaspoon red pepper flakes

1/3 cup dry white wine

1 cup tomato sauce

1/2 cup coarsely chopped fresh parsley

PREP TIME: 10 minutes • **COOK TIME:** 10 minutes • **SERVES:** 6

1 Cook the pasta according to the package directions. While it cooks, scrub and clean the mussels.

2 Heat the oil over medium heat in a large pot with a lid and cook the garlic for 1 minute, until pungent. Add the pepper flakes and wine, then the mussels, and put the lid on.

3 Cook about 4 minutes, until the mussels open. Discard any that don't open. Add the tomato sauce to the pot.

4 Place the drained pasta on a serving platter and pour the mussels over it along with the pan juices and liquid. Sprinkle with the parsley and serve immediately.

VARIATION
Linguine with Mussels and Peppers
Core, seed, and dice 3 red bell peppers and put them in a large pot with 3 tablespoons olive oil, 3 minced cloves garlic, and a sprinkle of red pepper flakes. Cook for about 10 minutes, until the peppers are softened, then stir in 3/4 cup tomato sauce. Meanwhile cook the mussels and shuck them into a pot, reserving the juice. Add mussels, their juices, and cooking liquid to the pepper mixture, toss with the drained pasta, and serve.

FIX IT FAST
Mussels may seem intimidating if you've never cooked them before, but they're easy. The only trick to know is that the "beard" must be removed. It's a little tag that looks like seaweed on one side. Pull it out gently and discard it *just before* cooking, because mussels die a few hours after being debearded.

TOP SECRET
Mussels, like clams, do not need to be boiled to be cooked; all they need is a quick blast of heat of any kind—grill, sauté pan, wok, or steamer—and they'll open right up. Any mussels that don't open should be fed to the compost pile; they're dead.

Linguine in Red Clam Sauce

Not sure whether you're a red or white clam sauce fan? The lines aren't as clearly drawn as the face-off between lovers of New England versus lovers of Manhattan clam chowder. One thing's certain: There's an easy way to find out.

1 pound dried linguine

2 tablespoons extra-virgin olive oil

1 yellow onion, chopped

3 cloves garlic, minced

1/2 teaspoon red pepper flakes

1 can (28 ounces) diced tomatoes (with juice)

1/2 teaspoon dried oregano

3 cans (6 1/2 ounces each) clams (with juice)

1/2 cup red wine

2 tablespoons tomato paste

Salt and pepper, to taste

1/4 cup chopped fresh parsley

PREP TIME: 10 minutes • **COOK TIME:** 10 minutes • **SERVES:** 6

1 Prepare the linguine according to the package directions. While the pasta cooks, heat the oil in a large heavy pot over medium-high heat.

2 Add the onions and cook for 3 to 4 minutes, or until softened but not browned. Add the garlic and pepper flakes and cook for 2 minutes before stirring in the tomatoes (with juice), oregano, clams (with juice), wine, and tomato paste. Bring to a boil, reduce the heat, and simmer for 5 to 6 minutes, just until the sauce starts to thicken. Season with salt and pepper.

3 Place the drained linguine on a large serving platter. Pour on the sauce and toss gently. Sprinkle with the parsley.

VARIATION

Linguine in White Clam Sauce

Omit the onions. While the linguine boils, slice the garlic instead of mincing it and use 3 tablespoons olive oil instead of 2. Skip the tomatoes and tomato paste. Use 1 cup full-bodied white wine, such as Chardonnay, instead of the red wine. Instead of canned clams, dump 1 1/2 pounds rinsed whole littleneck clams into the pot and clap on the lid. Steam for 4 minutes, until the clams open, discarding any that don't. Stir in 2 tablespoons butter and salt and pepper.

TOP SECRET

Canned clams are fine but if you have access to fresh clams, by all means, use them. How to open them? Here's a trick: Place the whole clams in their shells in the freezer for 15 to 20 minutes. The intense cold relaxes the muscles of the clams so you can slide a knife in and open them with much less force.

SEAFOOD SUPREME
Fish Fillets in a Package

En papillote is what the French call little parchment paper or foil packages of baked fish. You can fill the packets with shredded softer vegetables such as zucchini and onions, or keep them very simple, with just a little butter and herbs. Either way, you'll have a very simple, very elegant dish. Although parchment paper makes a lovely looking package, foil makes a tight, reliable seal.

4 sole fillets
(8 ounces each)
or catfish, tilapia,
or any delicate fish

Unsalted butter
or extra-virgin
olive oil

1 medium zucchini,
shredded

2 shallots,
thinly sliced

2 tablespoons
chopped fresh
thyme leaves

1 lemon,
thinly sliced

Salt and pepper,
to taste

PREP TIME: 15 minutes • **COOK TIME:** 25 minutes • **SERVES:** 4

1 Preheat the oven to 350°F. Lay four 18-inch squares of foil or parchment paper on a baking sheet.

2 Place a fillet on each, dot with butter or drizzle with olive oil, and divide the zucchini, shallots, thyme, and lemons evenly among the packets, finishing with a sprinkle of salt and pepper.

3 Fold the packages in half and twist the edges together to seal them. You want the seam to be tight so the steam stays inside.

4 Bake for 20 to 25 minutes, until packages are puffed up with steam. Serve individual packets on each plate and tear open with forks.

VARIATION
Sea Bass Packages with Vegetables

Use sea bass or snapper instead of the sole. Instead of zucchini and shallots only, dice a variety of vegetables or cut them into matchsticks. Before drizzling with the oil, mound the vegetables onto each piece of foil or parchment paper. Try celery, carrots, leeks, broccoli florets, halved grape tomatoes, slivers of red onion, and garlic. Pour on 1 to 2 tablespoons (no more!) white wine. Lay the fish on top of the vegetable mounds and sprinkle with salt. Instead of chopped thyme, put a little bundle of thyme sprigs on the fish and add a pat of butter on top of the herbs. Omit the lemon.

TOP SECRET

Fish and lemon go hand-in-hand, right? Wrong. Lemon (and any citrus fruit) can actually "cook" seafood, so unless you're making seviche (cold seafood salad made by marinating fish and shrimp in citrus), add lemon at the end of the cooking process. Fish and shrimp "cook" in citrus in 20 minutes, so if you cook them additionally, they'll be very, very tough.

Stir-Fried Shrimp with Snow Peas

When pink shrimp is stir-fried with tender green vegetables such as snow peas or fresh spinach leaves, you can have a beautifully color-coordinated meal. It's also ready really fast, provided that the rice (or noodles) is already cooked, so start it before you prepare the stir-fry ingredients. If you use peeled raw shrimp, you can have this dish on the table before a Chinese restaurant would even have time to deliver.

2 teaspoons cornstarch

3 tablespoons water

1 tablespoon cooking oil

1 tablespoon grated fresh ginger

1 clove garlic, minced

1 pound medium raw shrimp, peeled

2 cups snow peas

1/4 cup chicken stock

2 tablespoons soy sauce

2 scallions, thinly sliced

PREP TIME: 10 minutes • **COOK TIME:** 10 minutes • **SERVES:** 4

1 In a cup, mix the cornstarch with the water and set aside.

2 Heat the oil over high heat in a large nonstick skillet or a wok. Add the ginger and garlic and stir-fry for 30 seconds, then add the shrimp and stir-fry for 1 minute. Stir in the snow peas, stock, soy sauce, and cornstarch mixture.

3 Cook for 1 to 2 minutes, until the peas are bright green, the shrimp is opaque, and the sauce is thickened. Stir in the scallions, toss well, and serve immediately.

VARIATION

Garlic Shrimp with Balsamic Glaze

Stir-fry the garlic, omitting the ginger. Instead of snow peas, stock, soy sauce and cornstarch, pour in 1/4 cup balsamic vinegar and 1 tablespoon brown sugar. Cook for 2 to 3 minutes, until the shrimp is opaque, and the vinegar has boiled down to a syrupy glaze. Lift the shrimp onto a serving platter and pour the glaze over all. Sprinkle with chopped parsley instead of scallions and serve.

TOP SECRET

Ever try to get that delicious, incomparable flavor in your home stir-fries that you get in a Chinese restaurant? That elusive component found in the best Chinese cooking is called Wok Hay—or Breath of a Wok—and actually comes from a combination of things: freshness of ingredients, heat, and iron, which means that if you have access to a real Chinese cast-iron or carbon steel wok, use it! Heat it dry to the point that a small wisp of smoke emanates from the surface of the wok. Turn it off, add oil, turn it back on high, and proceed with cooking. Do not try this technique with a nonstick wok, however; the coating will melt and release toxins into the air.

SEAFOOD SUPREME
Crab Salad

Jumbo lump crabmeat is something of a costly investment—anywhere from $15 to $20 a pound in most stores—but it's so good that it seems worth its weight in gold. This easily doubled recipe serves two, perhaps for a special celebratory lunch.

1/4 cup Greek yogurt

3 tablespoons mayonnaise

2 tablespoons fresh lemon juice

2 teaspoons Dijon mustard

Salt and pepper, to taste

8 ounces jumbo lump crabmeat (about 1 cup)

1 scallion, thinly sliced

1 stalk celery, diced

PREP TIME: 15 minutes • **COOK TIME:** 0 minutes • **SERVES:** 2

1 Blend the yogurt, mayonnaise, lemon juice, and mustard in a small bowl. Season with salt and pepper.

2 Add the crab, scallions, and celery and toss together very gently to avoid breaking up the crab. Refrigerate for 20 minutes before serving, to allow the flavors to mingle.

VARIATIONS

Seafood Salad

Substitute sour cream for the yogurt and stir in 2 tablespoons chopped fresh dill. Instead of crab, gently blend in 1/2 cup flaked salmon, 1/2 cup tiny shrimp, and a handful of green peas (you can thaw frozen ones under warm water and use directly in the salad). Taste and add more lemon juice or salt, as needed.

Surimi Pasta Salad

Instead of crab, make the salad with chopped surimi (see "Top Secret" below), adding a little more mayonnaise and lemon juice, if needed. Toss the salad with 3 cups cooked small pasta shells and sprinkle with chopped chives.

DID YOU KNOW?

Jumbo lump crab meat is the meat that comes from the crab's hind legs, the largest chunks of meat. Lump crab is the smaller bits and pieces picked from the rest of the crab, so you won't get the big succulent chunks as in jumbo, but it will cost significantly less. Crab meat is also available, less expensively, in a pasteurized version, but the high-heat processing does impair the flavor; you just don't get that fresh briny sweetness that tastes so good in salad. If you're making a heated crab dish or soup, though, go for pasteurized.

TOP SECRET

If you want to replace the crab in this dish with imitation crab, you have no reason for concern: Imitation crab is in fact *not* a fake food—it's processed and shaped pollock. The Japanese invented surimi, and it appears frequently in their cooking. It is increasingly available in U.S. supermarkets, because it's inexpensive and tasty fish protein that really does taste crablike.

Shrimp and Sausage Paella

In Spanish restaurants, paella looks fabulously elaborate and complicated. In fact, it's a simple dish of rice and meat that looks all the more thrilling thanks to its presentation in a large, flat, two-handled skillet—the *paella* pan from which the dish takes its name. Happily, you don't have to own a paella pan to make a paella. Any large skillet will do.

1 tablespoon extra-virgin olive oil

8 ounces Spanish chorizo, diced (about 2 cups)

2 medium onions, chopped

1 large red bell pepper, cored, seeded, and sliced into long strips

1 teaspoon hot Spanish paprika (*pimentón*)

Salt and pepper, to taste

4 cups chicken stock

1 1/2 cups white rice

1 1/2 pound large raw shrimp, peeled

PREP TIME: 20 minutes • **COOK TIME:** 30 minutes • **SERVES:** 6

1 Heat the oil in a heavy large skillet over medium heat. Add the chorizo and cook it slowly, until it begins to render its fat. Then add the onions, peppers, and paprika and cook until the onions are tender and lightly browned. Season with salt and pepper.

2 Add the stock and the rice and bring to a boil. Reduce the heat, cover, and simmer, stirring occasionally, for about 15 minutes, or until the rice is tender.

3 Push the shrimp onto the surface of the rice. Cover and cook for about 5 minutes longer, until the shrimp turns pink.

VARIATION

Chicken and Shrimp Paella

Use 2 tablespoons olive oil, and instead of chorizo, brown 6 chicken drumsticks well before adding the vegetables. Stir 1 cup green peas into the rice before nestling the shrimp onto the surface.

TOP SECRET

Spanish paella chefs have a secret ingredient up their sleeves for making food rich and smoky...without any smoke. They use a smoked Spanish paprika called *pimentón*, which stands head and shoulders above the flavorless red powder you may have sprinkled on your deviled eggs. Available at better supermarkets, it's an addictively hot, smoky-sweet flavor whose depth and complexity can't be replaced by anything else. Also use it on scrambled eggs or hummus, or sprinkled on dips.

HOW TO MAKE THE WORLD'S BEST PARTY DISH

Some folks like pigs in blankets, and others like chips and salsa. When you're feeding a crowd, lasagna is often the way to go, but so is a casserole. But what is singularly the best, easiest-to-make, impressive party dish out there? It's paella! The only limit to a creative paella is pan size; if you have a gigantic pan, just set it over a round grill like a giant burner. There are a few secrets to making a great paella:

1 Don't rush. Cook the chorizo or spicy sausage slowly; when the olive oil begins to turn red from the spices in the sausage, add the rest of the vegetables.

2 Add the stock directly to the pan, pouring it in slowly, and stirring to keep the vegetables from sticking to the bottom of the pan.

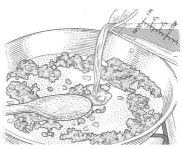

3 Pour the rice in directly on top of the broth and stir very gently.

Most important, don't peek once you've covered the pan!

SEAFOOD SUPREME

Grilled Whole Stuffed Trout

Whole fish on the grill makes for a dramatic presentation and moist, tender flesh. You don't need to stuff it with much, but a few fresh herbs and aromatics truly do permeate the flesh as the fish cooks. It's very helpful to brush liberal amounts of oil on the grill rack and also on the surface of the fish.

4 whole trout (about 12 ounces each), cleaned with heads left on

Salt and pepper, to taste

8 sprigs of fresh thyme

Handful of fresh chives

2 lemons, cut into narrow wedges

Oil, for brushing

PREP TIME: 3 minutes • **COOK TIME:** 15 minutes • **SERVES:** 4

1 Prepare the grill, allowing the coals to burn to medium hot, gray with a red underglow, or preheat a gas grill on high for 10 minutes with the lid down, then turn off the second side.

2 Sprinkle the inside of each fish generously with salt and pepper. Loosely stuff the fish with thyme and chives, and fit 1 or 2 lemon wedges into each.

3 Brush the surface of the grill rack and the outside of the fish liberally with oil. Lay the fish on the rack over direct heat and grill for 2 minutes per side, then move to indirect heat and grill for 6 minutes on each side, until browned and cooked through. Peek inside the cavity of one and see if the flesh is opaque yet, as larger fish will need a few extra minutes of cooking time. Eat immediately.

VARIATION
Planked Trout
Soak cedar planks in water overnight. Brush them lightly with olive oil and lay portions of fish on them. Place them on the grill, making sure to leave at least 3 inches between them, and cover the grill. Fillets that are 1 inch thick should take 10 to 15 minutes.

TOP SECRET

When cooking large fish whole, it helps to slash the exterior to let the heat penetrate faster and more easily. Using the sharp edge of a chef's knife, scrape along the surface of the skin from tail to head to feel for and remove any remaining scales (they may be invisible to the eye, but you'll feel them under the knife). Then slash three long angled cuts spaced down the length of the fish. Don't cut quite through to the center of the fish. Do this on both sides, and be sure to rub a little oil and salt into the slashes before cooking.

Grilled Tuna Steaks with Tomato Relish

Some recipes call for marinating the fish prior to cooking, but tuna is already such a flavorful, fatty fish that cooking it plain is often preferable. Also, marinating won't add moisture in the case of fish— you need to preserve the moisture that's already in there by not overcooking it. It's very easy to turn $15 worth of tuna steaks into cat food, so give the tuna extra attention and err on the side of undercooking.

RELISH

3 plum tomatoes, halved

1 small red onion, diced small

Zest and juice of 1 lime

2 tablespoons capers

Salt and pepper, to taste

TUNA

4 tuna steaks (8 ounces each), cut about 1 inch thick

Extra-virgin olive oil, for brushing

Salt and pepper, to taste

PREP TIME: 2 minutes • **COOK TIME:** 8 minutes • **SERVES:** 4

1 Prepare a charcoal grill, allowing the coals to burn to a hot fire, glowing red, or preheat a gas grill on high with the lid shut for 10 minutes.

2 *For the relish:* Squeeze the seeds and excess liquid from the tomatoes. Dice the tomatoes and add to a medium bowl. Mix in the onions, lime zest and juice, and capers. Season with salt and pepper.

3 *For the tuna:* Brush the steaks with oil and sprinkle with salt and pepper. Brush the grill rack with oil. Lay the steaks on the rack and cook for 4 minutes on one side and 2 minutes on the other.

4 Serve with the relish on the side.

VARIATION

Salade Niçoise

Although authentic Salade Niçoise is made with a can of drained tuna, chefs like to serve a fancier version with fresh cooked tuna, and grilled steaks are ideal. Top a handful of mixed baby greens with diced cooked potatoes and thin green beans cooked tender-crisp. Add a handful of black olives, some sliced red onions, and some chopped tomatoes. Dress with a few tablespoons of olive oil mixed with red-wine vinegar and Dijon mustard and lay a cooled, grilled tuna steak on top.

TOP SECRET

There is a fine line between raw and overcooked when it comes to seafood, and fresh tuna is no exception. How do you get that lovely perfect layer of pink when preparing this persnickety fish? Simple: Cook it for a longer time on the first side, and a much shorter time— 50% shorter—on the second. When you remove it from the heat, let it stand for about 2 additional minutes; it will continue to cook, but it will also retain its lovely rosy color—and its tenderness.

SEAFOOD SUPREME

Bacon-Wrapped Grilled Scallops

In honor of rumaki, that old cocktail party standard of bacon-wrapped chicken livers, this bacon-wrapped scallop is moist, tasty, and practically foolproof since the bacon keeps the mollusk moist. If you're using wooden skewers instead of metal, they must be soaked in water prior to threading on the food.

20 large sea scallops (about 1 1/2 pounds)

10 strips smoked bacon, cut in half

20 whole small white mushrooms, wiped clean

2 tablespoons butter

1 clove garlic, minced

2 tablespoons chopped fresh parsley

2 tablespoons fresh lemon juice

Freshly ground black pepper

PREP TIME: 10 minutes • **COOK TIME:** 6 minutes • **SERVES:** 4

1 Prepare a charcoal grill and let the coals burn to a hot fire, glowing red, or preheat a gas grill on high with the lid down for 10 minutes.

2 Wrap each scallop once around with a half-strip of bacon, and thread onto 4 skewers alternating with the mushrooms.

3 Grill for 5 to 6 minutes, turning frequently to cook evenly on each side. Remove the skewers to a warm serving platter.

4 In a small saucepan, melt the butter over very low heat and stir in the garlic and parsley. Don't brown or sizzle the garlic; just infuse the butter with garlic flavor. Add the lemon juice, and grind in some pepper. Stir the sauce and pour immediately over the scallop skewers.

VARIATION

Bacon-Wrapped Kebabs

Alternate the bacon-wrapped scallops on skewers with shrimp and whole cherry tomatoes instead of mushrooms. Drizzle with olive oil and sprinkle well with salt and pepper. Grill until the shrimp is pink and the tomatoes are softened. Squeeze the lemon juice over the kebabs and serve at once.

TOP SECRET

When skewering two things that cook at different rates—such as mushrooms (which cook quickly) and bacon-wrapped scallops (which cook less quickly)—it's important to make sure that you keep turning the skewers so that nothing burns or undercooks.

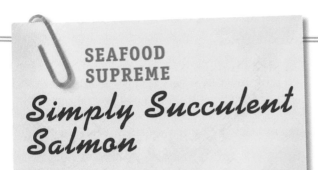

SEAFOOD SUPREME

Simply Succulent Salmon

This very traditionally French way of cooking fish creates a protective coating that seals in the moisture of the salmon while lending rich flavor. Of course, it's still important to avoid overcooking the fish, but you'll be amazed how such a simple technique yields such big rewards.

3 tablespoons mayonnaise

1 tablespoon Dijon mustard

2 tablespoons chopped fresh parsley

1 teaspoon grated orange zest

4 salmon fillets (about 1 1/2 pounds)

1/2 teaspoon salt

1/8 teaspoon freshly ground black pepper

PREP TIME: 5 minutes • **COOK TIME:** 15 minutes • **SERVES:** 4

1 Preheat the oven to 500°F. Coat a baking sheet with cooking spray.

2 In a small bowl, whisk together the mayonnaise, mustard, parsley, and orange zest.

3 Sprinkle the salmon with the salt and pepper. Coat each fillet with some of the mayonnaise mixture and set on the baking sheet.

4 Roast for 10 to 12 minutes, or until the fish flakes easily with a fork.

VARIATION

Yummy Tender Chicken Breasts

This technique works just as well on chicken (and pork or other types of fish). Adjust the seasonings, as desired; add garlic and rosemary for the chicken and try chopped sage for the pork.

TOP SECRET

Mayonnaise is not just for tuna salad anymore! Blended with a bit of Dijon mustard and then brushed onto fish, it not only adds a wallop of flavor but it literally seals the flesh, keeping it deliciously moist and succulent. Try this secret on absolutely any fish.

SEAFOOD SUPREME
Dill-Drizzled Poached Salmon

Cool and refreshing, this recipe tastes like springtime on a plate. Diced cucumbers add juicy crunch to the sour cream dill sauce that's dolloped over salmon poached in white wine. For the richest flavor, buy wild Alaskan salmon in season from May to September.

SALMON
1 1/2 cups water

1 cup
dry white wine

2 scallions, sliced

8 black peppercorns

4 salmon
fillets (about
1 1/2 pounds)

Fresh dill sprigs

SAUCE
3/4 cup sour cream

1/3 cup peeled,
diced cucumber

2 tablespoons
snipped fresh dill

1 tablespoon fresh
lemon juice

1/4 teaspoon salt

1/8 teaspoon
freshly ground
black pepper

PREP TIME: 15 minutes • **COOK TIME:** 10 minutes • **SERVES:** 4

1 *For the salmon:* Pour the water into a large nonstick skillet. Stir in the wine, scallions, and peppercorns. Put the salmon in the skillet in a single layer. Bring to just a boil over high heat.

2 Reduce the heat to medium-low, cover, and simmer for about 6 minutes, or until the fish flakes easily with a fork.

3 *For the sauce:* Stir the sour cream, cucumbers, snipped dill, lemon juice, salt, and pepper in a medium bowl. Refrigerate if not serving immediately.

4 Carefully transfer the fish with a slotted spatula to a large platter. Add the dill sprigs. Serve hot or chilled with the sauce.

VARIATION
Poached Salmon in Spicy Dill Sauce
Stir 2 teaspoons prepared horseradish into the sauce for extra zing.

TOP SECRET
Gone are the days when sour cream was just for strawberries or blintzes; it does amazing double-duty as a dense and luscious cream sauce in this recipe. Feel free to use the low-fat or nonfat versions, but the full fat is the best.

Crispy Citrus Tuna

Their beefy texture makes tuna steaks a favorite with confirmed meat-eaters. In this tangy recipe, the seasoned cornmeal seals in the tuna's juicy flavor. Who could resist?

SAUCE

1 1/2 cups fresh orange juice

2 tablespoons dry white wine (optional)

2 tablespoons cornstarch

2 large oranges, peeled and sectioned

TUNA

2 tablespoons chopped fresh cilantro

2 tablespoons cornmeal

Salt, to taste

1/4 teaspoon freshly ground black pepper

4 tuna steaks (1/2 inch thick, 6 ounces each)

4 teaspoons extra-virgin olive oil

PREP TIME: 15 minutes • **COOK TIME:** 9 minutes • **SERVES:** 4

1 *For the sauce:* Whisk the orange juice, wine (if using), and cornstarch in small saucepan until smooth. Bring to a boil over medium-high heat and cook, stirring, for about 2 minutes, until it boils and thickens. Remove from the heat and stir in the oranges. Keep warm.

2 *For the tuna:* Mix the cilantro, cornmeal, salt, and pepper in a pie plate. Coat both sides of the tuna steaks with the cornmeal mixture, pressing firmly so it adheres.

3 Heat 2 teaspoons of the oil in a large cast-iron skillet over medium-high heat until hot but not smoking. Sear the tuna until done to taste, 2 to 3 minutes on each side for medium-rare. Add the remaining 2 teaspoons of oil just before turning the fish. Serve with the sauce.

VARIATION

Cornmeal-Crusted Swordfish

For variety, try this recipe with fresh swordfish, and replace the orange in the sauce with lemon.

TOP SECRET

Everybody has this pantry staple.... Cornmeal is the perfect way to add a bit of crunchy coating to fish (and chicken or steak, for that matter). Opt for the finely ground variety.

SEAFOOD SUPREME
Baja Fish Tacos

Fish tacos make a light, refreshing entrée, and briefly simmering the fish in bottled picante sauce keeps it moist.

4 skinless mahi-mahi fillets (about 1 pound), halved lengthwise

1 tablespoon Mexican seasoning, such as McCormick's

1 teaspoon unsweetened cocoa powder

1 tablespoon olive oil

1 cup medium spicy picante sauce

3/4 cup thinly sliced Vidalia or other sweet onion

1 tablespoon chopped fresh cilantro

1 tablespoon fresh lime juice

1/8 teaspoon salt

8 fresh corn tortillas (6-inch)

1/2 cup sour cream

PREP TIME: 15 minutes • **COOK TIME:** 15 minutes • **SERVES:** 4

1 Combine the fish, seasoning, and cocoa powder in a large bowl and toss well to coat.

2 Heat the oil in a large nonstick skillet over medium-high heat. Add the fillets, skin-side down, and cook for about 4 minutes, until lightly browned, turning once. Stir in the picante sauce and reduce the heat to medium. Simmer, turning occasionally, for 6 to 8 minutes, or until the fish flakes easily with a fork.

3 Meanwhile, combine the onions, cilantro, lime juice, and salt in a small bowl and mix well.

4 Heat the tortillas according to the package directions. Place 1 piece of fish, 1 tablespoon of the sauce, and a quarter of the onion mixture on each tortilla. Top each with 1 tablespoon sour cream.

VARIATION
Cheesy Baja Tacos
For added richness and color, top each taco with 1 tablespoon shredded cheddar cheese. Or, to help the cheese melt, scatter it over the warm tortilla and then top it with the hot fish.

TOP SECRET
Adding prepared cocoa powder to premade Mexican seasoning adds amazing depth of flavor to the dish.

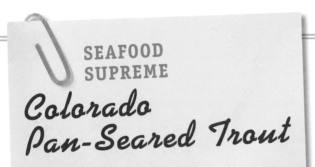

Colorado Pan-Seared Trout

One of the most beloved fish in the world, trout takes extremely well to pan-frying. Look for freshly caught fish, preferably with head and tail intact. (A nice fishmonger will remove them for you.)

1/2 cup freshly grated Parmesan cheese

1/2 cup crushed bacon-flavored crackers

1/2 cup cornmeal

1/4–1/2 teaspoon garlic salt

Pinch of freshly ground black pepper

2 eggs

1/2 cup milk

4 lake trout fillets (about 2 pounds), rinsed and patted dry

1/2 cup vegetable oil

Lemon wedges and/ or snipped fresh chives or parsley (optional)

TIME: 10 minutes • **COOK TIME:** 10 minutes • **SERVES:** 4

1 In a shallow bowl, combine the Parmesan, crackers, cornmeal, garlic salt, and pepper.

2 In another shallow bowl, beat together the eggs and milk.

3 Dip the fish in the egg mixture, then gently roll in the crumb mixture.

4 Heat the oil in a 12-inch skillet until hot. Add the fish in a single layer and fry for 5 to 7 minutes, turning once, until the fish flakes easily with a fork. Add the lemon and/or chives or parsley, if using, before serving.

VARIATION
Lake Trout Française
These fillets taste great with just a squeeze of lemon, but you can gild the lily by serving it with a quick aioli. Mix together 1/2 cup mayonnaise, 1 tablespoon fresh lemon juice, 1 tablespoon extra-virgin olive oil, and 2 minced cloves garlic.

TOP SECRET
This recipe takes a cue from an old Southern trick... using crackers as a coating! In this case, ratchet up the flavor by using bacon-flavored crackers. Yum!

7 ONE-DISH MEALS
FOR EVERY OCCASION

Everyone loves dishes like fried chicken and French toast, but one-dish meals are hands-down favorites of home cooks everywhere. Who doesn't love a cozy casserole that you can assemble ahead of time or pull out of the freezer when guests suddenly show up? The slow cooker is also a good place to start for one-dish meals, and if yours has been collecting dust for years, take it out! After a tiring day at work, we all have times when we need to get something on the table without a lot of effort, and this is where one-dish meals come in. Even professional chefs call this their family meal, which is actually what they're serving their staffs early in the evening before dinner service. Nine times out of ten, it's a one-dish meal!

Baked Tomato Shrimp over Orzo

An amazingly fast dish for how elegant and delicious it is, this baked shrimp over orzo, a rice-shaped pasta, may make you feel like you're visiting a Greek island.

2 tablespoons extra-virgin olive oil

1 pound orzo

4 cups water or chicken stock

1 teaspoon salt

1 medium yellow onion, diced

1 clove garlic, minced

1 can (28 ounces) diced tomatoes (with juice)

1 1/2 pounds raw medium shrimp, peeled

1/2 cup crumbled feta

Pepper, to taste

PREP TIME: 5 minutes • **COOK TIME:** 15 minutes • **SERVES:** 6

1 Preheat the oven to 400°F. In a medium saucepan over medium-high heat, heat 1 tablespoon of the oil and add the orzo. Toss to coat lightly with oil, then cook for 1 to 2 minutes, until the orzo is lightly browned. Add the water or stock and salt; cover. Bring to a boil, then reduce the heat to medium-low, cover and cook for 15 minutes, until the liquid is absorbed.

2 Meanwhile, heat the remaining 1 tablespoon oil in a large ovenproof skillet. Cook the onions for 3 to 4 minutes until just translucent. Stir in the garlic and cook for 1 minute until fragrant. Add the tomatoes (with juice) and simmer for 10 minutes, until the sauce starts to thicken. Taste and add salt, if needed.

3 Stir in the shrimp and sprinkle with feta. Bake for 12 minutes, until the feta melts and the shrimp is pink.

4 Spoon the orzo onto a serving dish and pour the shrimp over. Sprinkle with pepper and serve.

VARIATION

Spicy Feta Shrimp

Doctor the sauce by adding 1/2 cup dry white wine, 1/4 cup chopped fresh basil, and 1/2 teaspoon red pepper flakes along with the can of tomatoes.

DID YOU KNOW?

A whole block of feta cheese will keep for weeks without souring if you keep changing the water. Store feta in a sealed container with water to cover. Every 3 days, pour off the water and replace with fresh water.

TOP SECRET

Like loves like; in other words, if you are using an ingredient from a specific area or region, odds are that other ingredients from the same area are a good mate. Take feta, which comes from the Mediterranean: It's a natural for Mediterranean flavors, like lemon, tomato, thyme, garlic, olive oil, and seafood.

Chicken Potpie

If your idea of chicken potpie is the kind that comes out of a freezer box, you'll be surprised how good, and how simple, the homemade version is, all the way through to making your own flaky and tender pie crust to top it.

FILLING

4 chicken breasts, bone-in

Salt, to taste

1 chicken stock cube

1/2 cup (1 stick) unsalted butter

1 large yellow onion, diced

1 stalk celery, thinly sliced

2 large carrots, peeled and diced small

1/2 cup all-purpose flour

1/4 cup heavy cream

Salt and pepper, to taste

1 package (10 ounces) frozen peas

PASTRY

3 cups flour

1 teaspoon salt

1/2 teaspoon baking powder

1 cup (2 sticks) unsalted butter

1/2 cup cold water

1 egg yolk, beaten

PREP TIME: 20 minutes • **COOK TIME:** 1 hour • **SERVES:** 6

1 *For the filling:* Bring a medium saucepan of salted water to a boil and put in the chicken. Simmer gently for 30 minutes, spooning off any scum that rises. Remove the chicken to a plate, reserving the cooking liquid, and discard the skin and bone. Cut the meat into cubes.

2 Dissolve the stock cube in 4 cups of the reserved cooking liquid, discarding the rest. In a large stew pot over medium-low heat, melt the butter and add the onions, celery, and carrots. Cook until softened but not browned, about 15 minutes. Stir in the flour and cook, stirring, for 2 minutes. Slowly whisk in the hot chicken stock and cook for 2 minutes, whisking constantly, until thickened. Stir in the cream and season with salt and pepper. Add the cubed chicken and peas and stir gently to combine.

3 *For the pastry:* Combine the flour, salt, and baking powder in a food processor. Add the butter and pulse until the mixture is like cornmeal. With the motor on, slowly drizzle in the water just until the dough forms a ball. Wrap in plastic wrap and chill for 20 minutes in the freezer.

4 Preheat the oven to 350°F. Spoon the filling into a shallow 2-quart casserole dish. Roll the dough to 1/4-inch thickness and fit it over the top, pressing firmly to seal it all around the edges of the dish. Cut several slits in the top with the tip of a sharp paring knife. Brush with the egg and sprinkle with salt. Put the casserole on a baking dish and bake for 1 hour, until the filling is bubbling and the crust is a deep gold.

TOP SECRET

This dish (along with shepherd's pie, cottage pie, and the like) was born out of the need to use up leftovers, so this is an ideal way to use up the meat stripped off a rotisserie chicken, or anything that's leftover.

Broccoli Rabe, Chicken, and Pasta Bake

This dish, born out of a refrigerator full of leftovers (spicy greens, leftover chicken, grate-able cheese) is rustic enough to be eaten on a cold and blustery night in front of a roaring fire and gorgeous enough to be fed to a hungry crowd. The proportions here are just a guideline, so add more of anything as you see fit.

3 tablespoons extra-virgin olive oil

2 cloves garlic, minced

1 bunch broccoli rabe, blanched in boiling water, drained, and chopped

1 cup shredded or diced leftover chicken

2 cups cooked tubular pasta, such as penne or ziti

1/8 teaspoon red pepper flakes

Salt, to taste

1/4 cup breadcrumbs

2 tablespoons freshly grated Parmesan cheese

PREP TIME: 20 minutes • **COOK TIME:** 20 minutes • **SERVES:** 4–6

1 Preheat the oven to 350°F. In a large, ovenproof skillet, heat 2 tablespoons of the oil over medium-high heat until shimmering, and add the garlic. Sauté for 2 minutes, and add the broccoli rabe. Toss well to coat.

2 Blend in the chicken, pasta, red pepper flakes, and salt, and toss well so that everything is evenly combined.

3 Sprinkle evenly with breadcrumbs and Parmesan, and moisten with the remaining tablespoon of oil. Bake for 20 minutes, until the top is golden and crispy. Serve immediately.

VARIATION

Tuna Casserole Bake

Replace the broccoli rabe with frozen peas (no need to thaw), the chicken with canned tuna, and the pasta with egg noodles. Add a 12-ounce can of cream of mushroom soup to the pan along with the pasta, blend well, and proceed with the rest of the recipe.

LEFTOVER LUXURIES

This recipe is already a leftover luxury, but if you have leftovers of the dish itself, serve them cold atop a bowl of leafy greens, such as baby spinach or arugula. Delicious and packable for work for school.

TOP SECRET

Broccoli rabe, also known as rapini, can be extremely bitter. How do chefs sweeten it? Simple: Give it a minute-long dunk in a pot of boiling salted water, and the bitterness will disappear, like magic. And if you're boiling noodles from scratch for this recipe (instead of using pre-cooked leftover noodles), boil them in the same pot that you've blanched the rabe in. The result will be a lot more flavor (and one less pot to wash).

Pork Fried Rice

In American Chinese restaurants, fried rice is often an entrée, packed with bits of meat and vegetables. It may seem tricky to get it just so at home, with every grain separate and gleaming, but once you master the secret, you'll turn to this dish again and again as a quick supper.

2 tablespoons vegetable oil

3 eggs

1 teaspoon toasted sesame oil

1 small yellow onion, diced

4 scallions, thinly sliced

3 cloves garlic, minced

1 cup cubed cooked pork

1 cup frozen peas

Salt, to taste

4 cups cold cooked rice

1 tablespoon soy sauce

PREP TIME: 8 minutes • **COOK TIME:** 10 minutes • **SERVES:** 4

1 In a large nonstick skillet over medium heat, heat 1 tablespoon of the vegetable oil until shimmering. Beat the eggs lightly in a cup with the sesame oil and pour into the pan. Cook, lifting and turning the eggs with a heat-proof spatula, until just scrambled, about 2 minutes. Spoon into a small bowl and set aside.

2 Pour in the remaining vegetable oil and add the onions, scallions, and garlic. Cook 2 minutes, until the onions just start to take on color. Stir in the pork and peas and sprinkle with salt. Cook 1 minute, then stir in the rice, breaking up any clumps and tossing frequently.

3 Cook until heated through, about 5 minutes, then stir in the soy sauce and eggs. Serve at once.

VARIATION

Ham and Pineapple Fried Rice with Ginger

Omit the scrambled egg. Cook 1 tablespoon minced fresh ginger with the garlic, and use ham cubes in place of the pork. At the very end, along with the soy sauce, stir in 1 cup diced fresh pineapple and heat through for 1 minute. Serve with chili-garlic sauce on the side.

TOP SECRET

When you set out to make fried rice at home, it's absolutely crucial that the rice is day-old and cold in the refrigerator or the recipe simply will not work, so plan ahead in order to have enough leftovers. If you already have leftover roast pork or pork chops, it's worth cooking and chilling the rice separately just to make this delicious dish.

THE KING OF ONE-DISH MEALS

Most of us think of fried rice as that surefire, delicious comfort food that we order as takeout from the local Chinese restaurant. The truth is that virtually every culture lays claim to a version of the dish, and while our tendency is to think of it as strictly Asian, it isn't. What is true about fried rice is that it's the perfect vehicle for all manner of culinary creativity: If you have a batch of cold, leftover rice in your fridge, you've got the basis for a great, one-dish meal. Here are some less-obvious add-ins that may be lurking in your fridge or pantry. For Asian-style fried rice, stick with soy sauce as a base; for everything else, use extra-virgin olive oil in place of vegetable oil.

1 Cooked ham (any kind), diced or torn into small bits

2 Roast turkey, diced

3 Imitation crabmeat

4 Frozen or fresh spinach

5 Cooked bacon, crumbled

6 Red, white, or sweet onions, diced

7 Ground beef, cooked and drained

8 Tomatoes, canned or fresh, chopped

9 Salmon, canned or fresh, flaked

10 Smoked salmon, flaked

11 Ground pork, cooked and drained

12 Canned black beans, drained

13 Canned chickpeas, drained

14 Cooked grains (quinoa, bulgur, millet, barley)

15 Roasted or grilled vegetables

16 Roasted chicken, pulled off the bone

17 Goat cheese

18 Curry

19 Cooked sausage or hot dogs, diced

20 Barbecued pork or beef, diced

Baked Eggplant Parmesan

Most eggplant Parmesan dishes start with deep-frying the eggplant, which is delicious but laden with fat since eggplant slices act just like a sponge when they're placed in oil. This version begins with eggplant slices dredged in flour and baked until golden, then layered with cheese and tomato sauce. It takes a bit of time, but it's not difficult and the results are well worth the effort.

2 eggs

2 tablespoons milk

3/4 cup flour

3/4 cup Parmesan cheese

2 teaspoons dried whole oregano

Salt and pepper, to taste

2 large eggplants (2 1/2 pounds total), cut in 1/2-inch-thick slices

2 tablespoons extra-virgin olive oil

1 medium onion, diced

2 cloves garlic, minced

2 cans (28 ounces each) whole tomatoes (with juice)

2 cups shredded mozzarella

PREP TIME: 15 minutes • **COOK TIME:** 1 hour • **SERVES:** 6

1 Preheat the oven to 400°F. Line 2 baking sheets with lightly oiled parchment paper or foil. In a shallow bowl, whisk the eggs with the milk. On a deep plate, toss the flour with 1/2 cup of the Parmesan, 1 teaspoon of the oregano, and a sprinkle of salt and pepper.

2 Dip each slice of eggplant in the egg, then in the flour, and place on the baking sheets. Bake for 15 to 20 minutes, until browned, then flip and bake for 15 to 20 minutes longer, until browned and tender.

3 Meanwhile, heat the oil in a large skillet over medium heat and cook the onions for 10 minutes, until tender and lightly browned. Add the garlic and cook for 1 minute. Stir in the tomatoes (with juice), crushing them with the back of a spoon. Add the remaining teaspoon of oregano and bring to a boil. Reduce the heat and simmer for 20 minutes, until thickened.

4 When the eggplant is done, spread 2 cups of the tomato sauce in a 9 x 13-inch dish. Place half the eggplant over the sauce and top with 2 more cups tomato sauce, and 1/2 cup mozzarella. Repeat with remaining eggplant and sauce, and top with the remaining mozzarella. Top with the remaining 1/4 cup Parmesan and bake for 25 minutes, or until browned and bubbling.

TOP SECRET

Eggplant is packed with water that has to be forced out before the baking or frying process begins. Sprinkle each slice liberally with Kosher salt and layer them in a colander. Set in the sink to drain for at least 30 minutes. The eggplant may brown slightly, but it will also release a notable quantity of brown liquid, allowing your purged slices to fry up faster and easier. Rinse lightly and pat dry with paper towels before cooking.

Lentils and Chorizo with Rosemary

If you like beans, odds are you like lentils, too—and if you don't, this is the recipe to introduce them to your family. Meaty, hearty, rich, and deeply complex in flavor, it can be either a filling one-bowl meal or an elegant side dish to roast chicken. It's good hot in winter or room temperature in summer and dressed with a splash of red-wine vinegar.

2 tablespoons extra-virgin olive oil

1 large yellow onion, chopped

4 ounces chorizo, diced

2 cloves garlic

3 stalks celery, finely sliced

2 large carrots, peeled and finely diced

2 cups brown or green lentils

4 cups water or chicken stock

2 cups red wine

2 bay leaves

3 sprigs of rosemary

1 tablespoon hot Spanish paprika (*pimentón*)

Salt and pepper, to taste

PREP TIME: 10 minutes • **COOK TIME:** 35 minutes • **SERVES:** 6

1 In a large heavy stewpot, heat the oil over medium-high heat and cook the onions with the chorizo until the onions are softened and lightly browned, about 7 minutes.

2 Add the garlic, celery, and carrots and cook, stirring, 2 to 3 minutes, until the vegetables are softened. Stir in the lentils, water or stock, wine, bay leaves, rosemary, and paprika and season lightly with salt and pepper.

3 Bring to a boil and cook for about 1/2 hour, or until the lentils are tender. Add a bit more water or stock, if necessary. The finished lentils should not be soupy, but should have a bit of juicy sauce. Remove the bay leaves, season with salt and pepper, and serve.

VARIATION

Bacon Lentils with Rosemary

Replace the chorizo with 6 slices of diced thick-cut smoked bacon and cook it with the onions until the bacon is cooked through and crisp, spooning off the excess fat. Replace the Spanish paprika with 2 tablespoons chopped fresh rosemary leaves.

TOP SECRET

If you remember lentils as those bland things you ate in the 1960s and 1970s (remember lentil nut loaf?), you'll want to know how French chefs make sure that their lentils are packed with flavor. Lentils actually favor smoke, as do some greens (like collards and kale). Whether you choose to use smoky meat (bacon, chorizo, ham, or sausage) or just Spanish paprika, cooking lentils with a smoky companion will forever change the way you—and your guests—think about them.

Baked Stuffed Peppers

Cinnamon and cloves add an exotic flavor to these stuffed peppers, but you could also add a pinch of ground ginger, mace, cardamom, or allspice as well. The filling can be prepared up to 2 days in advance, but the important thing here is to cook the peppers until they're truly soft, so you're not scooping the melting and fragrant filling out of a half-cooked and unyielding vegetable.

4 large bell peppers (about 8 ounces each)

1/4 cup olive oil

1 large yellow onion, chopped

1 pound lean ground beef

1 can (14 ounces) diced tomatoes (with juice)

1/2 teaspoon ground cinnamon

1/4 teaspoon ground cloves

1 cup cooked white rice

Salt and freshly ground black pepper, to taste

1/4 cup dried bread crumbs

PREP TIME: 10 minutes • **COOK TIME:** 30 minutes • **SERVES:** 4

1 Preheat the oven to 425°F and bring a large pot of water to a boil over high heat. Cut off the stem end of the peppers and scoop out the seeds and membranes. Add the peppers to the boiling water and bring back to a boil. Cook rapidly for 12 to 15 minutes, until slightly softened.

2 Meanwhile, heat 2 tablespoons of the oil in a large skillet over medium-high heat. Add the onions and cook for about 4 minutes, until softened. Add the beef and cook, stirring, until crumbled and no longer pink, about 5 minutes. Add the tomatoes (with juice), cinnamon, cloves, and rice. Cook and stir for about 3 minutes, or until the liquid is absorbed. Season with salt and pepper.

3 Remove the peppers from the water and drain on paper towels. Pack each of the peppers with 1 cup filling.

4 Arrange in a shallow baking dish and sprinkle the tops with breadcrumbs. Drizzle with the remaining oil and bake for 10 to 15 minutes, or until nicely browned.

VARIATION

Stuffed Tomatoes

Replace the cinnamon and cloves in the filling with 2 tablespoons sliced fresh basil leaves. Scoop the seeds and most of the flesh and juices from 2 large ripe summer tomatoes. Chop the scooped-out tomato flesh and add to the filling. Skip the boiling water, and pack the filling into the tomatoes. Bake for 25 minutes, until the tomatoes are tender and the filling is hot.

TOP SECRET

Here's a secret trick to keeping lopsided bell peppers or tomatoes upright during the baking process: Place them in the separate cups of a muffin tin before baking.

Tomato and Sausage Risotto

This risotto is notable for using tomatoes for the liquid instead of the usual chicken stock, making it a heartier dish. Serve it with lots of extra Parmesan for dusting, and don't be shy about stirring in that final tablespoon or two of butter: That last fillip of fat is every chef's secret weapon for flavor.

1 can (28 ounces) diced tomatoes (with juice)

4 cups water

1 tablespoon olive oil

1 pound sweet Italian sausage

1 large yellow onion, diced

2 cloves garlic, minced

1 1/2 cups Arborio rice

1 cup dry white wine

1 box (10 ounces) frozen chopped spinach, thawed and squeezed dry

1/2 cup grated Parmesan cheese

2 tablespoons unsalted butter

Salt and pepper, to taste

PREP TIME: 5 minutes • **COOK TIME:** 25 minutes • **SERVES:** 6

1 Heat the tomatoes (with juice) and water in a large saucepan over medium-low heat. In a large skillet over medium heat, add the oil and squeeze the sausages out of their casings. Cook the sausage, breaking it up with a spoon, until no longer pink. Add the onions and garlic and cook for 3 to 4 minutes, until softened.

2 Add the rice and stir until each grain is coated with fat, about 2 minutes. Pour in the wine and stir for about 2 minutes, or until it's mostly absorbed.

3 Stir in a ladleful of tomatoes and cook, stirring often, for 4 minutes, until absorbed. Continue adding tomato sauce, about 1 cup at a time and stirring often, until all the liquid is absorbed and the rice is tender, about 25 minutes altogether. With the final ladle of tomatoes, stir in the spinach and cook until heated through.

4 Stir in the Parmesan and butter and season with salt and pepper. Serve with extra Parmesan for dusting.

TOP SECRET

There are two tricks to making a great risotto; patience and the right rice. Don't ever attempt to make this ancient dish with regular long-grain rice because it will turn mushy, not creamy, when cooked in this manner. Second, use a heavyweight pot that distributes heat evenly. Melt the butter, oil, or fat slowly, add the rice, stir, and don't add any liquid until all of the grains are coated with fat. The very minute that the rice stops absorbing liquid, you'll know that it's done.

Old-Fashioned Stuffed Cabbage

It seems like everyone's mom and grandmother has a stuffed cabbage recipe, but if yours didn't pass one down, here's a basic recipe to get you started, just ready for your own family's tastes to be imprinted on it.

1 large head Savoy cabbage

2 tablespoons extra-virgin olive oil

1 medium onion, diced

1 carrot, peeled and grated

1 stalk celery, thinly sliced

1 1/2 teaspoons salt

1/2 teaspoon pepper

1 pound lean ground beef

1/2 cup raw white long-grain rice

2 tablespoons tomato paste

4 cups tomato juice

PREP TIME: 30 minutes • **COOK TIME:** 1 hour • **SERVES:** 6

1 Bring a large pot of salted water to a boil, and trim the core out of the cabbage. Set the whole cabbage into the boiling water and cook for 3 to 4 minutes, until the leaves have softened. Carefully lift it out and run under cold water until cool enough to handle. Gently separate the leaves to keep them intact.

2 Heat the oil in a large skillet and cook the onions, carrots, and celery for about 10 minutes, until soft. Transfer to a large bowl and stir in the salt and pepper. Cool for 10 minutes, then stir in the meat, rice, and tomato paste. It's easiest to mix with your hands so that the meat is evenly distributed.

3 Put about 3 tablespoons of ground beef filling in the bottom of a large cabbage leave. (If there is a very large vein, as there will be in some of the outer leaves, trim it out with a sharp paring knife.) Fold the sides in over the filling and roll, tucking in the ends. Continue, using all the leaves and filling. You may need 2 smaller leaves to make a roll as you get into the center of the cabbage. Lay the rolls in even layers in a large, heavy pan.

4 Pour the tomato juice over the rolls. Bring to a boil, then reduce the heat to low and cover. Simmer gently for about 45 minutes.

LEFTOVER LUXURIES

Cabbage rolls in tomato sauce freeze very well. Cook as directed, then layer into a casserole dish, pour the sauce over, cover tightly with a double layer of foil, and freeze for up to 4 months. To reheat, place covered pan in a 350°F oven and bake for 1 hour, until the sauce is bubbling and rolls are heated through.

TOP SECRET

Stuffed cabbage rolls are terrific served right out of the pot. But they are a heck of a lot better the next day. This fact seems to be true also for stews, soups, and even chili. Why? When the flavors have time to "rest," they also tend to mellow, mingle, and deepen. If you are able, make this dish the night before you want to serve it, and you will be rewarded.

Slow Cooker Lamb and Turnip Stew

Unlike beef stew, which really needs the meat to be browned first, lamb stew is ideally suited to the slow cooker, which brings it to tender perfection. Season with a generous hand. This Irish stew should be pale, but not bland.

2 pounds round-bone lamb chops

2 medium onions, sliced

2 carrots, sliced

2 medium potatoes, peeled and cubed

6 small or 4 medium turnips, peeled and cubed

1 teaspoon salt

1 teaspoon chopped fresh thyme leaves

1/2 teaspoon pepper

2 beef stock cubes

Water

PREP TIME: 5 minutes • **COOK TIME:** 8 hours • **SERVES:** 6

1 Layer the lamb chops in the slow cooker with the onions, carrots, potatoes, and turnips, sprinkling with salt, thyme, and pepper as you work.

2 Crumble the stock cubes on top and add water to cover, stirring the stock cubes in slightly. Put the lid on and cook on low for 8 to 10 hours or on high for 4 to 5 hours.

VARIATION

Slow Cooker Beef Stew

Replace the lamb with stew beef cubes. Leave out the turnips and add an extra carrot and potato (or two). Sprinkle the beef cubes lightly with flour, salt, and pepper and brown them on all sides in a skillet with 2 tablespoons oil before tipping them into the slow cooker. Pour a little water into the pan and swish any remaining pan juices around, then add to the slow cooker along with 1/2 cup red wine.

LEFTOVER LUXURIES

Pull the meat off the bone, chop into cubes, and toss with wide, flat noodles, like pappardelle, or egg noodles, along with the sauce.

TOP SECRET

If your slow-cooked meals all wind up soupy, here's a tip that will help keep things from falling apart. If your dish includes vegetables such as onions, there's no need to add any additional liquid to the pot; the onions will give off plenty as they cook.

Curried Chicken and Rice with Spinach

You can use any chicken parts here, or even halved chicken breasts, if that's what you have on hand, but the moist, dark meat of chicken thighs stands up well to the curry flavor.

2 tablespoons vegetable oil

2 pounds skinless chicken thighs

1 large onion, diced

1 1/2 cups white rice

1 can (15 ounces) diced tomatoes (with juice)

3 cups water

2 tablespoons mild curry paste

1 chicken stock cube

1 teaspoon salt

1/2 teaspoon pepper

1/2 pound baby spinach leaves

Fresh cilantro, for garnish

PREP TIME: 10 minutes • **COOK TIME:** 30 minutes • **SERVES:** 6

1 Heat the oil over medium-high heat in a large skillet and brown the chicken pieces on all sides. Push the chicken to one side and add the onions to the pan and cook for about 8 minutes, until translucent.

2 Add the rice and stir until the grains are coated with the oil. Stir in the tomatoes (with juice). Add the water, curry paste, stock cube, salt, and pepper. Bring to a boil and then reduce the heat.

3 Cover loosely and simmer gently for 20 minutes. Add the spinach, cover the pan again, and cook another 15 minutes, until the liquid has been absorbed, the spinach and rice are tender, and the chicken is cooked through. Garnish with the cilantro.

VARIATION

Coconut Chicken and Rice

Leave out the tomatoes and add instead the same amount of unsweetened coconut milk. Reduce the water to 2 cups and add 1 box (10 ounces) frozen peas instead of spinach.

LEFTOVER LUXURIES

Even if you have curry powder or paste left over from this dish, it won't go to waste. For a quick soup that's especially good if you have a cold, blend 1 teaspoon hot curry paste into a bowl of hot chicken stock. Top with chopped green onions and sip slowly.

TOP SECRET

Whether or not you use hot or mild curry paste or powder, the true secret to this flavorful dish is freshness: If you're working with curry powder or paste that is more than 6 months old, replace it. The delicate aromatic oils in curry evaporate quickly, leaving you with little more than brown sawdust.

Cottage Pie

Cottage pie, virtually synonymous with Shepherd's Pie (which calls for lamb), is the term used in the British Isles for the version made with beef. The dish is more than the sum of its parts, warming and soothing in a way that ground beef and potatoes do not individually. Use a deep casserole dish; shallow ones make you spread the potatoes too thin and the gravy leaks out.

1 pound lean ground beef

1 medium yellow onion, diced

2 medium carrots, peeled and grated

2 tablespoons unsalted butter

2 tablespoons flour

1 1/2 cups water

1 beef stock cube

1 cup frozen peas

2 tablespoons Worcestershire sauce

1 teaspoon salt

1/2 teaspoon pepper

6 cups mashed potatoes

1/2 cup grated cheddar cheese

PREP TIME: 15 minutes • **COOK TIME:** 30 minutes • **SERVES:** 6

1 Preheat the oven to 375°F. Cook the ground beef in a skillet over medium-high heat, breaking it up as you cook. Spoon the meat into a bowl, leaving the excess fat in the pan, then pour off the fat and discard it.

2 Add the onions and carrots to the pan with the butter and cook for about 8 minutes, until they are softened and translucent. Return the meat to the pan and sprinkle the flour over all, stirring to combine.

3 Add the water and stock cube and bring to a boil. Reduce the heat and add the peas, Worcestershire sauce, salt, and pepper. Let simmer for about 5 minutes, or until the sauce thickens slightly.

4 Pour the meat mixture into a deep 3-quart casserole dish and smooth the mashed potatoes over the top, spreading them all the way to the edges. Sprinkle with the cheese and bake for 25 to 30 minutes, until bubbling and browned.

VARIATION
Shepherd's Pie
Replace the ground beef with ground lamb (ground pork is also good) and add 1/4 cup ketchup or tomato sauce with the Worcestershire.

TOP SECRET

Use a fork to make bumps and waves in the surface of the mashed potatoes before sprinkling with cheese. These peaks and crests will brown darker than the rest, making an appealing and appetizing contrast on the surface of the finished dish.

THE SECRETS TO SLOW COOKING

Slow cookers are the busy person's life-saver and a terrific way to make a one-pot meal with a less expensive and tougher cut of meat. But there's a difference between an okay slow-cooked dish and a really fabulous one; here are some secret tips that will help you make the yummiest slow-cooked dishes on the block.

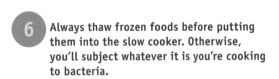

1 Don't add extra liquid. Unless you're making a stew requiring the addition of wine or stock, put the ingredients in dry, especially if it contains a lot of vegetables.

2 If you have time, brown the meat before you add it to the slow cooker. Caramelizing the surface of the meat will add a wallop of flavor to the dish and will also keep the meat from falling apart.

3 If you live in the mountains or at a high altitude, add an extra 1/2 hour of cooking time to the recipe.

4 Don't put a ceramic insert directly into the slow cooker housing straight from the freezer. The abrupt change in temperature can crack the insert.

5 Fattier foods, like roasts and pork shoulders, will cook faster than less-fatty foods, because fat retains heat better than vegetables. Adjust the cooking time accordingly.

6 Always thaw frozen foods before putting them into the slow cooker. Otherwise, you'll subject whatever it is you're cooking to bacteria.

7 Cooking for 1 hour on high is the equivalent of cooking for 2 hours on low.

8 Remove the skin from any poultry you're slow cooking, otherwise the fat will actually melt into the sauce and turn it rancid.

9 Only fill a slow cooker one-half to two-thirds full; otherwise its contents won't cook evenly.

10 Add dairy products—cream, yogurt, milk—during the last 30 minutes of cooking, or they will separate.

Pita Pizza with Pepperoni and Broccoli

Pizza-lovers get disheartened by fake homemade versions, such as the kind made on refrigerator biscuits or those big dry packaged crusts. But flat pita bread—the kind without a pocket—is terrific! Hot pita has the chewy, breadlike taste of a proper crust, and you can top it with anything from blanched vegetables to heaps of cheese and pepperoni.

1 small head broccoli, trimmed into small florets

6 flat pita breads, white or whole-wheat

Extra-virgin olive oil

1 can (8 ounces) tomato sauce

1 1/2 teaspoons dried oregano

4 ounces sliced pepperoni

1/2 cup black olives

2 cups shredded mozzarella

PREP TIME: 10 minutes • **COOK TIME:** 10 minutes • **SERVES:** 6

1 Preheat the oven to 350°F. Drop the broccoli in a saucepan of boiling water for 4 minutes, then drain.

2 Brush each pita with olive oil on the front and back. Lay the pitas on a baking sheet and spread each one with 2 to 3 tablespoons of the tomato sauce. Sprinkle 1/4 teaspoon of the oregano on each.

3 Divide the broccoli, pepperoni, and olives evenly among the pitas and scatter the cheese evenly over all.

4 Bake for 10 minutes, or until the cheese is melted and bubbly.

VARIATION
Pita Pizza with Artichokes and Clams
Leave out the black olives and substitute a 6-ounce can of drained clams for the pepperoni. Use a 6-ounce jar of drained and coarsely chopped artichoke hearts instead of the broccoli florets.

TOP SECRET
Pita pizza never has to be soggy or droopy. What's the secret to keeping the crust crisp? There are two: First, brush the pita with olive oil to keep it from drying out. Second, less is more, so limit yourself to only three toppings and avoid the urge to pile it on!

Quick-and-Easy Spicy Shrimp and Rice Gumbo

Here's a quick and healthy stew you can make in the microwave. For sharper flavor, increase the hot red-pepper sauce to 3/4 teaspoon.

1 large yellow onion, coarsely chopped

1 small green bell pepper, cored, seeded, and coarsely chopped

2 cloves garlic, minced

2 tablespoons olive oil

1 can (15 ounces) no-salt-added stewed tomatoes (with juice)

1 cup chicken stock

1 package (10 ounces) frozen sliced okra

1/2 teaspoon hot red-pepper sauce

1/4 teaspoon dried oregano, crumbled

1 pound medium shrimp, peeled and deveined

1 cup quick-cooking white rice

2 tablespoons minced fresh parsley

1 teaspoon fresh lemon juice

PREP TIME: 10 minutes • **COOK TIME:** 16 minutes • **SERVES:** 4

1 In an ungreased 2 1/2-quart microwavable baking dish with a lid, combine the onions, peppers, garlic, and oil. Cover and microwave on high for 4 to 5 minutes, or until the onion is glassy, stirring midway.

2 Break up the tomatoes with a fork and stir into the baking dish. Add the stock, okra, red-pepper sauce, and oregano. Cover and microwave for 12 minutes, or until the okra is tender, stirring every 4 minutes. Add the shrimp, cover, and microwave for 2 1/2 to 3 minutes, or until the shrimp is cooked through and pink.

3 Add the rice and stir until well-moistened. Cover and microwave for 2 minutes. Let stand, covered, in the microwave for 3 minutes, then stir in the parsley and lemon juice.

VARIATION
Quick and Simple Jambalaya
Cut 2 chorizo or spicy sausage links into rounds and add with the shrimp.

TOP SECRET
Good quality frozen vegetables will last up to 6 months in the freezer, so it always pays to have them on hand. They're often as tasty as fresh ones.

Golden Rice Pilaf

Almost any liquid can be used as the cooking liquid for rice. Chicken broth, tomato juice, beer, apple juice...they all lend signature flavors. Here, rice gets a delicious special treatment to heighten its flavors. Serve this delicious dish with chicken, turkey, or fish.

1 cup diced celery

3 tablespoons chopped onion

1 tablespoon grated orange zest

1/4 cup unsalted butter or margarine

1/2 teaspoon salt

3 tablespoons fresh orange juice

1 1/3 cups water

1 1/2 cups uncooked instant rice

PREP TIME: 10 minutes • **COOK TIME:** 15 minutes • **SERVES:** 4

1 In a 3-quart saucepan, sauté the celery, onions, and orange zest in the butter or margarine for about 5 minutes, or until tender but not brown. Add the salt.

2 Combine the orange juice and water in a measuring cup and add it to the celery mixture. Bring to a boil.

3 Stir in the rice. Remove from the heat, cover and let stand for 10 minutes. Fluff with a fork.

VARIATION

Spicy Golden Pilaf

To add a mildly spicy aroma, toss a cinnamon stick and a knob of peeled ginger into the cooking water. Remove both before serving.

TOP SECRET

Someone once said that a day without orange juice is a day without sunshine and they were right! But it's not just for breakfast anymore. Using a bit of OJ in poaching water or when making rice lends an incomparably yummy flavor that will have your family asking, "Hey, how did you do that?"

Polenta with Smoked Cheese

Smoked cheese lends fantastic aroma to nutty-tasting polenta. This easy-to-make side dish also gets a shot of salty chewiness with bits of chopped olives.

2 cups instant polenta

3 1/2 cups water

Small bunch of sage, oregano, basil, or parsley

1/2 pound smoked mature cheese such as smoked cheddar or smoked fontina, shredded or diced (about 2 cups)

1 1/2 teaspoons black or mixed peppercorns, crushed

8 pitted black olives (preferably oil-cured), finely chopped

PREP TIME: 10 minutes • **COOK TIME:** 20 minutes • **SERVES:** 4

1 Combine the polenta and water in a large saucepan. Bring it to a boil over high heat, then reduce the heat and let simmer for about 10 minutes, stirring the polenta frequently with a large wooden spoon or paddle to remove any lumps, until it becomes thick and starts to stiffen.

2 Meanwhile, strip the leaves from the herb stalks and chop them finely.

3 Stir in the herbs, cheese, peppercorns, and olives. Beat vigorously until the cheese is incorporated and the mixture begins to leave the sides of the saucepan when stirred.

4 Serve immediately or let stand to stiffen further, 5 to 10 minutes. It will remain hot.

VARIATION

Red Pepper and Parmigiana Polenta

Use only basil and replace the cheese with a cup of grated Parmesan. Instead of the peppercorns, add 1 teaspoon red-pepper flakes. Omit the olives.

DID YOU KNOW?

If you don't want to serve polenta soft, harden it in the refrigerator in a cake pan. It can be sliced into squares, reheated, or even grilled (which makes a perfect base for salad).

TOP SECRET

The secret key to making polenta is to give it plenty of flavor. Smoked cheese lends a warm, earthy fragrance to it. If you opt for the Parmesan instead, don't skimp, otherwise the polenta will be bland.

Smoky Santa Cruz Pepper Chili

This chili uses four kinds of hot peppers and three kinds of meat. The result is dynamite.

1/2 pound bacon, diced

2 1/2 pounds beef stew meat, cut into 3/4-inch cubes

1 1/2 pounds pork stew meat, cut into 3/4-inch cubes

2 medium onions, chopped

6–8 cloves garlic, minced

1–2 tablespoons chopped, seeded fresh poblano chiles

1–2 tablespoons chopped, seeded, and deveined fresh jalapeño peppers (wear gloves when handling)

2–3 teaspoons cayenne pepper

1 1/2 teaspoons dried oregano

1 teaspoon salt

1 teaspoon ground cumin

1 can (15 ounces) tomato puree

1 can (15 ounces) beef broth

7 plum tomatoes, cored, seeded, and chopped

PREP TIME: 30 minutes • **COOK TIME:** 1 1/2 hours • **SERVES:** 8

1 In a Dutch oven or soup pot over medium heat, cook the diced bacon until crisp. Transfer it to paper towels to drain. Drain the fat from the pot, reserving 3 tablespoons.

2 Add the beef, pork, and onions to the pot and sauté in the drippings until the meat is browned and onions are softened. Drain off the fat. Add the garlic, poblanos, jalapeños, cayenne, oregano, salt, and cumin and sauté for 2 minutes.

3 Stir in the tomato puree, broth, and tomatoes and bring to boil. Reduce the heat and simmer, covered, for about 1 hour, or until the meat is cooked through and tender.

VARIATION

California Veggie Chili

Replace the bacon with vegetarian bacon, the meat with 3 cups crumbled tempeh, and the beef broth with vegetable broth.

TOP SECRET

The secret ingredient in this amazingly flavorful chili is an all-time favorite that rarely gets used in this popular dish: bacon! The smokier the bacon, the better this chili will be.

Aloha Chili

This chili comes from Hawaii, complete with meat, beans, and pineapple!

2 pounds
ground beef

1 large onion,
finely chopped

1 can (16 ounces)
kidney beans,
rinsed and drained

1 can (16 ounces)
pork and beans
(with liquid)

1 can (20 ounces)
pineapple chunks
(with juice)

1 cup ketchup

1/4 cup packed
brown sugar

1/4 cup
white vinegar

PREP TIME: 5 minutes • **COOK TIME:** 20 minutes • **SERVES:** 8

1 In a large saucepan over medium heat, sauté the beef and onions until the meat is browned and onions are tender. Drain off the fat.

2 Stir in the kidney beans, pork and beans (with liquid), pineapple (with juice), ketchup, brown sugar, and vinegar. Bring to a boil, then reduce the heat and simmer, covered, for about 20 minutes, or until heated through.

VARIATION

Corny Beef Chili
Add a drained 16-ounce can of corn with the kidney beans.

TOP SECRET

What fruit is the perfect foil for meat dishes? Pineapple! Whether you're making a stew, a meat pizza, or chili, the addition of pineapple chunks with its juice not only adds flavor but also adds a perfect texture that will make it a favorite go-to ingredient every time.

Spicy Chicken Chili

The inspiration for this recipe is posole, a classic Mexican stew made with pork.

1 can (4 ounces) green chiles (with liquid) or 3 dried ancho chiles

1 clove garlic, sliced

2 pounds skinless, boneless chicken breasts

6 cups chicken stock

1 large yellow onion, finely chopped

2 teaspoons ground cumin

1 bay leaf

1/2 teaspoon dried thyme, crumbled

3 cloves garlic, minced

1/4 teaspoon salt

1 can (16 ounces) hominy (with liquid)

1/4 cup minced fresh cilantro or flat-leaf parsley

PREP TIME: 20 minutes • **COOK TIME:** 45 minutes • **SERVES:** 4

1 If using dried chiles, place them in a small saucepan, add 1 cup boiling water, and soak for 15 minutes. Drain and reserve the soaking liquid, then, wearing gloves, halve the chiles and remove the seeds, stems, veins, and skins.

2 In a blender, puree the canned chiles or dried chiles (and reserved juice) with the sliced garlic.

3 In a 4-quart Dutch oven over medium-high heat, combine the chicken, stock, onions, cumin, bay leaf, thyme, minced garlic, and salt. Bring to a boil, then reduce the heat and simmer, covered, for 15 minutes. Transfer the chicken to a plate. When it's cool enough to handle, cut it into bite-size pieces.

4 Add the hominy and pureed chilies to the pan and bring to a boil over medium heat. Reduce the heat and simmer, uncovered, for 15 minutes. Add the chicken and simmer, uncovered, for 4 minutes, or until heated through. Remove the bay leaf and stir in the cilantro or parsley. Ladle into bowls and garnish each serving with tortilla chips, avocadoes, and scallions (optional).

VARIATION

Black Bean Posole

If you prefer a more subtle flavor, omit the hominy and use canned black beans in its place.

TOP SECRET

You might prefer your microwave and your friends might love their food processor, but the best tool when you're making a raw sauce—that is, a chile sauce—is an old-fashioned blender. Why? The food processor has too much surface area and you'll wind up with chunks of the chilies instead of a puree. The tighter the surface area, the tighter the puree.

Spicy White Chili

Light, white, but still flavorful and spicy, this new twist on an old favorite is sure to become a dinnertime staple.

1 tablespoon vegetable oil

2 medium onions, chopped

4 cloves garlic, minced

2 cans (4 ounces each) chopped green chiles

2 teaspoons ground cumin

1 teaspoon dried oregano

1/4 teaspoon cayenne pepper

1/4 teaspoon ground cloves

2 cans (15 ounces each) chicken broth

4 cups cubed cooked chicken

3 cans (16 ounces each) Great Northern beans, rinsed and drained

2 cups shredded Monterey Jack cheese

Sour cream, for garnishing (optional)

Cored, seeded, and sliced jalapeños, for garnishing (optional)

PREP TIME: 20 minutes • **COOK TIME:** 30 minutes • **SERVES:** 6

1 Heat the oil in a 3-quart saucepan over medium heat. Add the onions and sauté for about 5 minutes, or until tender.

2 Stir in the garlic, chilies, cumin, oregano, cayenne, and cloves and sauté for about 2 minutes longer, until the chilies are tender.

3 Add the broth, chicken, and beans. Bring to a boil, reduce the heat, and simmer, uncovered, for 15 minutes.

4 Remove from the heat and stir in the cheese until melted. Garnish with sour cream and jalapeños, if using.

VARIATION
Juarez White Chili
Replace the chicken with pork loin.

TOP SECRET

The simplest way to make this dish quickly and easily on a busy work night is to use canned chicken. Stock up on it for this dish and also for tacos, casseroles, and other great and simple meals.

8 VERY VEGGIE ENTRÉES

Gone are the days when eating a vegetarian meal translated into chowing down on "lentil nut loaf." Today, vegetarian dishes are not only healthy and packed with nutrients but also they can be mouthwateringly delicious. From the days when being a vegetarian meant you had to eat nothing but chopped vegetable salads and undercooked whole grains, meat-free cooking has taken a huge swing to the exciting and the flavorful. Rather than making a big deal about the lack of pot roast, the recipes here are designed to be so full of flavor that there will be no need to point out the absence of meat to anyone at the table. After all, there's no absence of protein—or of substance and style.

Chickpea Stew with Tomatoes and Zucchini

Flavorful, low-fat, and full of fiber, this stew is also conveniently fast. It's delicious served over hot cooked rice, with hot sauce on the side for those who like it.

1 cup instant couscous

2 tablespoons extra-virgin olive oil

1 small onion, chopped

2 cloves garlic, minced

1/2 teaspoon grated fresh ginger

2 small zucchini, trimmed and diced

1 can (15 ounces) chickpeas, drained

1 can (14 ounces) diced tomatoes (with juice)

2 teaspoons ground cumin

1/4 teaspoon cayenne

Salt and pepper, to taste

PREP TIME: 5 minutes • **COOK TIME:** 15 minutes • **SERVES:** 4

1 Prepare the instant couscous according to the package directions and keep warm.

2 Heat the oil in a large skillet over medium-high heat. Add the onions, garlic, and ginger and cook, stirring often, for about 4 minutes, or until the onions are softened.

3 Add the zucchini and cook, stirring, for 3 to 4 minutes, until softened. Add the chickpeas, tomatoes (with juice), cumin, and cayenne. Reduce the heat to low, then cover and simmer for about 5 minutes, until the sauce is slightly thickened. Season with salt and pepper.

4 Spoon the couscous onto warmed plates and top with the stewed chickpeas. Serve hot.

VARIATIONS

Moroccan Chickpea Stew

Add 1/2 teaspoon cinnamon and 1/2 teaspoon turmeric to the stew. Stir in a handful of golden raisins and a few chopped dried apricots. Serve over hot couscous.

Spanish Chickpea Stew

Add 1/2 cup pitted and chopped black olives and 1/2 teaspoon smoked paprika along with the cumin.

TOP SECRET

Canned chickpeas are fast food at its best. But if you have dried chickpeas, all the better for holding together in a stew. Soak them in water overnight, then simmer them in water until tender, and proceed with the recipe.

Lentil Stew

Make this on the stovetop if you're going to be around, or let it simmer in a slow cooker all day if you're not. It's astonishingly easy, and the result is an elaborately delicious and filling stew, packed with protein and nutrients and a lot of fiber to boot. Serve it with sourdough bread to pick up the hint of tanginess from the lemon juice that you squeeze in just before serving.

2 yellow onions, diced

2 stalks celery, thinly sliced

2 large carrots, peeled and diced

4 cloves garlic, minced

3 cups brown lentils

1 can (16 ounces) chopped tomatoes (with juice)

1 teaspoon whole dried oregano

1 bay leaf

2 teaspoons salt

1 teaspoon pepper

2 quarts cold water

3 tablespoons fresh lemon juice

PREP TIME: 5 minutes • **COOK TIME:** 1 1/2 hours • **SERVES:** 6

1. Combine the onions, celery, carrots, garlic, lentils, tomatoes (with juice), oregano, bay leaf, salt, and pepper in a large stewpot and cover with the water. Bring to a boil, reduce the heat, cover loosely, and simmer gently over a very low heat for 1 1/2 hours. (If using a slow cooker, leave on high for 8 hours.)

2. When the stew is thick and the lentils and vegetables are tender, stir in the lemon juice and adjust salt and pepper, if needed. Add more lemon juice, if desired.

VARIATION
Lentil Stew with Potatoes and Spinach
For an even heartier dish in cold weather, peel and dice 2 russet potatoes and add them with the other vegetables. About 20 minutes before the end of cooking, add 1 box (10 ounces) of frozen chopped spinach. (If you add the spinach along with the other vegetables, it will be overcooked and too dark by the end.) Crumble feta cheese over each bowl when serving.

TOP SECRET
The shot of acid at the end of cooking makes a huge difference in lightening and brightening this earthy, finished dish, so be sure to add it at the very end so the heat doesn't dull the flavor. You can use lemon or lime juice or any type of vinegar, although red-wine vinegar is particularly well-suited to lentils.

14 THINGS TO DO WITH A CAN OF CHICKPEAS

That sad, lonely can of chickpeas sitting on your pantry shelf...who knew that it had so many uses? The truth about chickpeas is that while they're beloved far and wide by vegetarians everywhere, they're meaty consistency is ideal for stretching dishes, or introducing vegetarian cuisine to carnivores. Here are some terrific ways to use up what you're storing:

1 Make hummus.

2 Mash to a paste, add an egg, a clove of garlic, and salt. Fry, pancake-style, until golden brown. Top with salad.

3 Toss with cubed avocadoes and diced onions and tomatoes and stuff into a pita.

4 Dry thoroughly, drizzle with olive oil and salt, and roast in the oven at 300°F until crunchy. Instant munchies.

5 Flatten with the underside of a heavy skillet, add garlic and hot sauce, form into patties, and make chickpea burgers.

6 Add sautéed onions, hot peppers, ginger, and scallions, and drizzle with the juice of 1 lemon and chopped parsley.

7 Toss with tubular pasta, olive oil, garlic, and minced red bell peppers.

8 Toss with cubed tofu, sliced ginger, red bell peppers, sesame oil, and scallions.

9 Mix it with 3 beaten eggs and feta cheese to make an omelet.

10 Toss with bottled vinaigrette for an instant, protein-packed salad.

11 Heat the beans and use as a bed for poached eggs.

12 Fold it into leftover curry to stretch the dish to another meal, or meals.

13 Lightly mash and fold into egg salad with a pinch of cumin and a drizzle of hot sauce.

14 Dry thoroughly, roll in granulated sugar and cinnamon, and bake until crunchy.

VERY VEGGIE ENTRÉES

Jazzed-Up Beans and Tortillas

This recipe is like a jazzy, soupier version of refried beans, but one that requires a lot less fat and a lot less time. The cinnamon is an unusual addition that makes all the difference, along with that final dot of butter to round out the flavors—and don't skip it, either!

1 tablespoon extra-virgin olive oil

1 medium yellow onion, diced

2 cloves garlic, minced

2 cans (16 ounces each) pinto beans, drained

1 can (16 ounces) diced tomatoes (with juice)

1 1/2 teaspoons ground cumin

1 teaspoon ground cinnamon

Salt and pepper, to taste

2 tablespoons unsalted butter

12 corn tortillas

Sour cream, for serving

Bottled salsa, for serving

PREP TIME: 5 minutes • **COOK TIME:** 10 minutes • **SERVES:** 4

1 Heat the oil in a large skillet over medium-low heat. Add the onions and garlic and cook for about 5 minutes, until just tender and golden. Pour in the beans, tomatoes (with juice), cumin, and cinnamon and stir, mashing the beans with the back of a spoon. Simmer for 10 minutes, until the sauce is thickened. Season with salt and pepper and stir in the butter.

2 Wrap the tortillas in a clean kitchen towel that you have dampened with cold water. Lay the wrapped tortillas on a plate and heat in the microwave on high for 1 to 2 minutes, until hot.

3 Serve the beans in deep bowls with warm tortillas, sour cream, and salsa.

VARIATION

Spicy Souped-Up Beans

Cook 1 cored, seeded, and diced bell pepper and 2 seeded diced fresh jalapeños with the onions and garlic. Add 1 teaspoon chili powder and 1 tablespoon chopped chipotle in adobo with the tomatoes.

TOP SECRET

Ground cumin gives Mexican (and Indian) food its unmistakable earthiness. But for an even greater hit of flavor, sprinkle the amount called for in the recipe in a dry cast-iron pan and toast it very lightly before using. This will release oils and incomparable flavor.

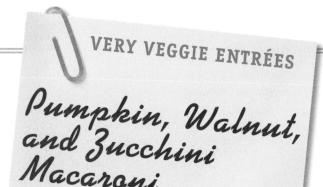

Pumpkin, Walnut, and Zucchini Macaroni

A recipe that shouts autumn, with warm colors and flavors, from the orange pumpkin and bright red pepper to the plump whole-wheat pasta, rounded out with Parmesan cheese. If you're trying to get more fiber into your daily diet, here's an excellent way to do it.

1 pound whole-wheat macaroni

2 tablespoons extra-virgin olive oil

1 medium yellow onion, diced

1 clove garlic, minced

1 medium zucchini, thinly sliced

1 red bell pepper, cored, seeded, and diced

1 can (15 ounces) pumpkin puree

1 1/2 cups vegetable stock or water

1/2 cup whole milk

1 teaspoon rubbed sage

1/2 teaspoon cayenne

Salt and pepper, to taste

1/4 cup toasted chopped walnuts

1/2 cup grated Parmesan cheese

PREP TIME: 8 minutes • **COOK TIME:** 20 minutes • **SERVES:** 6

1 Cook the pasta according to the package directions.

2 Heat the oil in a large skillet over medium-low heat and cook the onions and garlic for about 5 minutes, until just tender.

3 Add the zucchini, bell peppers, and sage. Cook, stirring, for 3 to 4 minutes, or until the vegetables soften. Add the pumpkin, stock or water, milk, sage, and cayenne and simmer for about 10 minutes, until the sauce is thickened. Taste and add salt and pepper, as needed.

4 Stir the drained macaroni into the sauce. Toss with the walnuts and Parmesan and serve with extra Parmesan.

VARIATION

Baked Pumpkin Pasta

Preheat the oven to 350°F. Don't simmer the sauce after adding the cayenne; instead, toss with the drained macaroni and pour into a buttered 3-quart baking dish. Top with 1 cup whole-wheat breadcrumbs tossed with the walnuts and Parmesan and drizzle with a few tablespoons olive oil. Bake for 40 minutes, until bubbling and browned.

TOP SECRET

Virtually every supermarket in America now carries a wide range of whole-wheat pasta. But for the best taste, go with lighter whole-wheat pasta; the color will actually tell you whether the pasta will be similar in texture to regular white pasta, or nuttier and more toothsome. Choose the former, and look for lighter tan whole-wheat pastas rather than darker, richer ones.

Egg-cellent Egg Salad

Egg salad sounds so ordinary—until you make some, and remember how good it can be. What's more, it's an easy, inexpensive, and filling protein. Don't use too much mayo (you may want to start with 2 tablespoons and add another only if necessary), and do use a bit of scallion or onion to bring out the best flavor in the eggs.

4 large eggs

3 tablespoons mayonnaise

1/4 teaspoon celery seed

1 scallion, thinly sliced

1 teaspoon white-wine vinegar

1/4 teaspoon paprika

Salt and pepper, to taste

PREP TIME: 5 minutes • **COOK TIME:** 10 minutes • **SERVES:** 4

1 Bring a medium saucepan of water to a boil and carefully lower the eggs in with a spoon. Cook for 10 minutes, then carefully pour out the water and cover the eggs with cold water until they are cool enough to handle.

2 Peel the eggs and put them in a medium bowl. Mash them with a fork until chunky.

3 Add the mayonnaise, celery seed, scallions, vinegar, and paprika, stir with the fork, and season with salt and pepper.

VARIATIONS

Mediterranean Egg Salad
Toss the egg salad with 1/4 cup roasted red pepper strips or 1/4 cup chopped sun-dried tomatoes packed in oil, along with 2 tablespoons chopped fresh basil leaves. Mound on toasted walnut bread with crunchy romaine leaves.

Curried Egg Salad
Add 1 teaspoon mild curry powder. Make sandwiches on toasted cinnamon-raisin bread.

Tofu Egg Salad
Substitute 1 cup diced tofu—preferably a firm or medium variety rather than the silken one, which may turn to mush—for the eggs. Season extra strong, perhaps with a bit more salt and lemon juice and a dash of Dijon mustard.

TOP SECRET

Don't be tempted to add celery here, because it will just add water to the salad. Instead, use a small amount of celery seed: A little goes a long way, and every chef knows that this is what will add the greatest flavor to this favorite salad!

Ratatouille Pasta with Goat Cheese

Goat cheese is the chef's shortcut to flavor—the tangy creaminess and the rich mouthfeel of it can't be replicated by any other ingredients. Here it melds together the ingredients of ratatouille into one fantastic whole.

1 pound fettuccine

1 tablespoon extra-virgin olive oil

1 medium yellow onion, chopped

1 clove garlic, minced

2 small zucchini, thinly sliced

1 small red bell pepper, cored, seeded, and diced

1 small green bell pepper, cored, seeded, and diced

4 large fresh tomatoes, cored and chopped, or 1 can (15 ounces) diced tomatoes (with juice)

Salt and pepper, to taste

1 log goat cheese (5 ounces)

3 tablespoons chopped fresh basil leaves

PREP TIME: 10 minutes • **COOK TIME:** 20 minutes • **SERVES:** 6

1 Cook the fettuccine according to the package directions.

2 In a large skillet over medium, heat the oil and cook the onions, garlic, zucchini, and peppers for about 10 minutes, until softened and slightly browned.

3 Stir in the tomatoes and bring to a simmer. Reduce the heat and cook for 7 to 8 minutes, until the vegetables are tender and the sauce is lightly thickened. Taste and season with salt and pepper.

4 Toss the ratatouille with the drained fettuccine. Cut the goat cheese into chunks and, just before serving, mix the goat cheese and the basil with the pasta.

VARIATION

Fettuccine with Caramelized Onions and Goat Cheese

Omit the zucchini, bell peppers, and tomatoes. Cook 2 thinly sliced large yellow onions with 2 cloves minced garlic in 3 tablespoons olive oil until sweet and caramelized. Stir in 1 teaspoon thyme leaves instead of the basil. Season with salt and lots of pepper, and toss with the pasta and goat cheese.

TOP SECRET

A sealed log of goat cheese will stay fresh in the refrigerator for about 2 weeks. Once you open it, pack any remaining goat cheese into a small container such as a bowl or cup and smooth the surface flat with the back of a spoon. Cover the whole surface of the cheese with a few tablespoons of olive oil and seal the container tightly with a lid or plastic wrap. This airtight seal will keep the cheese fresh for many more days than just covering the cheese with plastic wrap.

Fried Falafel

In Egypt, falafel—fried chickpea patties—packed in a pita with veggies and sauce, is a lunch food as standard as hamburgers and fries for Americans.

1 cup dried chickpeas

1 small yellow onion, quartered

1 tablespoon ground cumin

1 teaspoon chili powder

1 teaspoon salt

1/4 teaspoon baking soda

1 cup fresh flat-leaf parsley leaves

2 tablespoons fresh lemon juice

Vegetable or grapeseed oil, for frying

PREP TIME: 24 hours (includes soaking) • **COOK TIME:** 20 minutes • **SERVES:** 4

1 Soak the beans in water overnight, being sure to keep them fully covered in water—they will triple in size. Drain and put them in the food processor with the onions, cumin, chili powder, salt, baking soda, parsley, and lemon juice.

2 Carefully bring 2 inches of oil to 375°F in a large, heavy saucepan over medium heat (check with a deep-frying thermometer). Shape heaping tablespoons of the falafel mixture into balls and slide into the hot oil. Fry for 3 to 4 minutes, or until golden on all sides.

3 Drain on paper towels and serve.

VARIATIONS

Baked Falafel

Preheat the oven to 350°F and wipe 2 tablespoons olive oil all over the bottom of a rimmed baking sheet. Shape the falafel mixture into egg-shaped balls and lay them on the baking sheet, turning them once to coat a bit with the oil. Bake for 10 minutes, then turn each ball and bake for an additional 10 minutes, until golden brown.

Black Bean Falafel

Replace the chickpeas with a 15-ounce can of drained black beans and add 1/4 teaspoon hot sauce.

TOP SECRET

For surefire (or no-fire) frying, use an oil with a high smoking point, like grapeseed, vegetable, or canola oil. These are all flavor-neutral, which will not add additional taste to your dish.

THE CHEATING CHEF AT HOME

STOCK UP THAT PANTRY!

Vegetarian cooking has more than a few things going for it. First, it's (usually) healthy. Second, it's delicious. Third (and perhaps best of all), it's inexpensive. Compare the cost of a dinner for four involving beef and dinner for four involving vegetarian dishes, and do the math: There's no question about it. Vegetarian cooking is a good way to watch not only your waistline but also your wallet. One trick to surefire veggie cookery is to always have your pantry filled with the right combination of ingredients. Here are some must-haves.

Beans
dry beans will keep for 1 year; canned beans will keep for 2 years

Black beans

Chickpeas

Cannellini beans

Black-eyed peas

Lima beans

Kidney beans

Pinto beans

Cranberry beans

Grains
store 1 pound in airtight containers for up to 4 months; store overage in the freezer for up to 1 year

Quinoa

White Rice

Brown Rice

Wild Rice

Sticky Rice

Bulgur

Barley

Kasha

Flours
store 1 pound in airtight containers for up to 4 months; store overage in the freezer for up to 1 year

Unbleached white flour

White whole-wheat flour

Whole-wheat flour

Buckwheat flour

Chickpea flour

Rye flour

Cake flour

Wondra (store in its own container)

Oils
store away from light

olive oil

sesame oil

grapeseed oil

canola oil

vegetable oil

walnut oil

Nuts
store small quantities for 3 to 4 months; store overage in freezer for up to 8 months

raw unsalted almonds

unsalted pecans

unsalted pine nuts (pignoli)

unsalted cashews

unsalted hazelnuts

unsalted walnuts

Pastas
store for 6 to 8 months, unopened; store opened pasta in ziplock bags for up to 6 months. Whole-wheat won't last as long as white

Spaghetti

Penne

Elbow macaroni

Lasagna

Fettuccine

Farfalle (bow ties)

Angel hair spaghetti

Canned Goods
store for up to 1 year

Whole plum tomatoes

Artichoke hearts (unmarinated)

Hominy

Tomato paste

Chipotle chiles in adobo

Pickled jalapeños

Miscellaneous

Breadcrumbs, unseasoned

Canned fish (tuna, salmon, sardines, anchovies)

Soy sauce

Hot sauce (store in fridge after opening)

Ketchup (store in fridge after opening)

Mustard (store in fridge after opening)

Worcestershire sauce (store in fridge after opening)

Salsas (store in fridge after opening)

Creamy Pasta Primavera

This is so jam-packed with fresh spring vegetables that you won't mind all that cream—but if you prefer, make a lower-fat version by swapping in half-and-half instead.

1 pound spaghetti

2 tablespoons extra-virgin olive oil

1 small red onion, diced

4 cremini mushrooms, thinly sliced

2 small, slender Japanese eggplant, diced

1 medium zucchini, diced

1 medium yellow squash, diced

1/2 pound asparagus, trimmed diagonally into 1-inch pieces

3 small tomatoes, seeded and diced

1 cup cream

Salt and pepper, to taste

1/2 cup fresh basil leaves, thinly sliced

1/2 cup Parmesan cheese

PREP TIME: 10 minutes • **COOK TIME:** 15 minutes • **SERVES:** 6

1 Cook the spaghetti according to the package directions.

2 Meanwhile, heat the oil in a large skillet over medium heat. Add the onions and mushrooms and cook for 3 minutes, until they start to soften. Add the eggplant, zucchini, squash, and cook 10 to 12 minutes, until all the vegetables are softened and lightly browned. Add the asparagus and cook for another few minutes.

3 Stir in the tomatoes and cream and bring to a boil. Cook for 4 to 5 minutes, until the tomatoes are softened (but still in chunks, not cooked all the way down) and the sauce is slightly thickened. Season with salt and pepper, to taste.

4 Pour over the drained pasta, sprinkle with the basil and Parmesan, and serve immediately, tossing lightly to mix in the basil as you serve.

VARIATION

Green Primavera

Swap in farfalle (bow ties) for the spaghetti. Leave out the eggplant and yellow squash and, in their place, add thin green beans (haricots verts) and green peas or sugar snap peas. Along with the basil and Parmesan, sprinkle the top with a handful of chopped fresh chives.

TOP SECRET

Cutting basil flat tends to bruise it and make dark marks in the sensitive leaves. Don't chop basil until the last possible minute before you use it, and when you do, roll several leaves together like a little cigar and slice into very thin ribbons. Use a downward thrust and a slight push forward with your knife for the cleanest, smoothest cut. This technique results in julienne (or chiffonade, if the ribbons are thread thin), and it exposes the maximum of the herb's delicate essential oils to your taste buds.

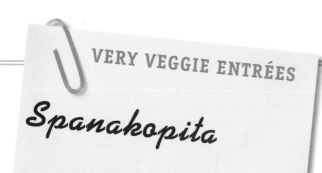

Spanakopita

With frozen phyllo pastry available in nearly any grocery store you visit, there's no excuse not to make this Greek bakery favorite at home. The super-professional look of the golden, flaky pastry will amaze your friends and family—and you'll be astonished at the ease with which this classic dish can be thrown together.

2 tablespoons extra-virgin olive oil

1 large yellow onion, diced

Salt and pepper, to taste

6 large eggs

3 boxes (10 ounces each) frozen chopped spinach, thawed and squeezed dry

6 scallions, thinly sliced

2 cups crumbled feta cheese (about 8 ounces)

1/2 cup grated Parmesan cheese

1 1/2 teaspoons freshly grated nutmeg

1 box (1 pound) frozen phyllo pastry, thawed (about 16 sheets)

1/2 cup (1 stick) butter, melted and cooled slightly

PREP TIME: 25 minutes • **COOK TIME:** 1 hour • **SERVES:** 6

1 Preheat the oven to 375°F. Heat the oil in a large skillet over medium heat and cook the onions for about 10 minutes, until softened and golden. Season liberally with salt and pepper.

2 Beat the eggs in a large bowl and stir in the spinach, scallions, feta, Parmesan, and nutmeg. Add the onions.

3 Lightly grease a 9 x 13-inch baking dish. Unwrap the phyllo and cover it with a clean kitchen towel that has been thoroughly wet and then squeezed out. Working quickly, brush a sheet of phyllo with butter, then lay it in the bottom of the pan at one end. Continue until you have layered 8 sheets of phyllo overlapping across the bottom of the dish, letting the extra hang over the sides. Spoon in the filling, then layer another 8 sheets of buttered phyllo across the top. Fold all the phyllo in over the top and brush well with the remaining butter.

4 Using a sharp paring knife, cut lightly through the first few layers of phyllo, marking out diamond-shaped serving pieces (this eases cutting of the finished dish). Bake for 1 hour, until the phyllo is golden brown and crisp. Serve warm or at room temperature.

TOP SECRET

Here's a trick to get every last bit of liquid out of spinach. Open a thawed box of spinach and place the rectangle on a dinner plate. Set a second plate on top, bottom-side down as if you were stacking them in the cupboard, and hold them over the sink while you squeeze the two plates together as hard as you can. Tilt the plates so all the liquid drains out. (This works best if the plate bottoms are completely flat, not the kind with a rim underneath—though that type still gets good results.)

Sweet Potato and Black Bean Enchiladas

Rich, filling, and packed with the flavors of the American Southwest, this dish can be made ahead, frozen, and reheated.

2 large
sweet potatoes

3 tablespoons
vegetable oil

3 tablespoons flour

1/3 cup
chili powder

4 cups
chicken stock

1 can (6 ounces)
tomato paste

1 teaspoon
dried oregano

1 1/2 teaspoons
ground cumin

Salt and pepper,
to taste

12 large
corn tortillas

2 cans (15 ounces
each) black beans,
drained

2 cups (8 ounces)
grated Monterey
Jack cheese

3 tablespoons
chopped
fresh cilantro

4 scallions,
thinly sliced

Sour cream,
for serving

PREP TIME: 20 minutes • **COOK TIME:** 20 minutes • **SERVES:** 6

1 Preheat the oven to 350°F. Scrub the sweet potatoes and prick all over with a fork. Microwave on high for 10 minutes, until tender.

2 Heat the oil and flour in a large, heavy skillet over medium heat, stirring constantly, for 1 minute. Stir in the chili powder and cook for 1 minute. Add the stock, tomato paste, oregano, and cumin and bring to a boil. Reduce the heat and simmer gently for 15 minutes, stirring occasionally.

3 Scoop out the sweet potato flesh into a medium bowl and mash it with a fork, seasoning with salt and pepper. Pour 1 cup of the sauce in the bottom of a 9 x 13-inch baking dish. Wrap the tortillas in a damp clean kitchen towel and microwave for 1 to 2 minutes, until hot and soft.

4 Working quickly, lay a hot tortilla on a work surface and smear with a spoonful of sweet potatoes. Spoon some beans up the center and sprinkle with some cheese, a bit of cilantro, and some scallions. Roll the tortilla like a burrito and lay it, seam-side down, in the baking dish. Repeat. Pour the remaining sauce over all and bake for 20 minutes, until heated through and bubbling. Top with any remaining cilantro and scallions and serve with sour cream on the side.

TOP SECRET

Sure, you can cook sweet potatoes the way you would white potatoes. But the secret to getting every ounce of sweetness out of them is in your microwave! The microwave concentrates their flavor and brings a touch of caramelization to the orange flesh.

Crispy Black Bean Tacos with Slaw and Feta

These simple tacos are a flavor explosion in the mouth, from the tangy lime slaw to the salty bursts of feta. Hot sauce or bottled salsa is the finishing touch.

1 can (15 ounces) black beans, drained

1 teaspoon ground cumin

3 tablespoons fresh lime juice

3 tablespoons salsa

1 teaspoon minced chipotles in adobo

Salt and pepper, to taste

1/4 cup extra-virgin olive oil

3 cups finely shredded cabbage or packaged coleslaw mix

2 scallions, thinly sliced

1/4 cup chopped fresh cilantro

8 corn tortillas

1/2 cup crumbled feta cheese

Hot sauce or salsa, for serving

PREP TIME: 10 minutes • **COOK TIME:** 5 minutes • **SERVES:** 4

1 Mash the beans coarsely in a medium bowl with cumin, 1 tablespoon of the lime juice, salsa, and chipotles and season with salt and pepper.

2 Mix 1 tablespoon of the olive oil and the remaining 2 tablespoons of lime juice in another medium bowl. Add the cabbage, scallions, and cilantro and toss to coat. Season with salt and pepper.

3 In a large nonstick skillet, heat the remaining 3 tablespoons olive oil over medium-high heat. Lay a tortilla in the oil and let it cook for 1 to 2 minutes, until golden and crisp but still soft. Fold the taco in half with tongs, and transfer to a paper towel–lined plate. Continue with the remaining tortillas, adding a bit more oil to the pan, as needed.

4 Spoon some of the bean mixture into each and pack each taco with some of the cabbage mixture and feta. Serve with hot sauce or additional salsa on the side.

VARIATION

Crispy Tacos with Guacamole

Skip the cabbage mixture and feta and top the bean mixture with shredded iceberg lettuce, diced tomatoes, and guacamole made by mashing 1 ripe avocado with the juice of 1 lime, salt, and 1 finely sliced scallion. Top with salsa and sour cream, if desired.

TOP SECRET

Forget out about those stiff-as-cardboard hard taco shells and make your own. The taste of fresh masa—corn flour specific to Mexican food—will elevate this dish from good to great!

Mushroom Bourguignon

Who says that only meat-eaters get to enjoy the rich taste of a stew slow-cooked with red wine? Here, the chunks of beef are replaced by big meaty chunks of portobello mushrooms. Serve over fluffy mashed potatoes or buttered wide egg noodles, sprinkle the whole plate with chopped fresh parsley, and you'll never miss the meat.

2 tablespoons extra-virgin olive oil

3 tablespoons unsalted butter, softened

2 pounds portobello mushroom tops, sliced 1/4 inch thick

1 large yellow onion, thinly sliced

1 carrot, diced small

4 cloves garlic, minced

2 teaspoons chopped fresh thyme leaves

1 teaspoon chopped fresh rosemary leaves

2 cups red wine

1/4 cup tomato paste

2 cups vegetable stock

1 package onion soup mix

1 1/2 cups frozen pearl onions

2 tablespoons flour

Salt and pepper, to taste

PREP TIME: 10 minutes • **COOK TIME:** 40 minutes • **SERVES:** 6

1 Heat 1 tablespoon of the oil and 1 tablespoon of the butter in a large, heavy stewpot over high heat. Put the mushrooms in the pan and brown the outsides quickly, about 3 minutes. Remove to a plate.

2 Reduce the heat and add the remaining 1 tablespoon olive oil. Add the sliced onions, carrots, garlic, thyme, and rosemary to the pot and cook for 10 minutes, stirring now and then, until the onions are lightly browned and vegetables have softened.

3 Stir in the wine, bring to a boil, and cook for about 6 minutes, or until the wine is reduced by half. Add tomato paste, stock, and onion soup mix, and stir in the mushrooms along with any juices on the plate. Return to a boil, lower the heat, and cook for 20 minutes, until the mushrooms are tender. Stir in the pearl onions.

4 On a small plate, knead the remaining 2 tablespoons butter with the flour and drop this paste into the pot. Lower the heat and simmer for 10 more minutes, stirring to smooth out the flour and butter. Season with salt and pepper and serve hot.

VARIATION
Wild Mushroom and Pepper Bourguignon

Add 1 cored, seeded, and diced red bell pepper along with the onions, and replace the portobellos with chopped mixed wild mushrooms (cremini, shiitake, oyster, chanterelle). Cook as above, and stir in 1/2 cup heavy cream at the end, just before adding the butter and flour.

TOP SECRET

Julia Child would never do it, but she was never a restaurant chef! The trick to getting the fullest vegetable flavor here is the addition of a package of onion soup mix. Add it, stir, and let it do its magic.

VERY VEGGIE ENTRÉES

Soba Noodle Salad

Soba noodles usually are served in soup in Japan, but as they have become increasingly available in American supermarkets, soba salads have gotten popular. That's because the noodles are heartier and more flavorful than simple semolina pastas—and the buckwheat means that they tend to have more nutrition than white-flour pasta.

1 package
(12 ounces)
soba noodles

3 tablespoons
fresh lime juice

1/4 cup soy sauce

1 tablespoon
sesame oil

1 tablespoon
grapeseed or
canola oil

1 tablespoon grated
fresh ginger

1 clove garlic,
minced

1 bunch broccoli,
trimmed into
florets

1 cup sugar
snap peas, blanched

2 tablespoons
sesame seeds

1 red bell pepper,
cored, seeded, and
thinly sliced

1 yellow bell
pepper, cored,
seeded, and
thinly sliced

4 scallions,
thinly sliced

PREP TIME: 15 minutes • **COOK TIME:** 10 minutes • **SERVES:** 4

1 Cook the noodles according to the package directions.

2 Meanwhile, whisk together the lime juice, soy sauce, sesame oil, grapeseed or canola oil, ginger, and garlic.

3 For the last 2 minutes of cooking time for the noodles, add the broccoli and sugar snap peas to the cooking water. Rinse the cooked noodles, broccoli, and peas under cold running water and drain well. Place into a large bowl and combine with the lime dressing.

4 Toast the sesame seeds by tossing them in a dry pan over medium heat for 1 to 2 minutes, until they smell fragrant. Immediately pour them over the noodles. Add the bell peppers and scallions and toss to combine. Serve at once, or chill for several hours.

VARIATION
Mango and Cucumber Soba Salad
Add 1 teaspoon sugar and the grated zest of a lime to the dressing. Skip all the vegetables and instead add a large thinly sliced seedless (or English) cucumber and a large diced ripe mango. Toss in 1 cup chopped fresh mint leaves and 1/2 cup sliced fresh basil leaves. Top the salad with 1 cup roasted peanuts instead of the sesame seeds and serve at once.

TOP SECRET
Blanching—cooking vegetables in hot water for a few minutes and then plunging them into cold water—is a chef's trick for keeping them bright, healthy, and crispy. Blanch any raw vegetables that you'd like to include in a salad—pasta or otherwise.

Chickpea and Ginger Soup

This soup is chock-full of healthy goodness, making it a fast, filling, and diet-friendly lunch when paired with a sandwich. It's also a good light supper on a day when you may have overindulged at lunch!

2 cans (15 ounces each) chickpeas (with liquid)

2 tablespoons extra-virgin olive oil

2 cloves garlic, minced

2 tablespoons grated fresh ginger

1 jalapeño pepper; seeded and deveined (wear gloves when handling)

1 teaspoon ground cumin

Salt and pepper, to taste

3 tablespoons fresh lime juice

3 tablespoons chopped fresh cilantro

Hot sauce, to taste

PREP TIME: 5 minutes • **COOK TIME:** 12 minutes • **SERVES:** 4

1 Put the chickpeas in a blender or food processor with their liquid and pulse until smooth.

2 Heat the oil in a medium saucepan over medium heat and add the garlic, ginger, and jalapeño. Cook for about 1 minute, then toss into the blender with the chickpeas. Pulse until smooth.

3 Pour the chickpea mixture into the saucepan and add the cumin. Simmer for about 10 minutes to allow the flavors to combine, then season with salt and pepper. Stir in the lime juice and cilantro and add hot sauce (the vinegar in the hot sauce helps brighten the flavor). Serve hot.

VARIATION

Spicy Hummus Soup with Egg

Stir 1/2 to 1 teaspoon red pepper flakes and 1 teaspoon ground coriander into the soup while heating. Just before serving, stir in 1/4 cup chopped roasted red pepper strips or jarred pimientos and top each serving with a dollop of plain yogurt and a spoonful of hard-boiled egg that has been mashed with a fork.

FIX IT FAST

Have you ever had a batch of hummus go wrong, where you've forgotten to drain the can of chickpeas or added too much garlic or salt or lemon juice to the food processor? This soup is precisely what to do with a failed batch.

TOP SECRET

Lime juice and cilantro mimic each other's flavor, so if you don't have one, just use a bit more of the other.

VERY VEGGIE ENTRÉES

Cauliflower and Potato Curry

Boiled potatoes and cauliflower wouldn't feel like much of a meal—but bathe it in a rich curry sauce and suddenly you have a hearty and filling Indian-style stew.

3 tablespoons
vegetable oil

1 large yellow
onion, diced

2 cloves garlic,
minced

1 jalapeño pepper,
seeded, deveined,
and chopped
(wear gloves
when handling)

1 tablespoon grated
fresh ginger

1 teaspoon
ground cumin

1/4 teaspoon
turmeric

1/4 teaspoon
cayenne

1 teaspoon salt

1 small head
cauliflower, cut into
florets

4 medium Yukon
Gold potatoes,
diced

4 cups water

2 tablespoons
fresh lemon juice

PREP TIME: 10 minutes • **COOK TIME:** 30 minutes • **SERVES:** 6

1 Heat the oil in a large heavy skillet over medium heat and cook the onions, garlic, jalapeño, and ginger for 10 minutes, stirring occasionally, until softened and browned.

2 Stir in the cumin, turmeric, cayenne, and salt and cook for 2 minutes, until the spices are pungent.

3 Add the cauliflower and potatoes and 4 cups water. Bring to a boil, reduce heat, and simmer for 20 minutes, until the vegetables are tender. Remove the lid and cook 5 minutes more to thicken the sauce. Season with lemon juice.

VARIATIONS

Red Potato Curry with Cauliflower and Peas

Instead of Yukon Golds, use red potatoes and dice them with the peels still on. Add a 10-ounce box of frozen peas during the last 5 minutes of cooking. The color contrast is lovely, with the yellow sauce, white cauliflower, red potato skins, and green peas.

Butternut Squash Curry with Cauliflower and Peas

Replace the potatoes with 1 cup cubed butternut squash and add a 10-ounce box of frozen peas during the last 5 minutes of cooking.

TOP SECRET

If you need to remove salt from a soup or stew, throw in several chunks of potato and simmer gently, then remove and discard the potato—much of the salty taste will have been removed. Conversely, if you're trying to cut down on salt, season a potato dish only just before serving, so you taste the freshly added salt instead of hiding a lot of sodium away in the vegetables during long cooking.

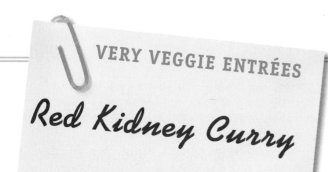

VERY VEGGIE ENTRÉES

Red Kidney Curry

Known as *rajma* in India, where it's a popular dish in the Punjab region, this is like a spicy red-bean chili. But it's nonetheless a curry, an easy one built entirely out of spices already in your cupboard—and thus it's terrific served over rice or with hot naan bread.

1/4 cup extra-virgin olive oil

1 medium yellow onion, diced

1 jalapeño pepper, seeded, deveined, and diced (wear gloves when handling)

3 tablespoons chopped fresh ginger

3 cloves garlic, minced

1 teaspoon salt

1 teaspoon ground cumin

1 teaspoon ground coriander

1/2 teaspoon ground turmeric

1/4 teaspoon cayenne

1 can (15 ounces) diced tomatoes

1 tablespoon red-wine vinegar

2 cans (15 ounces each) red kidney beans, drained and rinsed

PREP TIME: 10 minutes • **COOK TIME:** 20 minutes • **SERVES:** 6

1 Heat the oil in a large heavy pan over medium heat. Add the onions, jalapeños, ginger, and garlic and cook for 1 minute. Add the salt, cumin, coriander, turmeric, and cayenne and cook for 2 minutes, stirring frequently, until the spices smell pungent.

2 Add the tomatoes, vinegar, and beans and bring to a boil. Reduce the heat and simmer for 15 minutes, until the sauce is thickened.

VARIATION

Creamy Red Kidney Curry
Just before serving, stir in 3/4 cup plain full-fat yogurt.

TOP SECRET

Mash about half of the beans with the back of a wooden spoon to thicken the sauce. For a more authentic Indian flavor, stir in 1 teaspoon garam masala, a mild, fragrant spice mix readily found in supermarkets.

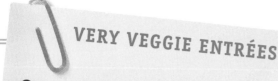

Broccoli and Red Pepper Quiche

Starting with a ready-made pie crust makes this fast and easy, but you don't have to be bound by frozen or refrigerated crust. Try lining a 9-inch pie pan with thawed puff pastry for a flakier finish.

3 eggs

1/2 cup whole milk

1 package (3 ounces) cream cheese, softened

1 package (10 ounces) frozen chopped broccoli, thawed and drained

1 jar (4 ounces) roasted red peppers, drained and chopped

1/2 cup grated Gruyère cheese

1/4 cup grated Parmesan cheese

6 green onions, thinly sliced

Salt and pepper, to taste

1 deep-dish 9-inch frozen pie crust

PREP TIME: 10 minutes • **COOK TIME:** 25 minutes • **SERVES:** 6

1 Preheat the oven to 400°F. In a medium bowl, beat the eggs, milk, and cream cheese until smooth.

2 Mix in the broccoli, red peppers, Gruyère, Parmesan, onions, and salt and pepper. Pour into the crust and bake for 25 minutes, until the filling is set and the crust is golden.

VARIATIONS

Spinach Quiche
Leave out the broccoli and red peppers and stir in a thawed and drained 10-ounce box of frozen chopped spinach and 1/2 teaspoon freshly grated nutmeg.

Mushroom and Red Pepper Quiche
Omit the broccoli and instead add 8 ounces of thinly sliced white mushrooms cooked in 2 tablespoons butter until golden.

TOP SECRET
Do wet pies such as quiche or pumpkin pie mix jiggle and spill when you transfer them to the oven, even when you set them on a baking sheet first? Here's a trick you need. When you're ready to bake, pull the oven rack out slightly with an oven mitt. Put a baking sheet on the rack, set the pie plate lined with the crust on the sheet, and pour the batter in. Slide the baking sheet and rack back in and shut the door. Have everything ready so you don't need to hold the oven door open too long, and move fast. The few moments of heat you lose will be worth the spills you save!

Not Your Mother's Bean Salad

If Mom's version consisted of opening cans of beans and tossing them with bottled vinaigrette—then this isn't it. Bursting with fresh summer flavor, this is a bean salad to make when you've just returned home from a farmer's market and you're wondering what to do with all those beans.

3 large ripe tomatoes

2 cups young, tender green beans, halved diagonally

2 large ears ripe corn

3 tablespoons olive oil

1 clove garlic, minced

1/4 teaspoon red pepper flakes

2 tablespoons white-wine vinegar

Salt and pepper, to taste

1/2 cup thinly sliced fresh basil leaves

PREP TIME: 10 minutes • **COOK TIME:** 10 minutes • **SERVES:** 6

1 Bring a pot of salted water to a boil and slide the tomatoes in. Cook for 2 minutes, then lift them out with a slotted spoon and leave the water boiling. Rinse the tomatoes in cold water, which will cause the skins to split. Peel and discard the skins.

2 Cook the green beans in the water for 3 minutes. Remove them with a slotted spoon into a colander and rinse in cold water. Meanwhile, break the corn ears in half and drop into the boiling water for 2 minutes. Remove and run under cold water.

3 In a large bowl, whisk together the oil, garlic, pepper flakes, and vinegar. Coarsely chop the tomatoes into the bowl, catching the juices. Add the beans, and slice the cooked corn off the cobs, adding the corn to the bowl. Taste and add salt and pepper, as well as extra vinegar, if desired. Top with shredded fresh basil leaves.

VARIATION

Hot Bean Salad

Heat the olive oil in a large skillet over medium heat and cook a chopped medium onion until just softened. Add the dressing ingredients, chopped tomatoes and simmer. Add the remaining ingredients, except for the basil, and heat through. Pour into a serving dish. Top with basil and drizzle with lemon juice before serving.

TOP SECRET

To remove corn kernels from the cob, cut the top off the ear of corn to make a flat bottom, then stand the ear of corn in a bowl. Slice downward with a sharp chef's knife, being careful not so cut too far inward or you'll include the hard, inedible base of each kernel. Rotate the ear as you cut, making long even slices all the way around. When you're done, turn the knife around and drag the dull edge down the length of the corn to "milk" all the flavorful juices.

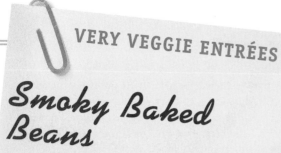

Smoky Baked Beans

Canned baked beans aren't vegetarian unless specified on the label, since so many of them contain bacon. But you can get a rich smoky taste without needing pork fat. Big, pillowy white cannellini absorb the flavors well and taste richer than smaller navy beans—but those work here, too. Use a hickory-smoke variety of bottled barbecue sauce to ratchet up the flavor.

1 large yellow onion, finely diced

2 cloves garlic, minced

1 cup bottled barbecue sauce

1/2 bottle dark beer

1/4 cup dark brown sugar

1/4 cup molasses

3 tablespoons Dijon mustard

3 tablespoons Worcestershire sauce

1 tablespoon soy sauce

2 teaspoons minced chipotles in adobo

4 cans (15 ounces each) cannellini beans, drained

PREP TIME: 5 minutes • **COOK TIME:** 1 hour • **SERVES:** 6

1 Preheat the oven to 350°F.

2 Stir together the onions, garlic, barbecue sauce, beer, brown sugar, molasses, mustard, Worcestershire sauce, soy sauce, chipotles, and beans in a deep, 3-quart baking dish.

3 Bake for 1 hour, until bubbling.

VARIATION

Maple Baked Beans

Combine the cannellini, 1 finely chopped onion, 1 cup ketchup, 3 tablespoons Dijon mustard, and 1 1/2 cups real maple syrup in the baking dish.

TOP SECRET

Contrary to popular belief, dried beans—if you choose to use them—do not last forever. If you have a bag sitting in your fridge that's more than a year old, use it as a paperweight. Cooking with old dried beans will result in a mushy finished dish.

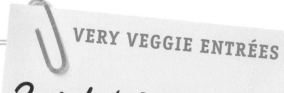

Quick 'n' Simple Lasagna Pie

When is a lasagna not a lasagna? When it's a pie! This noodle-free, couldn't-be-easier spin on an Italian savory tart can be made ahead of time and frozen, or baked and then frozen, for quick dinners on the fly. Use the vegetables here as a guideline; anything that's in season will work perfectly.

1 9-inch prepared pie crust

1 tablespoon extra-virgin olive oil

1 yellow summer squash, sliced in rounds

1 green zucchini, sliced in rounds

1/2 pound button mushrooms, sliced

1 medium onion, thinly sliced

2 cloves garlic, minced

2 cups prepared tomato sauce

1/2 cup mozzarella cheese

1/2 cup Parmesan cheese

PREP TIME: 30 minutes • **COOK TIME:** 30 minutes • **SERVES:** 6

1 Preheat the oven to 350°F.

2 Press the pie crust into a tart or pie tin and trim off the excess from the edges. Brush the surface of the pie crust with the olive oil, and bake for 3 minutes. Remove from the oven and let cool.

3 Place the pie tin on a baking sheet. Layer the squash, zucchini, mushrooms, onion, and minced garlic in any fashion (alternating layers, or arrange them like a mosaic). Pour the tomato sauce over all, taking care not to put in too much (or it will overflow).

4 Sprinkle with the two cheeses and bake until golden brown, about 30 minutes.

VARIATION
Sausage and Vegetable Pie
Crumble precooked vegetarian sausage directly into the vegetable mixture, and contiune with the tomato sauce.

TOP SECRET
They'll all want to know how you did it, but sometimes, a prepared pie crust is a chef's best friend. It pays to always have a few on hand, frozen. Use them for quiches, tarts, and even calzones.

9 PASTA!
THEY CALL IT MACARONI

If you have pasta in the cupboard, you have the makings for a simple, delicious meal. You don't even need an especially well-stocked pantry, since a filling pasta dinner can be as simple as angel hair tossed with olive oil and garlic, and perhaps a dusting of cheese. Pasta can take on many guises: With a few chefs' tricks up your sleeve for saucing and serving, you'll be dining in style—at top speed!

PASTA!

Puttanesca Pasta with Beans

Puttanesca is Italian for a style of pasta sauce named after women who practiced the world's oldest profession: In other words, people who might not have all day to linger over a simmering pot of tomato sauce. This version uses the white beans so favored by the Tuscans. Anchovies are optional, but their flavor adds depth to the sauce. If you have summer-fresh tomatoes, use 4 to 5 large ones instead of canned.

1 pound short tubular pasta shape, such as rigatoni or penne

2 tablespoons extra-virgin olive oil

1/2 cup pitted black olives, coarsely chopped

4 cloves garlic, minced

1 teaspoon red pepper flakes

1 can (28 ounces) diced tomatoes (with juice) or 4 large fresh tomatoes, diced

2 whole anchovies in oil or 2 teaspoons anchovy paste (optional)

1 teaspoon dried whole oregano

1 can (15 ounces) cannellini beans or other white beans, drained and rinsed

Salt, to taste

PREP TIME: 5 minutes • **COOK TIME:** 15 minutes • **SERVES:** 6

1 Cook the pasta according to the package directions until just done (still toothsome).

2 Heat the oil in a large skillet over medium heat and add the olives and garlic, giving them a quick stir. Add the pepper flakes and stir for less than a minute, until the garlic smells pungent.

3 Add the tomatoes (with juice). Stir in the anchovies or paste, if using, and the oregano and beans. Bring to a boil and let it bubble hard for about 5 minutes, until the sauce is slightly thickened. Season with salt.

4 Scoop some of the pasta cooking water into a cup and reserve. Drain the pasta and add it to the skillet. Loosen the sauce with some of the pasta cooking water. Toss well and serve.

VARIATION
Tuna Puttanesca
Skip the tubular pasta and cook spaghetti. Instead of beans, stir in 2 well-drained 6-ounce cans tuna packed in oil and 1 1/2 tablespoons capers, along with a handful of chopped flat-leaf Italian parsley.

TOP SECRET

Save that water! Most home cooks pour pasta cooking water down the drain without a second thought, but chefs treat it like liquid gold and always add a bit of it to the pasta sauce. Why? The starch that comes off the pasta into the water during the cooking process adds depth of flavor, texture, and unbeatable body to whatever sauce you combine it with. All you need is a cup and the difference will be immediately noticeable.

PASTA!

Spicy Peanut Noodles

Quick and savory, you can eat this dish cold on hot nights and hot on cold nights. It's filling and satisfying, and it can be ready as soon as the noodles are cooked, about 10 minutes. Spicy Peanut Noodles keep well in the refrigerator and are excellent eaten right out of the container while you stand in the doorway of the fridge.

1 pound Chinese egg noodles or vermicelli

1 cup peanut butter

1/2 cup hot water

1/4 cup cider vinegar

1/4 cup soy sauce

2 tablespoons sesame oil

1 clove garlic, minced

1 teaspoon sugar

1 teaspoon red pepper flakes

4 scallions, thinly sliced

1 large cucumber, peeled and cut into matchsticks

2 cups fresh bean sprouts

2 tablespoons chopped fresh cilantro

PREP TIME: 15 minutes • **COOK TIME:** 10 minutes • **SERVES:** 6

1 Cook the noodles according to the package directions.

2 Meanwhile, put the peanut butter, water, vinegar, soy sauce, oil, garlic, sugar, and pepper flakes in a blender and puree until smooth.

3 Drain the noodles and place in a large serving bowl. Add the scallions, cucumbers, bean sprouts, and cilantro, and pour the sauce over all. Toss well and garnish with fresh cilantro. Eat right away while warm or serve at room temperature.

VARIATION

Peanut Noodles with Chicken

Before adding the sauce, stir in 2 cups shredded cooked chicken. Toss gently with the sauce to avoid breaking up the chicken too much. Top the finished dish with 3 tablespoons roasted, salted peanuts.

LEFTOVER LUXURIES

Make a double batch of the spicy peanut sauce and store it in the refrigerator. Use it for a new batch of noodles or make a quick Asian slaw by pouring the sauce over cabbage shredded in the food processor. It also doubles as Indonesian gado-gado sauce to be poured over a hodgepodge salad of rice, hard-boiled eggs, bean sprouts, chopped green peppers, celery, and carrots.

TOP SECRET

Spicy peanut noodles are delicious, but somehow, they never come out quite the same way at home as they do in a restaurant, where they're smooth, unctuous, and creamy. How do restaurant chefs get that texture? They thin the sauce with hot water, as needed.

THE CHEATING CHEF AT HOME

PASTA SHAPES AND THE SAUCES THEY LOVE

Walk into any supermarket in America, and you'll find scads of types of pasta, in just a few shapes: strands, wide noodles, elbows, and tubes. But as imported pasta becomes more and more popular, the types available to us have become vast and often confusing. The fact is, certain pasta shapes work better with certain sauces than others. So if you think that your spaghetti is good with your mom's meat sauce, just wait until you try it with rigatoni! Here's a map:

Rigatoni
Ideal for dense, heavy, wetter sauces and for baked dishes.

Penne
Perfect for lighter tomato-based sauces.

Fusilli
Ideal for adding to luncheon salads.

Spaghetti
Perfect for lighter sauces and oil-and-garlic combinations.

Bucatini
Perfect for hearty, dryer sauces containing meat or ham.

Farfalle
A natural for seafood pastas in lighter, cream-based sauces.

Pappardelle
Withstands heavyweight ragus of lamb or duck.

Orecchiette
Goes best with dryer pasta sauces, like broccoli rabe with sausage and oil.

Radiatore
Most delicious when paired with heavier, wetter sauces.

Cappelli d'Angelo
Ideal in broth-based pasta sauces.

"Real" Tuna Noodle Casserole with Peas

Made with a can of condensed cream of mushroom soup, this is the stuff of thousands of forgettable weeknight suppers. Made with a homemade white sauce, topped with buttered crumbs, and baked till golden, it's quite another matter.

1 pound wide egg noodles

3 tablespoons unsalted butter

2 tablespoons flour

1 cup whole milk

1/4 cup plus 2 tablespoons grated Parmesan cheese

1/4 teaspoon grated nutmeg

Salt and pepper, to taste

1 package (10 ounces) frozen peas

2 cans (6 ounces each) tuna, drained

3/4 cup breadcrumbs

2 tablespoons extra-virgin olive oil

PREP TIME: 15 minutes • **COOK TIME:** 20 minutes • **SERVES:** 6

1 Cook the egg noodles according to the package directions. Preheat oven to 350°F.

2 Meanwhile, heat the butter in a large saucepan over medium heat. Stir in the flour and cook for 1 to 2 minutes, stirring frequently. Whisk in the milk and cook until thickened, stirring constantly, about 4 minutes. Stir in 1/4 cup of the Parmesan and the nutmeg. Season with salt and pepper.

3 Stir the peas into the white sauce and simmer for 1 to 2 minutes, stirring often. Remove from the heat. When the noodles are done, drain and add them to the saucepan along with the tuna. Stir gently to avoid breaking up the tuna too much.

4 Tip into a buttered 3-quart baking dish. Top with the breadcrumbs and drizzle with the oil, then sprinkle with 2 tablespoons Parmesan. Bake for 20 minutes, until bubbling.

VARIATION
Salmon Noodle Casserole
Replace the tuna with a 15-ounce can wild salmon. Stir 2 tablespoons chopped fresh parsley into the noodles with the salmon.

TOP SECRET
If you don't have time to make a white sauce, yes, of course you can replace it with a can of condensed cream soup blended with 1/2 cup of whole milk.

PASTA!

Creamy Mushroom Fettuccine

Dried mushrooms are always available and their shelf life seems to be inexhaustible; add a little warm water, and they spring to life again. Among the best dried mushrooms are shiitakes; they have depth and earthiness, a perfume that permeates an entire dish and lingers deliciously on the palate. Serve this creamy dish with a tartly dressed salad.

1 1/2 cups water

2 ounces dried shiitake mushrooms

1 pound fettuccine

1/4 cup extra-virgin olive oil

1 medium yellow onion, thinly sliced

2 cloves garlic, minced

1/2 cup heavy cream

Salt and pepper, to taste

3/4 cup grated Parmesan cheese

PREP TIME: 10 minutes • **COOK TIME:** 20 minutes • **SERVES:** 6

1 Bring the water to a boil in a small saucepan. Add the mushrooms and let steep off the heat for 20 minutes.

2 Cook the pasta according to the package directions. Pour the mushroom soaking liquid through a strainer lined with a paper towel, reserving the strained liquid. Pick off and discard the stems, which are woody, and chop the mushrooms.

3 Heat the oil in a large skillet over medium heat. Add the onions and garlic and cook for 3 minutes, until slightly softened. Add the mushrooms and the strained soaking liquid and bring to a boil. Simmer for 10 minutes, until the sauce is reduced by half, then pour in the cream and heat through. Season with salt and pepper.

4 Place the drained pasta in a large bowl. Pour the sauce over and toss with the Parmesan. Serve immediately.

VARIATION

Fresh Cremini Pasta

Trim 1/2 pound (about 2 cups) fresh cremini mushrooms into thin slices and cook with the onions in 2 tablespoons olive oil and 2 tablespoons butter until golden. Use chicken stock instead of the soaking liquid.

TOP SECRET

Dried mushrooms can be rehydrated in any liquid—hot water, hot stock, wine—and the result will be a blast of flavor, so be sure to keep the soaking liquid for the recipe. The trick is to strain it well because bits of grit may emerge from the mushrooms. If you're only straining a small amount, pour the liquid through a coffee filter for sorting out the fine particles. Larger amounts can go through a paper towel–lined strainer. For most recipes, different types of dried mushrooms are interchangeable.

PASTA!

Picnic Pasta Salad

Cold salads made of pasta exploded on the American culinary scene in the 1980s and have never left. Like chili, every cook has a recipe for pasta salad, and this one is an excellent base. It also keeps well in the refrigerator and makes a good brown-bag lunch, especially since it often tastes better the second day.

1 bunch broccoli, trimmed into florets

1 large carrot, sliced into very thin half-moons

1 pound rotini or fusilli

1/2 cup extra-virgin olive oil

1/4 cup red-wine vinegar

1 tablespoon Dijon mustard

1 small clove garlic, minced

1 teaspoon dried oregano

1/4 cup pimiento-stuffed green olives, chopped

1/4 cup grated Parmesan cheese

PREP TIME: 10 minutes • **COOK TIME:** 12 minutes • **SERVES:** 6

1 Bring a large stock pot filled with salted water to a boil and add the broccoli and carrots. Cook for about 8 minutes, until the broccoli turns bright green and becomes tender. Remove to a bowl filled with ice water, drain well, and set aside.

2 Add the pasta to the same water, and cook, according to the package directions. Take care not to overcook. (If there was ever a time for al dente pasta, it's now.)

3 In a large bowl, whisk together the oil, vinegar, mustard, garlic, and oregano. Add the drained pasta and vegetables and toss lightly to coat. Stir in the olives and Parmesan. Serve at once or chill for up to 2 days. Store tightly covered in glass or plastic in the refrigerator.

VARIATION

Pasta Salad with Roast Chicken

Leave out the carrot and add 1 cup trimmed sugar snap peas; use lemon juice in the dressing instead of red-wine vinegar and substitute chopped black olives for the green. Shred the meat from one rotisserie chicken and toss with the pasta and dressing just before serving. This is best eaten the day it's made.

FIX IT FAST

Chilling pasta salad overnight dulls the flavors. When you look in the dish the next day, there may appear to be no dressing at all. That's because the pasta absorbs every drop of moisture in the bowl. To revive it, mix a second, smaller batch of dressing without the garlic and oregano (their flavors will have intensified as the dressing sits). Toss the pasta with the fresh dressing and allow it to sit 15 minutes at room temperature before serving.

TOP SECRET

Chefs always know how to add more zing to an otherwise bland dish, and this is just one way: Whenever you make a pasta dish that involves vegetables, blanch the vegetables first, drain them, and then cook the pasta in the same water. An amazing hit of flavor!

PASTA!

Penne with Roasted Eggplant

Roasting and pureeing eggplant and bell pepper results in a bright chunky sauce that's not very liquid, making this an ideal dish to transport to a potluck or picnic—and also easier to balance on a those flimsy paper plates!

1 medium eggplant (unpeeled), diced into 1-inch cubes

1 red bell pepper, cored, seeded, and chopped

1 pint grape tomatoes

3 cloves garlic

1/4 cup extra-virgin olive oil

1 teaspoon red pepper flakes

Salt and pepper, to taste

1 pound penne

1/2 cup fresh mint leaves

1/2 cup grated Parmesan cheese

2 tablespoons fresh lemon juice

2 tablespoons sliced fresh basil leaves

PREP TIME: 15 minutes • **COOK TIME:** 35 minutes • **SERVES:** 6

1 Preheat the oven to 400°F. In a large bowl, combine the eggplant, bell pepper, tomatoes, garlic, 2 tablespoons of the olive oil, and the red pepper flakes. Sprinkle with salt and pepper and lay out in an even layer on a baking sheet. Roast for about 35 minutes, until the eggplant is tender and browned.

2 Meanwhile, cook the penne according to the package directions. Reserve 2 cups of the pasta cooking water before draining the pasta.

3 Put the roasted vegetables in a food processor. Add the mint, the remaining 2 tablespoons of oil, the Parmesan, and lemon juice. Pulse to a chunky puree.

4 Put the drained pasta in a large serving dish and add the eggplant puree. Toss gently, adding the reserved pasta water a bit at a time until the dish is as saucy as you like. Sprinkle with the basil and serve hot or at room temperature.

VARIATION

Penne with Eggplant and Ricotta

Add an 8-ounce container of ricotta to the food processor when pureeing the vegetables.
Taste and season with additional salt and pepper and red pepper flakes, as desired. Toss with the penne.

TOP SECRET

Mint is what elevates this dish from the boring to the sassy. If you're saving mint to use a few sprigs in iced tea, you're not giving it half its due. A great deal of Middle-Eastern cooking uses mint in all sorts of savory ways, and it blends beautifully with the mild earthy flavor of eggplant, elevating both to more than the sum of their parts. Try mint in any dish where you might use basil, and see how it lightens and brightens the flavor.

PASTA!

Rigatoni with Baked Tomato Sauce

Using grape tomatoes adds a concentrated punch of sweetness in the off-season, but if it's summertime, use any red ripe tomato.

1 pound grape tomatoes, halved

1/3 cup breadcrumbs

1/3 cup grated Parmesan cheese

2 cloves garlic, finely chopped

Salt and freshly ground pepper, to taste

1/4 cup extra-virgin olive oil

1 pound rigatoni

1/4 cup loosely packed fresh basil leaves, torn

1/4 teaspoon red pepper flakes

PREP TIME: 10 minutes • **COOK TIME:** 20 minutes • **SERVES:** 6

1 Preheat the oven to 400°F. Grease a 13 x 9-inch baking dish and put the grape tomatoes, cut-side up, in the dish.

2 In a small bowl, combine the breadcrumbs, Parmesan, and garlic and toss with a fork to mix well. Sprinkle the crumb mixture over the tomatoes, then sprinkle with salt and pepper and drizzle with oil. Bake for about 15 minutes, until the tomatoes are tender and starting to brown.

3 Meanwhile, cook the pasta according to the package directions. Reserve 1 cup of the pasta cooking water and drain the pasta.

4 Toss the pasta with the tomatoes, adding a few tablespoons of cooking water to make a light sauce. Stir in the basil and red pepper flakes and serve sprinkled with Parmesan.

VARIATION
Baked Ziti

Skip the roasted tomatoes and make a simple tomato sauce from 1 diced onion cooked until tender in 2 tablespoons olive oil. Add a 28-ounce can of diced tomatoes (with juice) and simmer until lightly thickened. Season with salt and pepper. Stir in a 16-ounce container of ricotta and 2 cups shredded mozzarella. Mix with the cooked pasta, and pour into a lightly greased 9 x 13-inch baking dish. Top with 2 cups shredded mozzarella and bake at 350°F for about 30 minutes, or until bubbly and browned.

TOP SECRET

Many chefs cook pasta using the absorption method, rather than in big vats of water. You can do the same with baked ziti by adding a couple cups of water to the sauce before combining it with the raw pasta. Spread the saucy mixture into the baking dish, leaving off the final topping of cheese, and cover tightly with foil. Cook for 1 hour. Remove the foil, stir gently, and top with cheese. Bake for 10 minutes more, until the cheese is browned and the sauce is bubbling.

Creamy Macaroni and Cheese

A pound of cheese to a pound of macaroni sounds outrageously fatty, but it truly is the amount required to get that unctuous cheesy flavor that makes mac and cheese so comforting and delicious. The addition of cottage cheese gives this version a bit of backbone (and some extra protein), and lets you skip the usual step of making a white sauce.

1 pound macaroni

1 cup
cottage cheese

1 tablespoon
Dijon mustard

Pinch of cayenne

1/2 teaspoon
freshly
grated nutmeg

1/2 cup whole milk

4 cups grated
extra-sharp
cheddar cheese

Salt and pepper,
to taste

PREP TIME: 15 minutes • **COOK TIME:** 45 minutes • **SERVES:** 8

1 Preheat the oven to 375°F. Cook the pasta for 6 minutes in boiling water, until still firm. Lightly butter a 9 x 13-inch pan.

2 Put the cottage cheese, mustard, cayenne, and nutmeg in a food processor and puree until completely smooth.

3 Transfer to a large bowl and combine with the milk, 3 1/2 cups of the cheese, and the drained pasta. Season with salt and pepper. Pour into the prepared pan, cover tightly with foil, and bake for 30 minutes.

4 Uncover the pan and sprinkle with the remaining 1/2 cup of the cheese. Bake 15 minutes more, or until bubbly and golden. Cool for 10 minutes before serving.

VARIATION
Maverick Mac and Cheese
Don't cook the pasta! Add an additional 1 1/2 cups milk, for a total of 2 cups, and follow the directions above, cooking for an additional 15 minutes once you uncover the pasta. It's unusual to mix crunchy uncooked elbows in with the cheese mixture, but it works.

TOP SECRET
Anytime you want to forgo typically high-calorie white sauce, puree cottage cheese instead. To keep it freshest, store the container upside down in your refrigerator.

PASTA!

Spaghetti and Meatballs

It's all about the meatballs in this classic Italian-American dish. If they're good (and these will be!), the tomato sauce and spaghetti are almost an afterthought.

1 cup white breadcrumbs (about 4 slices)

1/2 cup buttermilk

3/4 pound ground pork

3/4 pound ground beef

1 small onion, very finely minced

2 tablespoons chopped fresh parsley

1/2 cup grated Parmesan cheese

1 teaspoon salt

1 extra-large egg, beaten

Vegetable oil

1 tablespoon olive oil

1 large yellow onion, diced

2 cloves garlic, minced

1/4 teaspoon red pepper flakes

1/2 cup red wine

1 can (28 ounces) diced tomatoes (with juice)

1 pound spaghetti

PREP TIME: 1 hour • **COOK TIME:** 1 hour • **SERVES:** 6

1 Put the crumbs and buttermilk in a large bowl and leave for 10 minutes. Add the pork, beef, onions, parsley, Parmesan, salt, and egg and mix gently. Form into 2 dozen meatballs, about 2 inches in diameter.

2 Brown the meatballs in batches in a large skillet with several tablespoons of vegetable oil, turning to brown all sides. Remove to a plate, and add a bit more oil, as needed, until all the meatballs are cooked.

3 In the same skillet, heat the olive oil and cook the onions and garlic for about 8 minutes, until softened. Add the red pepper flakes and wine and bring to a boil, stirring, for about 2 minutes, or until the wine is reduced by half. Stir in the tomatoes (with juice).

4 Gently lift the meatballs into the sauce, cover and simmer on low for 30 minutes. Meanwhile, cook the spaghetti according to the package directions. Serve the meatballs and sauce on the drained spaghetti with Parmesan cheese.

VARIATION

Spicy Meatballs and Spaghetti

Add 2 minced cloves garlic and 1 1/2 teaspoons Italian seasoning along with 1/2 teaspoon red pepper flakes to the meatball mixture. Simmer 3 pickled pepperoncini in the sauce.

TOP SECRET

When shaping the meatballs, pick up a portion of meat and form it very loosely into a shaggy ball, being very careful not to press—the rough edges will smooth off in the simmering. The result is light, fluffy meatballs that absorb the sauce and taste delicate in the mouth.

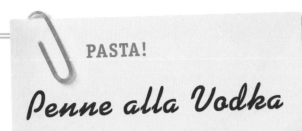

PASTA!

Penne alla Vodka

Some vodka sauce recipes call for a slight splash of vodka—this one calls for more. A big glug of vodka that is then reduced brings a lightness and brightness to the sauce, hence the continued popularity of this American-Italian classic.

1 pound penne

1 tablespoon butter

1 tablespoon extra-virgin olive oil

2 cloves garlic, minced

1 cup vodka

1 can (28 ounces) crushed tomatoes

Salt and pepper, to taste

1/2 cup heavy cream

1/2 cup sliced fresh basil leaves

Grated Parmesan cheese

PREP TIME: 15 minutes • **COOK TIME:** 15 minutes • **SERVES:** 6

1 Cook the penne according to the package directions.

2 Meanwhile, heat the butter and oil in a large skillet over medium heat. Add the garlic and cook for 1 to 2 minutes, until it is pungent but not brown. Pour in the vodka, bring to a boil, and cook until reduced by half, about 4 minutes.

3 Add the tomatoes and bring to a boil. Reduce the heat and simmer for 5 minutes. Season with salt and pepper.

4 Stir in the cream and basil and toss with the drained pasta. Serve at once with the Parmesan.

VARIATION

Penne alla Vodka with Pancetta

Dice 4 ounces pancetta (or thick-sliced bacon) and cook it in the butter and olive oil before adding the garlic.

TOP SECRET

Any tomato sauce will benefit from a hit of vodka. Why? The alcohol in the vodka reacts with the tomatoes' acid to create the flavor compounds known as esters, hence the lightness and brightness of the sauce over any regular tomato sauce. And if you're worried about the alcohol content, or flavor, fear not: By the time it finishes cooking, the sauce contains less than 1 percent alcohol.

Beef Lo Mein

Once you master making sizzling lo mein at home, you'll never need to order it from a Chinese takeout again. Chinese lo mein noodles are readily available in the Asian food section of the supermarket, which is where you'll also find oyster sauce and sesame oil.

8 ounces Chinese lo mein noodles

3/4 pound flank steak

3 tablespoons oyster sauce

1/2 teaspoon pepper

3 teaspoons sesame oil

2 tablespoons vegetable oil

4 cups chopped Napa cabbage

1 teaspoon sugar

1 1/2 teaspoons salt

2 tablespoons soy sauce

PREP TIME: 30 minutes • **COOK TIME:** 40 minutes • **SERVES:** 4

1 Cook the noodles in boiling salted water for 5 minutes until tender. Drain and rinse under cold water to stop the cooking. Drain well and set aside.

2 Slice the meat against the grain as thinly as possible. Place in a dish with the oyster sauce, pepper, and 1 teaspoon of the sesame oil.

3 In a large skillet, heat the vegetable oil over medium-high heat and cook the beef, stirring constantly, for 1 minute. Remove to a large bowl with a slotted spoon, leaving any oil in the pan. Add the cabbage, sugar, and salt. Cook, stirring, for 3 to 4 minutes, until the cabbage is just softened. Spoon the cabbage over the beef and set aside.

4 Turn the heat to high and, when hot, add the noodles. Cook, stirring, for 2 minutes. Add the soy sauce and the remaining 2 teaspoons of the sesame oil. Return the beef and cabbage to the pan and toss to blend and heat through.

VARIATION
Shrimp Lo Mein
Replace the beef with 1 pound medium shrimp, peeled.

TOP SECRET

Oyster sauce is crucial to add depth to the sauce. It's a dark, rich concoction that looks (and also tastes) like brown ketchup. Made of oysters, brine, and soy sauce, it adds meaty depth to the noodles, with no hint of seafood at all. If you can't find oyster sauce, add a couple tablespoons of fish sauce and ketchup instead.

PASTA!

Farfalle with Butternut and Sage Brown Butter

Roasted butternut squash has a rich sweetness that sings with the addition of nutty browned butter. Add the autumnal fragrance of sage and you have a warming pasta dish that you'll turn to again and again throughout the fall.

1 butternut squash (about 3 pounds), cut into 1-inch cubes

1/4 cup extra-virgin olive oil

Salt and pepper, to taste

1 pound farfalle

3 tablespoons butter

1 large shallot, finely chopped

1 tablespoon chopped fresh sage or 1 teaspoon dried

Grated Parmesan cheese

PREP TIME: 10 minutes • **COOK TIME:** 35 minutes • **SERVES:** 6

1 Preheat the oven to 400°F. Line a baking sheet with foil. Toss the squash with 1 tablespoon of the oil, then place it in one layer on the foil. Sprinkle with salt and pepper and roast for about 30 minutes, or until tender and browned.

2 Meanwhile, cook the pasta according to the package directions.

3 Melt the butter with the remaining 3 tablespoons of the olive oil in a small skillet over medium heat. Add the shallots and sage and cook for 2 to 3 minutes, until the shallots are softened and the butter is lightly browned.

4 In a large serving dish, toss the drained pasta with the squash and the butter mixture. Serve at once with Parmesan.

VARIATION

Farfalle with Butternut, Bacon, and Pecans

Cook 4 diced slices thick-cut bacon until crisp. Set aside and remove most of the bacon fat from the skillet before adding the butter and olive oil. Stir 1/2 teaspoon red pepper flakes into the oil while cooking the shallots, and add 1/2 cup chopped pecans for the last minute, tossing until they are toasted and lightly coated with oil. After combining the squash, butter, and pasta, sprinkle the bacon bits over all and serve with freshly grated Parmesan.

TOP SECRET

Butternut squash can be huge and tough-skinned and therefore difficult to cut up. Here are some chef tips to make the going easier: First, cut off the stem end and the bottom so that the squash stands flat. Then cut it in half lengthwise and scoop out the seeds. Then peel it and cube it. Why not peel it first? Peeling it will make the squash slippery and hard to maneuver, making it dangerous if you're using a sharp knife.

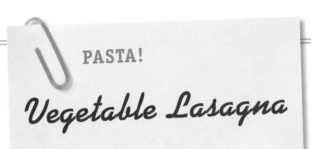

PASTA!

Vegetable Lasagna

You've never seen lasagna more stuffed with vegetables than this one. It may seem like all these vegetables won't fit in the pan, but use the deepest 9 x 13-inch pan you have—and the result is a dish overflowing with vegetable goodness.

2 tablespoons olive oil

1 onion, chopped

1 large carrot, shredded

2 cups white mushrooms, sliced

5 cloves garlic, minced

1 box frozen chopped spinach

1 teaspoon dried basil

1 1/2 teaspoons salt

1/2 teaspoon pepper

1/2 cup sliced fresh basil leaves

2 eggs, beaten

1 container (16 ounces) low-fat ricotta cheese

1 pound shredded mozzarella cheese

2 jars (28 ounces each) spaghetti sauce

12 no-boil lasagna noodles

PREP TIME: 30 minutes • **COOK TIME:** 1 hour 15 minutes • **SERVES:** 8

1 Preheat the oven to 375°F. Lightly grease a deep 9 x 13-inch baking dish.

2 Heat the oil in a large skillet over medium-high heat. Add the onions and carrots and cook, stirring, for about 10 minutes, or until the onion is translucent. Add the mushrooms and garlic and cook for 3 minutes, until softened. Stir in the spinach, dried basil, salt, and pepper. Cover and cook for 15 minutes, until the spinach is cooked through. Remove from heat and stir in the fresh basil.

3 In a medium bowl, mix the eggs with the ricotta and 2 cups of the mozzarella.

4 Spread one-half jar of the spaghetti sauce over the bottom of the dish. Place 4 lasagna noodles on top. Spread with half of the ricotta mixture, half of the vegetable mixture, and the remaining half of the first jar of sauce. Add 4 more lasagna noodles, spread with the remaining ricotta mixture and the remaining vegetables. Top with half the second jar of sauce. Add the remaining 4 lasagna noodles and the rest of the sauce. Sprinkle with the remaining 2 cups of mozzarella. Coat the dull side of a piece of foil with oil and cover the baking dish. Bake for about 1 hour, until bubbly. Uncover and cook for 10 minutes longer, or until the cheese is browned. Let rest 15 minutes before serving.

TOP SECRET

The best lasagnas are also the most flavorful, making this ancient dish a perfect vehicle for leftover meat, poultry, or veggies. Most Italian grandmas know this secret: Layer in ground or lightly cubed boneless chicken, pork, crumbled cooked sausage, leftover chopped veggies, and (heavens!) even cubed tofu and watch your guests smile.

PASTA!

Baked Ziti

This all-time favorite is a perfect make-ahead dish. It freezes well, and leftovers will keep for up to 4 days.

8 ounces ziti

1 cup part-skim ricotta cheese

1 1/2 cups shredded mozzarella cheese (about 6 ounces)

1 cup shredded sharp provolone cheese (about 4 ounces)

2 ounces pepperoni, cut into 1 1/4-inch pieces

2 cups prepared marinara sauce

PREP TIME: 15 minutes • **COOK TIME:** 45 minutes • **SERVES:** 4

1 Preheat the oven to 350°F. Coat an 8-inch-square baking pan with cooking spray.

2 Cook the pasta according to the package directions. In a colander, drain the pasta 1 to 2 minutes before it is fully cooked so that it is still slightly underdone. Rinse with cold water to stop the cooking, then drain it again.

3 In a medium bowl, whisk together the ricotta, 1 cup of the mozzarella, 3/4 cup of the provolone, and the pepperoni.

4 Pour half of the drained pasta into the baking pan. Top with 1 cup of the marinara sauce then spread with the ricotta mixture. Top with the remaining ziti. Spread with the remaining 1 cup of marinara sauce. Sprinkle with the remaining 1/2 cup mozzarella and 1/4 cup provolone. Bake for about 30 minutes, until bubbling and the cheese has completely melted.

VARIATION
Baked Eggplant Ziti
Add cubed eggplant to the pasta in step 4 and proceed with the recipe.

DID YOU KNOW?

This dish is ideal for entertaining and serving at parties. Assemble it the night before, wrap in plastic, then refrigerate until about 30 minutes before you need to bake it. Then just pop it in the oven.

TOP SECRET

Pepperoni is usually relegated to the antipasto platter or pizza. Adding diced cubes to pasta lends a subtle spicy aroma and a satisfying chew. The second secret ingredient—provolone cheese—adds a bit of sharpness to balance the milder, creamier ricotta and mozzarella cheeses.

PASTA!

Chicken Spaghetti Toss

This recipe was born out of an almost-empty refrigerator, which means that you can make it in a snap when the cupboard is almost bare. Plenty of Parmesan gives it a nice, nutty kick.

8 ounces spaghetti

5 green onions, chopped

2 cloves garlic, minced

2 tablespoons unsalted butter

2 tablespoons extra-virgin olive oil

1 1/2 pounds boneless, skinless chicken breasts, cubed

3 tablespoons fresh lemon juice

3 tablespoons minced fresh parsley

1 teaspoon salt

1 teaspoon lemon-pepper seasoning

Grated Parmesan cheese, to taste

PREP TIME: 10 minutes • **COOK TIME:** 20 minutes • **SERVES:** 4

1 Cook the spaghetti according to the package directions.

2 Meanwhile, in a large nonstick skillet, sauté the onions and garlic in the butter and oil for about 4 minutes, or until tender.

3 Stir in the chicken, lemon juice, parsley, salt, and lemon-pepper. Sauté for 15 to 20 minutes, or until the chicken juices run clear.

4 In a large bowl, toss the drained spaghetti with the chicken mixture. Top with the cheese.

VARIATION

Tuna Spaghetti Toss

Replace the chicken with 2 drained 12-ounce cans of chunk light tuna.

FIX IT FAST

If you don't have prepared lemon-pepper seasoning, simply replace it with 1/2 teaspoon grated lemon zest, 1/4 teaspoon freshly ground black pepper, and 1/8 teaspoon salt.

TOP SECRET

Some jarred spices are little more than sawdust, and others are worth their weight in gold. Lemon-pepper seasoning is one of them. Use it on pasta, fish, chicken, and even steak. Bonus: Many lemon-pepper seasonings are salt-free.

PASTA!

Linguine with No-Cook Tomato Sauce

This quick-and-easy sauce is bound to become your house favorite. It's bursting with fresh-from-the-garden flavor.

3 pounds plum tomatoes, seeded and chopped

2/3 cup chopped fresh basil

1/4 cup olive oil

1/4 cup chopped fresh flat-leaf parsley

2 tablespoons chopped fresh mint

2 teaspoons grated orange zest

3 cloves garlic, minced

1/2 teaspoon freshly ground black pepper

Salt, to taste

12 ounces linguine

1/4 cup grated Parmesan cheese

PREP TIME: 15 minutes • **COOK TIME:** 15 minutes • **SERVES:** 4

1 Mix the tomatoes, basil, oil, parsley, mint, orange zest, garlic, pepper, and salt in a medium bowl. Let stand for at least 30 minutes, or up to 2 hours, at room temperature.

2 Cook the pasta according to the package directions.

3 Add the drained pasta to a large bowl. Top with the sauce and sprinkle with the Parmesan.

VARIATION

Pasta Balsamico

Add 1 1/2 tablespoons balsamic vinegar to the sauce for extra zip. When mixing the hot pasta with the sauce, toss in 8 ounces cubed fontina, which will soften but not completely melt from the heat of the noodles.

TOP SECRET

The secret ingredient in this dish that gives it its round, yummy flavor is orange zest: Citrusy but full of oomph, it's the perfect foil for no-cook tomato sauce.

PASTA!

Creamy Salmon Fettuccine

Forget about bagels and cream cheese; smoked salmon and its favorite mate are wonderful together in this delicious and simple pasta dish. It's not for the diet-conscious, but it is a delicious treat every once in a while!

12 ounces fettuccine

2 tablespoons unsalted butter

2 tablespoons extra-virgin olive oil

1 red onion, finely chopped

3 ounces smoked salmon, chopped

1/2 cup cream cheese

2/3 cup heavy cream

1/4 teaspoon salt

1/8 teaspoon freshly ground black pepper

1 tablespoon chopped fresh dill

PREP TIME: 10 minutes • **COOK TIME:** 15 minutes • **SERVES:** 4

1 Cook the pasta according to the package directions.

2 Meanwhile, heat a large nonstick skillet over medium-high heat and add the butter and oil. Heat until the butter melts, then stir in the onions. Cook, stirring occasionally, for 2 to 3 minutes, until the onions start to soften.

3 Add the salmon and cook for 1 minute, or until opaque. Stir in the cream cheese and cook for about 45 seconds, stirring, until it melts.

4 Pour in the cream and cook for 1 minute, until hot. Remove from the heat and stir in the drained fettuccine. Toss until well-coated. Stir in the salt, pepper, and dill and serve.

VARIATION
Lighter Salmon Fettuccine
To lighten up this dish, use half the amount of oil and butter, use reduced-fat cream cheese, and substitute 2% milk for the cream. Avoid boiling the sauce because the lower fat content could cause it to separate.

TOP SECRET
The key to the powerful flavor in this lovely dish is not the salmon or the cream cheese—it's the onion... *red* onion, that is. Stronger in flavor than white or yellow onions, it also possesses a more mellow taste, which is why it's almost always paired with salmon and cream cheese.

Creamy Tortellini Soup

One of the easiest soups to put together, this old-fashioned dish comes straight from the heart of Italy (minus the yogurt).

1 package (1 pound) frozen cheese or meat tortellini

3 tablespoons olive or vegetable oil

1 medium yellow onion, coarsely chopped

5 cloves garlic, minced

4 cups chicken stock

1 package (10 ounces) frozen green peas, thawed and drained

2 cups low-fat plain yogurt, well stirred, or sour cream

1/4 teaspoon black pepper

1/3 cup minced fresh parsley

1/2 cup grated Parmesan cheese, for serving (optional)

PREP TIME: 10 minutes • **COOK TIME:** 10 minutes • **SERVES:** 4

1 Cook the pasta according to package directions. Drain, transfer to a large bowl, add 1 tablespoon of the oil, and toss.

2 In a large saucepan over medium heat, heat the remaining 2 tablespoons of oil. Add the onions and garlic and sauté for about 3 minutes, or until soft.

3 Increase the heat to high, add the stock and peas, cover, and bring to a boil.

4 Reduce the heat to low and whisk in the yogurt or sour cream. Add the tortellini and pepper and cook until heated through without boiling. Stir in the parsley. Serve with the Parmesan, if using.

VARIATION

Tortellini in Brodo

Omit the oil, garlic, and yogurt, and instead bring the chicken stock to a boil, lower the heat, and add the cooked tortellini directly to the pot. Add the peas, and serve with a dusting of pepper, parsley, and cheese.

TOP SECRET

Having a bag or two of frozen tortellini stashed away in your freezer is the ticket to a perfect, sophisticated dinner. Whether tossed with a marinara sauce or turned into a pasta salad, it's a no-fail way to wow your guests every time.

THE JOY OF NO-FAIL, NO-COOK PASTA SAUCES

One of the reasons that pasta is beloved as one of the world's favorite dishes, hands-down, is because it's so quick and easy to put together: some good tomato sauce, a few veggies, a grating of decent cheese, and you have the makings of a truly wonderful dish. If you happen to have a hankering for Asian food, you can toss some cooked lo mein noodles with a bit of soy sauce, some veggies, and a dash of sesame oil, and you have a great meal in a virtual instant.

But what if it's too warm out to make sauce? What if you just don't feel like going through the process of cooking sauce? Does this mean you have to rethink dinner? Nope. You just have to switch gears a little bit, and make one of these spectacular no-cook pasta sauces. Start with a base of freshly cooked hot or warm pasta, and proceed!

Pasta Portofino

Toss together 1/2 cup chopped pitted black olives, 1/2 cup extra virgin olive oil, 1/2 cup freshly grated Parmesan cheese, 3 diced plum tomatoes, 1/4 teaspoon red pepper flakes, 1/2 cup minced basil leaves in a bowl. Let stand for 10 minutes, and add one pound of room temperature pasta.

Pasta Romana

Quarter 1 cup canned, drained artichoke hearts and toss with 1/2 cup chopped pitted black olives, 1/2 cup extra-virgin olive oil, 2 tablespoons capers, 3 chopped garlic cloves. Add to one pound of cooked spaghetti, and top with grated Romano cheese.

Pasta Niçoise

In a large bowl, combine 1 1/2 cups chopped, pitted black olives, 1/4 cup lemon juice, 1/2 cup extra virgin olive oil, 2 tablespoons Dijon mustard, 1 tablespoon fresh thyme leaves. Let stand at room temperature for 30 minutes. Add a large can of drained tuna, 4 sliced hard-boiled eggs, and a teaspoon of anchovy paste. Toss well, and blend gently with one pound of cooked shells.

Pasta Ricotta Salata

In a large bowl, toss 2 cups crumbled ricotta salata cheese with 2 cups fresh chopped basil leaves. Add 1/2 cup olive oil and 2 cups cherry tomatoes, halved. Add in a pound of cooked and drained penne, and toss well.

Pasta Mozzarella Toss

Chop 1/2 pound fresh mozzarella into cubes. In a large bowl, toss it together with 1/2 cup extra-virgin olive oil, 1 cup pitted chopped black olives, and 1 cup chopped sun-dried tomatoes. Add a pound of warm pasta, toss well, and serve while the mozzarella melts.

10 SCRUMPTIOUS SIDES

The challenge of getting fresh vegetables to your table is a big one, especially if you live in an intemperate climate. But the good news is that it requires virtually no effort to put together a simple squash dish or to add some cukes and carrots to a green salad. If you must, opt for frozen vegetables instead of canned ones; they're very often frozen immediately after picking, and this locks in both flavor and nutrients. But if the idea of steamed, boiled, or even roasted vegetables sounds boring to you, quit thinking of veggies as a side and start thinking of them as a main course; give them proper seasoning to make them more tasty and appealing than any meat on the table. And when in doubt, serve mashed potatoes!

Mashed Potatoes

A mashed potato recipe just seems right—after all, potatoes come from the earth and, when you leave the skin on them, are packed with nutrients. To make really exciting, chef-worthy mashed potatoes, you certainly could use unsalted butter—and using whole milk helps a lot. But this recipe makes some top-secret adjustments that will make this favorite dish taste great.

5 pounds Yukon Gold potatoes, quartered

2 tablespoons unsalted butter

1 1/2 cups 2% milk

2 tablespoons low-fat sour cream

Salt and pepper, to taste

PREP TIME: 15 minutes • **COOK TIME:** 25 minutes • **SERVES:** 6

1 Put the potatoes in a large heavy saucepan and cover them with cold water. Bring to a boil, then reduce the heat and simmer for about 25 minutes, until tender.

2 Drain the potatoes. Return them to the pot and mash with a handheld potato masher. Add the butter, and as it begins melting, fold it into the potatoes with a wooden spoon or a rubber spatula. When it's incorporated, add the milk and sour cream, and continue to fold. Season with salt and pepper.

VARIATION
Basil Mashed Potatoes
Beat 1/3 cup freshly-made pesto into the mashed potatoes just after adding the milk, and omit the sour cream.

LEFTOVER LUXURIES
Roll 2 tablespoons cold mashed potatoes into a barrel shape. Dip them into beaten egg and then bread-crumbs, and panfry them in extra-virgin olive oil in a heavyweight pan over medium-high heat. Remove to a paper towel–lined plate when they're golden brown. Serve warm.

TOP SECRET
If you need to hold potatoes on the stove, pour 1/2 cup warm milk over the smoothed surface of the spuds and cover with a lid. They can sit that way on the back of the stove for 30 minutes with no loss of taste or texture. When ready to serve, beat in the milk.

Potato Salad with Green Beans

Potatoes for salad are best cooked with the skin on to keep them from getting mushy. Peel them when they're cool, and then the salad will come together quickly.

3 pounds redskin new potatoes

1/2 pound fresh green beans

1 clove garlic, minced

1/3 cup olive oil

3 tablespoons red-wine vinegar

2 tablespoons Dijon mustard

Salt and pepper, to taste

PREP TIME: 15 minutes • **COOK TIME:** 15 minutes • **SERVES:** 6

1 Scrub any dirt off the potatoes and put them in a large saucepan. Cover with cold water and add a couple teaspoons of salt. Bring to a boil over medium heat and cook for 10 to 15 minutes, or until tender and the skins just start to crack.

2 Meanwhile, remove the top and the tail of the green beans, and break into bite-size lengths. Before the end of the potato cooking time, add the green beans and cook until bright green but still crunchy.

3 In a medium bowl, whisk together the garlic, oil, vinegar, mustard, and salt and pepper until the dressing is thick and creamy.

4 Drain the beans and potatoes and place in a large serving bowl. Pour the dressing over all and toss well to coat.

VARIATION
Ballpark Potato Salad

Put 2 eggs in the water with the potatoes and bring to a boil. Remove the eggs after 10 minutes. Continue cooking potatoes until tender. Rinse the eggs and potatoes in cold water. When cool, cut up the potatoes, dice the eggs, and add 2 chopped stalks celery and 1 minced dill pickle. Dress with mayonnaise spiked with vinegar, yellow mustard, and a little pickle juice.

TOP SECRET

For the best potato salad, take a lesson from classic French home cooking and douse the potatoes with a good dose of red- or white-wine vinegar while they're still scalding hot, just after draining. This trick results in more complex layers of flavor.

Grilled Sweet Potato Salad

Sweet potatoes are ideal for grilling and, when topped with a potent vinaigrette, they make a winning side dish: sweet flesh and sharp dressing, creamy interior with a crispy grilled edge, all with a smoky undertone. If you're only accustomed to supersweet holiday preparations, this is a whole new angle.

6 medium sweet potatoes, peeled and cut into thick wedges

Vegetable oil, for grilling

Salt and pepper, to taste

3 scallions, thinly sliced

1/4 cup chopped fresh flat-leaf parsley

1/4 cup olive oil

2 tablespoons honey

2 tablespoons red-wine vinegar

1 tablespoon Dijon mustard

1 tablespoon chopped fresh rosemary

1 small shallot, minced

Dash of Worcestershire sauce

PREP TIME: 15 minutes • **COOK TIME:** 12 minutes • **SERVES:** 6

1 Put the sweet potatoes in a large saucepan and barely cover with cold water. Bring to a boil and cook for about 5 minutes, until just tender when pierced with a knife tip. Drain and cool.

2 Preheat a gas grill on high with the lid closed for 10 minutes. Brush the potatoes with vegetable oil and sprinkle with salt and pepper. Grill for about 3 minutes per side, until the outside edges are crisp and the potatoes are tender.

3 Put the potatoes on a serving platter and sprinkle with the scallions.

4 In a small bowl, whisk together the parsley, olive oil, honey, vinegar, mustard, rosemary, shallots, and Worcestershire sauce. Pour over the sweet potatoes while still warm.

VARIATION

Southwest Sweet Potato Salad

In the dressing, substitute 1 1/2 teaspoons ground cumin for the honey and chopped canned chipotle in adobo for the Dijon mustard. Grill 2 whole poblanos or Anaheim chiles with the sweet potatoes, then seed and chop the chiles. Combine the grilled potato wedges with the chopped chiles. Substitute cilantro for the parsley. Pour on the dressing and toss lightly. Serve at once.

TOP SECRET

Grilling sweet potatoes—or regular potatoes—works best if the potatoes are slightly precooked until just softened. If you cook the potatoes until they're tender, they will turn to mush and fall to pieces on the grill rack instead of becoming crisp outside and creamy within. Because adding a dressing (and also sitting around) softens the crisp exterior, this kind of salad is best eaten moments after you dress it.

Spinach Salad with Sesame-Orange Dressing

A simple starter salad packed with vegetables, this one is notable for having the rare low-fat dressing that actually tastes terrific. Reducing the orange juice to syrup makes a full-bodied base for the Asian accents. Baby spinach leaves are tender and easy to eat, but you can use this dressing for any salad greens.

1 cup fresh orange juice

2 tablespoons apple-cider vinegar

1 tablespoon soy sauce

1 tablespoon grated fresh ginger

2 teaspoons sesame oil

12 cups baby spinach leaves

1 medium carrot, grated

1 pint grape tomatoes, halved

1 small red onion, thinly sliced

1 tablespoon toasted sesame seeds

PREP TIME: 10 minutes • **COOK TIME:** 6 minutes • **SERVES:** 4

1 Bring the orange juice to a boil in a small saucepan and cook for 5 to 7 minutes, until reduced by half to a syrupy consistency. Remove from the heat and whisk in the vinegar, soy sauce, ginger, and oil. Set aside.

2 Divide the spinach among 4 serving plates and top with equal amounts of carrots, tomatoes, and onions. Sprinkle with sesame seeds and serve with dressing on the side.

VARIATION

Spinach Salad with Warm Bacon-Shallot Dressing

Skip the low-fat dressing and cook 4 slices thick-cut bacon until crisp. Remove the bacon from the pan and spoon out and discard all but 3 tablespoons of the fat. Cook 1 large diced shallot in the fat until just golden. Add 3 tablespoons apple-cider vinegar and a tiny pinch of sugar. Slice hard-boiled eggs and fresh white mushrooms thinly over the salad greens and vegetables, top with warm dressing, and give each plate several good grindings of fresh black pepper. Serve at once.

TOP SECRET

Once you've washed them, dry greens with paper towels. Put a dry paper towel in the bottom of a ziplock bag and heap the greens on top of it. Either remove all the air by zipping the bag almost all the way and then inhaling the air out of the bag as you seal it the final inch or two; or, partially seal the bag and blow a breath of air into the bag before sealing the final inch. Inhaling removes all the oxygen, making an airtight seal that preserves the greens for up to a week. Exhaling into the bag replaces the oxygen with carbon dioxide, also great for preservation.

STORING FRESH GREENS FOR THE LONG HAUL

Sometimes it pays to take advantage of great sales on big packages of fresh greens, or better still, to buy fresh greens at a farm stand or farmer's market at the height of their season. But very often, big bunches of greens go bad before you have the chance to finish them all. Here's the trick to keeping them in tip-top shape, for 2 whole weeks.

1 Fill your cleaned kitchen sink with cool, fresh water.

2 Make sure the greens are completely dry. If they're still attached to their core (romaine and butter lettuces generally are), remove the individual leaves.

3 Place the dry individual leaves in the sink, and submerge them. Let them float to the surface, and sit in the sink for 10 minutes.

4 Remove the leaves and dry them again completely between sheets of paper towels. Do not spin them in a salad spinner. Keeping them wrapped in dry paper towel, place them in large ziplock bags and store in your crisper.

Why Does This Work?

Greens are made up of thousands of moisture-holding cells, and when the surface of the leaf outweighs the internal cells in moisture content, they rot. When the internal cells are packed with water and the surface is dry, the leaves thrive on their internal moisture. This trick takes totally dry leaves, fills the cells with water, and then dries their surfaces again. The key is that the cells stay packed with water even when the surface is dry. The cellular moisture in the leaves keeps the lettuce in perfect shape, every time.

Greek Salad

In restaurants, Greek salads come with all sorts of garnishes such as croutons, anchovies, and stuffed grape leaves, but the hallmarks are the crumbled feta cheese and fragrant Kalamata olives, along with that wonderful oregano-scented dressing. Feel free to embellish, but here's the basic version to start.

DRESSING

1/2 cup extra-virgin olive oil

2 tablespoons red-wine vinegar

2 tablespoons fresh lemon juice

1/2 small clove garlic, minced

3/4 teaspoon whole dried oregano

1/8 teaspoon red pepper flakes

Pinch of sugar

Salt and pepper, to taste

SALAD

2 romaine hearts, chopped

1/2 seedless cucumber (also called English cucumber), peeled and diced

2 medium fresh ripe tomatoes, cubed

1 small red onion, thinly sliced

3/4 cup crumbled feta cheese (about 4 to 5 ounces)

1/2 cup Kalamata olives, pitted

PREP TIME: 10 minutes • **COOK TIME:** 0 minutes • **SERVES:** 4

1 *For the dressing:* Place the oil, vinegar, lemon juice, garlic, oregano, pepper flakes, and sugar in a blender and pulse to form a creamy emulsion. Season with salt and pepper.

2 *For the salad:* Place the lettuce in a salad bowl and toss cucumbers, tomatoes, and onions on top. Sprinkle with the cheese and olives.

3 Pour the dressing over all. Toss lightly and serve at once.

VARIATIONS

Italian Tomato Salad

The fastest tomato salad possible is sliced summer tomatoes topped with a few torn leaves of fresh basil. Put slices of soft, fresh mozzarella between the slices of tomato, and then you can drizzle with some extra-virgin olive oil.

Winter Cucumber Salad

In winter, cucumbers, red onions, and vinegar are far more flavorful than cottony winter tomatoes. Slice cucumbers and onions thinly. Toss with red-wine vinegar and a light sprinkle of sugar, salt, and pepper. Stir in a couple spoonfuls of sour cream.

TOP SECRET

If you don't have an olive pitter and you're faced with a bowl of olives with pits, here's the way to pit them in seconds. Place the olive on your cutting board and lay the flat side of your chef's knife over it. Give the knife a good whack with your other hand and voilà: The pit will pop right out.

Asian Ginger Slaw

This Asian-inspired dressing, pungent with both fresh and ground ginger, makes a nice low-fat change from mayonnaise-based versions. It tastes even better after a couple of days in the refrigerator.

1/2 cup apple-cider vinegar

3 tablespoons sesame oil

3 tablespoons soy sauce

1 tablespoon sugar

1 tablespoon ground ginger and 1 1/2 tablespoons minced fresh ginger

8 cups finely shredded green cabbage (about 1/2 head)

2 medium carrots, grated

1/2 cup peanuts, chopped

1/2 cup fresh cilantro, lightly chopped

PREP TIME: 10 minutes • **COOK TIME:** 0 minutes • **SERVES:** 6

1 In the bottom of a large mixing bowl, whisk the vinegar, oil, soy sauce, sugar, and gingers.

2 Add the cabbage and carrots and toss well to coat. Allow to sit at least 4 hours, or overnight.

3 Just before serving, garnish with the peanuts and cilantro.

VARIATION
Calico Slaw
Named after the bright patchwork of multi-colored vegetables, Calico Slaw is a good side dish for a summer supper. To the cabbage and carrot mixture, add 1 cup each finely diced red cabbage, and cored, seeded, and chopped red and green bell peppers. Dress with your favorite salad dressing.

DID YOU KNOW?
There is a vast difference between toasted sesame oil and plain sesame oil. The toasted variety is often used as a condiment in small drops because of its very concentrated flavor; plain sesame oil is ideal for salads.

TOP SECRET
Ginger is delicious, healthful, and packed with flavor. Too bad that peeling it is such a pain in the neck! Here's the way chefs do it: Hold the gingerroot in your left hand, and using a tablespoon, scrape up the skin, toward you. You'll skin it perfectly without losing a drop of the yummy flesh.

Sesame Broccoli

It was a sad day for veggies when a former American president proclaimed his hatred of broccoli—he plainly never had it with soy sauce and sesame oil!

1 large bunch broccoli, trimmed into long florets with stems

2 tablespoons soy sauce

1 tablespoon sesame oil

2 cloves garlic, finely minced

2 teaspoons sesame seeds

Pinch of red pepper flakes (optional)

Squeeze of lime juice (optional)

PREP TIME: 5 minutes • **COOK TIME:** 5 minutes • **SERVES:** 4

1 Bring a medium pot of water to a boil. When the water is boiling, drop in the broccoli and cook for about 5 minutes, until tender but still bright green (dark green is overcooked).

2 In a serving bowl, whisk together the soy sauce, oil, and garlic.

3 Toast the seeds quickly by swirling them in a dry skillet over high heat for about 30 seconds. Pour into the dressing immediately.

4 Drain the broccoli well and add it to the serving bowl. Toss to coat with dressing. Sprinkle with red pepper flakes and lime juice, if desired. This is as good at room temperature as it is hot.

VARIATION

Italian Broccoli

In a large skillet over medium-high heat, add 3 tablespoons olive oil and cook the broccoli spears for 1 to 2 minutes, until coated in oil. Add 4 sliced cloves garlic and 1 cup dry white wine, along with 1/4 teaspoon red pepper flakes. Simmer for 8 to 10 minutes, covered, until the stalks are tender and the liquid is reduced. Sprinkle with salt and pepper, to taste, and serve at once.

LEFTOVER LUXURIES

Chop leftover broccoli into smaller pieces (stems included) and toss with hot Asian noodles, such as soba noodles or Chinese vermicelli.

TOP SECRET

If you love lemon or lime juice with your broccoli, squeeze it on after the vegetable is cooked. Why? Adding lemon or lime juice too early will actually discolor the vegetable, turning it pale and wan.

Rapid Ratatouille

Ratatouille doesn't have to be the all-day stewing affair of a Provençal housewife. Ratatouille for two is superfast, because the small amount lets the vegetables soften very quickly. If you're going to double or quadruple the recipe (which you easily can), just don't expect it to be quite so rapid—cook larger amounts for at least 45 minutes, or until the vegetables are soft and creamy.

3 tablespoons extra-virgin olive oil

2 cloves garlic, minced

1 medium eggplant, coarsely diced

1 medium zucchini, thinly sliced into rings

1 medium red bell pepper, cored, seeded, and cut into thin strips

1 large fresh tomato or 1 cup canned whole tomatoes (with juice)

Salt and pepper, to taste

Handful of coarsely chopped fresh basil

PREP TIME: 5 minutes • **COOK TIME:** 12 minutes • **SERVES:** 2

1 Heat the oil over medium heat in a skillet. Add the garlic, eggplant, zucchini, and peppers. Stir until well-coated. Cook for 5 minutes, stirring occasionally.

2 If using a fresh tomato, coarsely chop it directly into the pan to catch the juices. If using canned, break them up with a spoon as you add them. Bring the mixture to a boil, reduce the heat, and simmer gently for 7 to 8 minutes, or until the vegetables are tender and the tomatoes are cooked down and slightly thickened. Season well with salt and pepper and stir in the basil just before serving.

VARIATION
Roasted Ratatouille

Toss all the diced vegetables (except the tomatoes) with the oil and garlic and sprinkle with salt and pepper. Spread in an even layer on a baking sheet and roast at 400°F for 15 to 20 minutes, or until tender and browned. Place the roasted vegetables in a large saucepan with the tomatoes and cook for 6 to 7 minutes, just until the tomatoes thicken slightly to a sauce. Season with salt, pepper, and basil and serve.

LEFTOVER LUXURIES

Leftover ratatouille is perfect for folding into an omelet or tossing with hot cooked pasta.

TOP SECRET

If you have the time while making a recipe, it pays to salt the eggplant and let it sit, if only for 10 minutes. Why? Eggplant is packed with water and soaks up oil like a sponge unless it is lightly salted, which draws the liquid out of it, drying it out. Toss cut-up eggplant in a colander with a tablespoon of salt and let sit in your sink. Rinse, drain, and proceed with the recipe.

Persian Carrots with Apricots

There are so many flavors swirling around in this appealing braised carrot dish that you won't know where to begin. From the natural sweetness of the carrots themselves to the citrusy kick of the dried apricots to the buttery garlic and the crunch of pistachios, this is more than a dull side dish.

2 pounds carrots, peeled and cut into 1/2-inch-thick half-moons

1 1/2 cups water

1/4 cup dried apricots, diced

Zest and juice of 1 lemon

4 cloves garlic, minced

2 tablespoons unsalted butter

Salt and pepper, to taste

1/4 cup shelled pistachios

PREP TIME: 10 minutes • **COOK TIME:** 15 minutes • **SERVES:** 6

1 In a large skillet over medium heat, add the carrots, water, apricots, lemon zest, and garlic. Bring to a boil, then reduce the heat and simmer, covered, for about 10 minutes, until the carrots are just tender.

2 Remove the lid and boil for 2 to 3 minutes, or until the remaining liquid just glazes the carrots. Stir in the butter and sprinkle with lemon juice. Season with salt and pepper, then pour into a serving dish. Sprinkle with the pistachios and serve hot or warm.

VARIATION

Sweet Carrots with Apricots

A notably sweeter, lightly creamy version that's great for serving alongside roast chicken or duck. Double the amount of apricots and leave out the garlic. Add 2 tablespoons honey along with the lemon zest. Instead of butter, stir in 1/4 cup full-fat yogurt or sour cream.

TOP SECRET

For a hit of even stronger apricot flavor, do what chefs do with fruit-based braises: Add a dollop of good-quality apricot preserves to the mix with the apricots. The result will be a fruitier flavor and a heavier syrup.

Oven-Roasted Sweet Tomatoes

It doesn't matter if it's the dead of winter; this surefire recipe for oven-roasted tomatoes will have you making this dish all year round. Sweet and unctuously gooey, the jammy result is delicious on its own, as an accompaniment to grilled fish or chicken, or spread on toasted garlic bread.

1 tablespoon extra-virgin olive oil

1 can (28 ounces) whole plum tomatoes

2 teaspoons sugar

Salt and pepper, to taste

PREP TIME: 5 minutes • **COOK TIME:** 45 minutes • **SERVES:** 6

1 Preheat the oven to 300°F. Cover a rimmed baking sheet with foil, and wipe it down with the olive oil.

2 Drain the can of tomatoes, taking care to not crush them. Place each tomato on the baking sheet, making a small slit in each one with a paring knife. Sprinkle with the sugar and place in the oven. After 20 minutes, remove the sheet and, using a small spatula, turn each tomato over.

3 Turn up the heat to 400°F and continue to roast for another 25 minutes. Remove the pan and carefully lift or scrape the tomatoes off and into a serving bowl. If there are any caramelized bits stuck to the baking sheet, make sure to include those.

4 Serve hot, at room temperature, or cold.

VARIATION

Sweet-and-Sour Oven-Roasted Tomatoes

Lightly drizzle the tomatoes with balsamic vinegar and brown sugar in place of white sugar.

TOP SECRET

If you can find them, San Marzano tomatoes take this dish from very good to extraordinary; chefs wouldn't think of using anything but San Marzanos, which are special paste tomatoes grown in the volcanic soil of Italy, making them packed with sweetness.

Fried Corn

Southerners call this dish fried even though the corn is, in fact, essentially braised and not fried at all. But that is its name and that is the dish that is gobbled down in thousands of homes across the Southern United States when corn is ripe.

6 ears corn

2 tablespoons butter

1/2 cup water

Salt and pepper, to taste

2 tablespoons chopped fresh flat-leaf parsley

PREP TIME: 15 minutes • **COOK TIME:** 25 minutes • **SERVES:** 4

1 Shuck the corn and remove the silks. Using a sharp knife, slice off the corn kernels onto a large plate. Turn over the knife and drag the dull edge down the length of each ear to scrape out all the milky juices onto the plate.

2 Heat the butter in a large skillet over medium-high heat, and just as it sizzles, add all the corn and juices you've scraped off. Cook and stir for 3 to 4 minutes to coat the kernels with butter, then add the water to the pan.

3 Simmer gently for 20 to 25 minutes, until the corn is tender and the milky sauce is lightly thickened. Season with generous amounts of salt and pepper, then sprinkle with the parsley and serve hot.

VARIATION
Indian Lime Corn

For a suave international take on Fried Corn, add 2 teaspoons mild curry powder along with the butter and cook for 1 to 2 minutes. Omit the water and drizzle with the juice of 2 limes. Sprinkle with cilantro instead of parsley.

TOP SECRET

Corn silk can seem impossible to remove when you're elbows deep in shucking a big batch of fresh corn. One thing works: a clean, dry terrycloth towel. Shuck, then wipe each ear down with the towel; the corn silk sticks to terrycloth as well or better than it does to your fingers. (Then shake out the towel outside.)

Green Beans with Sweet Onion Vinaigrette

When green beans are in season, it's also the time to find truly sweet-fleshed onions, such as Vidalia and Walla Walla. This vinaigrette brings out the sweetness of the onions and makes the best of fresh summer beans.

2 pounds fresh green beans

3 tablespoons olive oil

2 tablespoons white-wine vinegar

1 tablespoon Dijon mustard

1/2 large sweet onion, such as Vidalia or Walla Walla, finely chopped

Salt and pepper, to taste

PREP TIME: 5 minutes • **COOK TIME:** 8 minutes • **SERVES:** 6

1 Remove the top and the tail of the green beans, and slice in half diagonally.

2 Bring a large pot of salted water to a boil and add the green beans. Cook for about 8 minutes, or until just tender.

3 Meanwhile, in a medium bowl, stir together the oil, vinegar, and mustard. Add the onions and season with a little salt and pepper.

4 Drain the beans well. Pour the vinaigrette over the hot beans and marinate for at least 10 minutes before serving. Serve warm or at room temperature.

VARIATION

Green Beans with Pecan and Cranberry Vinaigrette

Add 1/2 cup chopped toasted pecans and 1/2 cup dried cranberries after you pour the onion vinaigrette over the beans.

TOP SECRET

Chefs say that to make vegetables taste really good, the cooking water must be "salty like the sea." Not a teaspoon or two of salt, but several tablespoons, so that the salty water actually adds flavor to the cooked vegetables. This technique works well with vegetables that you're boiling briefly, such as green beans and broccoli, but it's not ideal for starchy vegetables such as potatoes and lima beans, which will absorb too much sodium. If you're concerned that the vegetables you're cooking will be too salty, rinse them in cool water as you drain them, to take off any excess surface salt. Chances are that the veggies will have absorbed just the right amount.

Wilted Escarole

Wide and sturdy, dark green leaves of escarole make a tough and bitter green salad, but they cook down into silky sweetness. Use the outer leaves, the toughest, darkest ones. The inner leaves get too mushy.

1 pound dark green escarole leaves, limp and discolored spots trimmed

3 tablespoons extra-virgin olive oil

2 cloves garlic, minced

1 cup chicken stock

Salt and pepper, to taste

PREP TIME: 5 minutes • **COOK TIME:** 30 minutes • **SERVES:** 4

1 Wash the escarole in a large basin of cold water, lifting the leaves off the water and rinsing with fresh water to remove any grit. Slice into 3-inch pieces.

2 Put the oil in a large, heavy skillet over medium heat. Add the garlic and cook for 1 minute.

3 Add the escarole and cook for about 4 minutes, stirring constantly, until wilted. Pour in the stock and bring to a boil. Cover and cook, stirring occasionally, for about 30 minutes, or until tender and silky. If it gets too dry, add more stock or some water. If there's too much liquid, when you remove the cover, turn up the heat and simmer off the excess. Season with salt and pepper and serve hot.

VARIATION
Wilted Escarole and Beans
About 15 minutes into the cooking time, add a drained can of white beans. Season with lots of pepper.

LEFTOVER LUXURIES
Gently warm leftover greens in a nonstick pan, break an egg or two over the top, cover, and cook until the egg white is translucent and the yolk is cooked to your preference.

TOP SECRET
You can easily swap out spinach, kale, or collard greens for the escarole in most dishes, but the latter two are extremely hardy and will take longer to cook. The trick to cooking tougher greens quickly is to slice them into ribbons, and they'll cook as quickly as their tenderhearted cousins.

CHEATING CHEF AT HOME

ROAST, FRY, OR STEAM?

A Quick Guide to Simple Vegetable Cooking

Not every vegetable is delicious cooked by the same methods. For example, carrots can pretty much stand up to any style of cooking, but boil them, and you'll want to run in the opposite direction. Brussels sprouts, the scourge of nursery school students everywhere, are most delicious pan-roasted, but steam them, and you'll wind up with something you'd probably not want to feed to the pooch. Here's a short list of what to cook, and how.

Cabbage
Slice, panfry, or sauté in olive or sesame oil with a tablespoon of butter.

Brussels Sprouts
Roast at high heat with a drop of olive oil and a drizzle of soy sauce.

Carrots
Cook in a skillet on top of the stove with 1 tablespoon oil, 1/4 cup water, and 1 tablespoon sugar. Cook small carrots whole and cut larger ones into chunks or rounds. Also delicious roasted.

Broccoli
Oven-roast, panfry, or steam with a sprinkle of salt and a drizzle of olive oil. If steaming, check after 5 minutes to make sure they're fork-tender, then remove them from the heat immediately.

Hardy Greens *(chard, kale, collards, mustard greens)*
Sauté on top of the stove only in olive oil, sesame oil, or butter. If the leaves are tough and fibrous, remove the stem, roll the leaves up like a cigar and sliver them for quick cooking.

Tender Greens *(spinach, escarole, watercress)*
Steam quickly or sauté on top of the stove and drizzle with oil.

Eggplant
After salting and rinsing (see Top Secret, page 250), slice into rounds or cubes, roast in the oven, or sauté on top of the stove.

Winter Squash
Steam, roast, or panfry with a drizzle of olive or sesame oil.

Summer Squash *(zucchini or yellow squash)*
Steam or panfry with a bit of olive or sesame oil.

Beets
Roast on the grill or in an oven; let cool, peel, and drizzle with olive oil and salt.

Orange Roasted Beets

Never boil beets again! Roasting them concentrates their earthy sweetness and is much, much easier when it comes to prep.

3–4 medium beets (1 pound)

Extra-virgin olive oil

1 orange

Salt and pepper, to taste

Unsalted butter

PREP TIME: 3 minutes • **COOK TIME:** 1 hour • **SERVES:** 4

1 Preheat the oven to 375°F. Trim and scrub the beets. Put each on a square of heavy-duty foil and drizzle with oil. Using a Microplane or zester, zest the orange over the beets. Juice the orange and sprinkle over the beets, along with salt and pepper. Fold the foil tightly over each beet, making sure the seams are tightly crimped to keep the juice (and steam) in.

2 Place on a baking sheet and roast 45 to 60 minutes, or until a knife tip can easily pierce to the center. (With an oven mitt, you can gently squeeze a beet package to see how soft it is before piercing the foil.)

3 Cool until you can handle the beets. Peel off the skins, which will slough off easily under your fingers. Slice or cube and serve hot or warm with a bit of butter, more salt and pepper, and a dash of fresh orange juice.

VARIATIONS

Beet and Goat Cheese Salad
Cut the roasted beets into small cubes and toss with a vinaigrette made from a few tablespoons olive oil, a dash of red-wine vinegar, 1/2 teaspoon Dijon mustard, and salt and pepper, to taste. Spoon onto serving plates and crumble a few ounces of goat cheese on top. Scatter with some chopped fresh rosemary.

Romaine Salad with Beets and Walnuts
Toss the beets with the vinaigrette from the Beet and Goat Cheese Salad (variation above). Spoon the mixture on top of chopped leaves of crisp romaine hearts and toss with 1/2 cup toasted walnuts.

TOP SECRET
Hands stained fuscia from working with beets? After you're done preparing them, scrub your hands with soap—and milk—and the color will fade like magic.

Brussels Sprouts with Caramelized Onions

If all you've ever had was dull, boiled Brussels sprouts, you haven't even met this vegetable yet. Roasted, they reveal depths of sweetness and nuttiness that boiling water could never bring out. They may just become your new favorite. You'll certainly never want to boil them again.

1 1/2 pounds Brussels sprouts, trimmed

1 tablespoon extra-virgin olive oil

Salt and pepper, to taste

4 strips thick-cut bacon, diced

1 medium red onion, thinly sliced

PREP TIME: 10 minutes • **COOK TIME:** 35 minutes • **SERVES:** 8

1 Preheat the oven to 400°F. Toss the sprouts with the oil and salt and pepper. Place on a baking pan and roast for about 15 minutes, shaking the pan occasionally, until browned and tender.

2 Meanwhile, cook the bacon in a large skillet over medium heat for about 10 minutes, or until crisp. Spoon into a bowl and discard the excess fat, leaving about 2 tablespoons in the pan.

3 Add the onions to the pan and cook for about 15 minutes, or until deeply browned and caramelized. Put the sprouts in the pan and gently stir to reheat for about 5 minutes. Sprinkle with the bacon, season with salt and pepper, and serve warm.

VARIATION

Roasted Brussels Sprouts with Lemon, Walnuts, and Parmesan

Put 1/2 cup chopped walnuts on the baking sheet for the last 5 minutes of roasting time. When you remove the sprouts from the oven, toss with 1/4 cup grated Parmesan cheese, a dollop of olive oil, and the juice and zest of 1 lemon. Serve hot or at room temperature.

TOP SECRET

Many cooks peel the outer leaves off of sprouts and *then* slice off and cut an X in the bottoms. You want to first make a slice about 1/2 inch deep in the bottom of the sprouts and the larger, coarser, outer leaves of each sprout will simply fall away. Cutting the X in the bottom of sprouts is unnecessary when you're not boiling them. Instead, for roasting, cut each sprout in half.

Sautéed Brussels Sprouts

Golden-fried Brussels sprouts are not the ones you remember as a kid; crunchy, caramelized, and topped off with this surprise ingredient, they're sure to become one of your favorite taste treats.

1 tablespoon vegetable oil

1 pound fresh Brussels sprouts, rinsed, trimmed, and halved

1 cup seedless red grapes, halved

Salt and freshly ground black pepper, to taste

PREP TIME: 10 minutes • **COOK TIME:** 15 minutes • **SERVES:** 4

1 Heat the oil in a large nonstick skillet, then add the Brussels sprouts and toss well.

2 Add the grapes and cook over medium heat, stirring, for about 8 minutes, or until the Brussels sprouts are crisp-tender and the grape skins have split.

3 Season with salt and pepper and serve.

VARIATION

Balsamic Brussels Sprouts

For a delightfully different flavor, drizzle the sprouts with good-quality balsamic vinegar just before serving.

TOP SECRET

To get that nice, caramelized texture on your sprouts (or sautéed asparagus, for that matter), don't add sugar...add seedless grapes! As the grapes cook, they release natural sugars that help the sprouts crisp up as they cook. Delicious!

Moroccan Carrot Dip

Put a bowl of this dip out with crackers or pita chips, and it will disappear in minutes. The sweetness of cooked and pureed carrots makes a perfect backdrop for cinnamon, ginger, cumin, and paprika. A spoonful of honey adds just the right enhancement.

1 pound carrots, thickly sliced

1 teaspoon ground cinnamon

1 teaspoon ground cumin

2 cloves garlic, crushed

1 teaspoon ground ginger

1 tablespoon honey

1 tablespoon olive oil

1 teaspoon paprika

3 tablespoons vinegar or fresh lemon juice

Salt and freshly ground black pepper, to taste

PREP TIME: 15 minutes • **COOK TIME:** 20 minutes • **MAKES** 1 3/4 cups

1 Place the carrots in a large saucepan, cover with water, and bring to a boil. Reduce the heat and simmer for 20 to 25 minutes, or until they are very soft.

2 Rinse the carrots in a colander under cold running water, then drain thoroughly. Put them in a medium bowl and mash with a potato masher until mostly smooth.

3 Stir in the cinnamon, cumin, garlic, ginger, honey, oil, paprika, and vinegar or lemon juice. Blend well and season with salt and pepper.

VARIATION
Sweet-and-Hot Carrot Dip
Add a pinch of red pepper flakes with the other spices.

TOP SECRET
Carrots, especially supermarket carrots, are not always sweet. To help this dish along, don't add sugar...add honey! This miracle food will not only add flavor it will also add substance and weight to the dish.

Salmon Pâté

An elegant appetizer for a dinner party, this rich-hued pâté gets a flavor lift from lemon zest and chives, and a bit of bite from horseradish.

1 packet unflavored gelatin

1/2 cup cold water

1 can (14 ounces) salmon, drained, skin removed

3/4 cup plain yogurt

2/3 cup sour cream

2 tablespoons drained prepared horseradish

2 tablespoons grated onion

2 1/2 teaspoons grated lemon zest

1 tablespoon fresh lemon juice

3/4 teaspoon salt

1/3 cup minced chives

PREP TIME: 15 minutes • **COOK TIME:** 5 minutes • **MAKES** 4 cups

1 Sprinkle the gelatin over the water in a heat-proof glass measuring cup. Let stand for 5 minutes to soften. Set the measuring cup in a small saucepan of simmering water and heat for about 2 minutes, or until the gelatin has melted. Set aside to cool slightly.

2 Place the salmon in a food processor and pulse until smooth. Add the yogurt, sour cream, horseradish, onions, lemon zest, lemon juice, and salt and pulse until the mixture is blended.

3 Add the chives and gelatin mixture and pulse until combined. Transfer to a 4-cup bowl, crock, or decorative mold. Cover and refrigerate until set, at least 3 hours.

4 Serve directly from the bowl or crock. Or, if using a decorative mold, unmold onto a serving plate.

VARIATION
Tuna Pâté
Replace the salmon with good-quality tuna.

FIX IT FAST
Canned salmon works fine in this recipe, but if you have freshly cooked salmon, use that. When making your next salmon meal, cook an extra pound of salmon, let cool, then use in the recipe. It will keep in the refrigerator for about a week.

TOP SECRET
One of the unsung heroes of every chef's kitchen is horseradish. Too much may make your eyes water, but just the right amount can add a hit of spicy, herby flavor. It's especially wonderful with fish.

Tangy Potato Wedges

Move over French fries! This delicious potato side dish has a wonderfully different flavor that goes great with Italian, Mexican...or any type of food you cook.

1/4 cup unsalted butter, melted

1 tablespoon fresh lime juice

1 teaspoon grated lime zest

1 teaspoon dried thyme

3 large potatoes, each cut into 8 wedges

1/4 cup freshly grated Romano cheese

1/2 teaspoon salt

1/4 teaspoon paprika

PREP TIME: 10 minutes • **COOK TIME:** 20 minutes • **SERVES:** 6

1 Preheat the oven to 400°F. Grease a baking sheet.

2 In a large bowl, combine the butter, lime juice, lime zest, and thyme. Add the potatoes and toss to coat. Place the wedges, skin-side down, on the prepared baking sheet.

3 Combine the cheese, salt, and paprika in a small bowl. Sprinkle over the potatoes. Bake for 20 to 25 minutes, or until tender.

VARIATION

Spicy Potato Wedges

For a little more heat and punch, add 1 teaspoon red-hot sauce to the butter-lime mixture before adding the potatoes. You can also shake a little cayenne pepper onto the wedges before baking.

TOP SECRET

The hidden key to this great recipe is lime. It may go great with a margarita, but the truth is that this citrus fruit actually mimics both salt and spice, making it an ideal accompaniment to baked or roasted potatoes.

Dried Cherry Quinoa Pilaf

Grainlike quinoa (pronounced KEEN-wah) is not a grain at all, but the nutritious seed of a plant related to Swiss chard. It cooks up like rice and takes well to a variety of flavors. Here, it's made into an aromatic pilaf with thyme, walnuts, and a generous amount of dried cherries for chewy sweetness. Serve with pork or poultry.

2 teaspoons extra-virgin olive oil

1 large onion, finely chopped

2 cups quinoa, rinsed until the water runs clear

2 cups boiling water

Salt, to taste

1 teaspoon freshly ground black pepper

1/2 teaspoon thyme

1 cup dried cherries

1/2 cup toasted and coarsely chopped walnuts

PREP TIME: 10 minutes • **COOK TIME:** 30 minutes • **SERVES:** 12

1 Heat the oil in a large saucepan over medium heat. Add the onions and cook, stirring frequently, for about 7 minutes, or until golden brown.

2 Meanwhile, place the quinoa in a large skillet over medium heat and cook, stirring often, for about 5 minutes, until lightly toasted. Add to the onions.

3 Stir in the water, salt, pepper, and thyme. Return to a boil, cover, and gently boil for 10 minutes. Uncover and cook, stirring occasionally, for 10 to 12 minutes longer, until the liquid has been absorbed and the quinoa is tender.

4 Remove from the heat and stir in the cherries and walnuts. Serve hot, at room temperature, or chilled.

VARIATION
Roasted Hazelnut Quinoa
Instead of walnuts, add hazelnuts that have been roasted in a 200°F oven for 10 minutes and then chopped.

TOP SECRET
Grain recipes can be traditionally murky and muddy-tasting, and the way to avoid that is to pack them with flavor and texture. The secret here is dried cherries. Tart, tangy, and utterly delicious, they're a great foil for the earthy flavor of the quinoa and nuts. Add them to meat stews and you'll be glad you did.

11 BONKERS FOR BREAD!

Nothing says "home" and "welcome" like the smell of bread baking. Chefs consider "housemade" bread such an essential part of good restaurant cooking that the most high-end restaurants hire a baker whose sole job is to produce a flow of bread and rolls. Most of us don't have this leisure at home, and baking bread tends to become a rainy-day project, one that we'll get around to later since surely it must require lots of time and energy. It doesn't. Once you get over the fear of yeast and make bread baking part of your regular kitchen activities (especially during the cold months), you'll find that your efforts will repay a hundredfold.

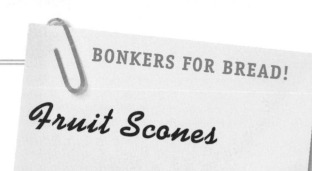

Fruit Scones

The fruit in the scones is actually raisins or currants. If you leave them out, you'll have plain scones. This is a deliberately wet dough for making drop or "rock" scones, so-called because of their craggy appearance.

1 3/4 cups flour

1/3 cup sugar

2 teaspoons baking powder

1/4 teaspoon salt

1/2 cup (1 stick) unsalted butter, cut into 8 pieces and chilled

1/2 cup whole milk

1 egg, beaten

1/2 cup raisins or currants

PREP TIME: 10 minutes • **COOK TIME:** 15 minutes • **MAKES** 12 scones

1 Preheat the oven to 375°F.

2 In a large bowl, stir the flour, sugar, baking powder, and salt. Add the butter and rub into the flour with your fingertips or a fork until the mixture is like coarse cornmeal. (You can also do this in a food processor.)

3 Add the milk, egg, and raisins or currants and stir briefly to combine. Drop a dozen shaggy mounds of dough onto a baking sheet and bake for 15 to 17 minutes, until just lightly golden. Eat hot.

VARIATIONS

Cream Scones

Replace the butter with 1/2 cup heavy whipping cream—it *must* be heavy whipping cream because that provides the necessary fat content to make the scones delicate.

Chocolate-Orange Scones

Add 1 teaspoon orange zest and chocolate chips to the batter in place of raisins.

Lemon-Poppy Seed Scones

Add the juice and zest of 1 lemon and 2 tablespoons poppy seeds to the dough in place of the raisins.

TOP SECRET

When you use currants or raisins, be sure to plump them first by soaking them in a little hot water for 15 minutes, then drain and pat dry with paper towels. It brings them (and aged raisins) miraculously back to life.

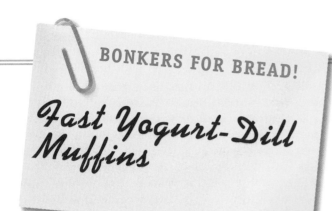

Fast Yogurt-Dill Muffins

A fragrant, savory muffin with a delicate crumb, these herby delights come together quickly to accompany a beef stew or bean soup. You can vary the herb used to suit the food you're serving with it: try rosemary, oregano, or fresh chives. Make extra sure not to overbeat these in the food processor or they'll be very tough. Like most muffins, these are best eaten the day they're made.

2 eggs

1 cup plain yogurt

1/2 cup (1 stick) butter, melted

2 cups all-purpose flour

2 teaspoons baking powder

1 tablespoon sugar

1/2 teaspoon baking soda

1/2 teaspoon salt

2 teaspoons dried dill or 2 tablespoons chopped fresh

PREP TIME: 5 minutes • **COOK TIME:** 15 minutes • **MAKES** 12 muffins

1 Preheat the oven to 400°F and line a 12-cup muffin pan with paper liners.

2 Pulse the eggs, yogurt, and butter in the food processor until well-blended. Measure in the flour, baking powder, sugar, baking soda, salt, and dill and pulse 4 to 6 times—no more—until the ingredients are just moistened and still lumpy.

3 Spoon the batter into the prepared cups and bake for 12 to 15 minutes, until the tops are puffed and golden. Serve hot.

VARIATION

Zucchini and Cheddar Yogurt Muffins

Add 1 peeled, grated small zucchini and 1/2 cup grated sharp cheddar cheese. Replace the dill with chopped fresh oregano or chives.

TOP SECRET

One of the best things about muffins (and many quick breads) is that they freeze beautifully, if you know how to save them. Put the muffins in a ziplock bag, press the air out, and store in the freezer for up to 4 months. Reheat directly from the freezer on a baking sheet in a 350°F oven for 10 minutes. Never reheat them in the microwave, though; it will make them tough and chewy.

Jalapeño Corn Muffins

Hearty corn muffins are even more versatile than tender white muffins, because sturdy cornmeal can take on stronger flavors such as chiles and cheese, and more solid ingredients, such as corn kernels and chopped green bell peppers. This recipe uses pickled jalapeños, but you could substitute a small can of drained milder diced green chiles.

2 eggs

1 cup buttermilk

1/2 cup (1 stick) butter, melted

1–2 pickled jalapeños, stemmed and seeded (wear gloves when handling)

1 1/2 cups yellow cornmeal, preferably stone-ground

1/2 cup all-purpose flour

2 teaspoons baking powder

1/2 teaspoon baking soda

1/2 teaspoon salt

PREP TIME: 5 minutes • **COOK TIME:** 20 minutes • **MAKES** 12 muffins

1 Preheat the oven to 425°F and line a 12-cup muffin pan with paper liners.

2 Place the eggs, buttermilk, and butter in the food processor work bowl. Put the jalapeños in the food processor and pulse until the liquids are well-combined and the jalapeños are finely chopped but not pureed.

3 Add the cornmeal, flour, baking powder, baking soda, and salt and pulse very briefly, 4 or 5 times, until ingredients are just combined.

4 Spoon the batter into the prepared cups and bake for 15 to 20 minutes, until golden brown. Serve hot.

VARIATIONS

Creamed Corn Muffins
Leave out the jalapeños, reduce the buttermilk to 1/2 cup, and add a 14-ounce can creamed corn.

Cheesy-Chile Muffins
Add 1/2 cup grated cheddar cheese along with the dry ingredients.

DID YOU KNOW?

Cornmeal turns rancid faster than most grains and flours in the average kitchen, thanks to the high oil content of the germ. Be sure that cornmeal is always stored in an airtight container, and, of all the grains, this is the one you should most likely keep in the refrigerator. Processed, degerminated cornmeal won't go bad as quickly, but the highly preferable flavor and texture of stone-ground cornmeal is best preserved in the fridge or freezer.

TOP SECRET

A jar of pickled jalapeños is every cook's and baker's friend. Tightly sealed, it will keep for nearly 6 months, and its flavor will mellow with age, providing warmth and awesome jalapeño flavor without the sting of the pepper.

THE SECRET GUIDE TO GRAINS AND FLOURS

Most of us, if we like to cook, have a pantry packed with assorted flours and grains. Guess what: They don't last forever, so even if you have a tin of flour tucked away someplace, you'll need to know how long you can keep it, because there's nothing worse than baking with rancid ingredients. Here's what you need to know about some of the more popular grains and flours on the market today.

Unbleached/ White Flour
Store in an airtight container in the refrigerator for up to a year or in your pantry for up to 8 months.

Cornmeal
Store in an airtight container in your refrigerator for up to 6 months.

Whole-Wheat Flour
Store in an airtight container in the freezer for up to 16 months.

Multi-Grain Flour
Store in an airtight container in the freezer for up to 1 year.

Bread Flour (also known as high-gluten flour)
Store in an airtight container in the freezer for up to 1 year.

Buckwheat Flour
Store in an airtight container in the refrigerator for up to 3months and in the freezer for up to 6 months.

Spelt Flour
Store in an airtight container in your freezer for up to 1 year.

Chickpea Flour
Store in an airtight container in your freezer for up to 8 months.

Quinoa
Store in an airtight container in your pantry for up to 3 months, in your refrigerator for up to 6 months, and in your freezer for up to 1 year.

Barley
Store in an airtight container in your freezer for up to 6 months.

Quick Tips for Instant Use

1. If you choose to freeze flours and grains, decant them into several smaller, single-use containers and label/date them.

2. Don't "defrost" flours or grains when you use them from the freezer.

3. When you bring home flour, immediately remove it from its paper packaging, and pour into a clean, airtight container.

4. If you suspect that you've had a flour or grain too long (but you can't remember *how* long), give it a sniff: If it's off, it will actually smell rancid.

BONKERS FOR BREAD!

Light-and-Sweet Cornbread

"Light" refers to the texture, achieved by using half white flour, half cornmeal. It's a softer, more tender bread than the grainy, all-cornmeal kind and lends itself to sweeter additions.

2 eggs

1/2 cup vegetable oil

1 cup buttermilk

1 1/2 cups all-purpose flour

1/2 cup yellow cornmeal

1/4 cup sugar

2 teaspoons baking powder

1/2 teaspoon baking soda

1/2 teaspoon salt

PREP TIME: 5 minutes • **COOK TIME:** 20 minutes • **SERVES:** 9

1 Preheat the oven to 450°F and lightly grease a metal 9 x 9-inch pan.

2 Place the eggs, oil, and buttermilk in a food processor and pulse to combine.

3 Add the flour, cornmeal, sugar, baking powder, baking soda, and salt and pulse briefly until just combined, with all the dry ingredients moistened but still slightly lumpy. Pour the batter into the prepared pan and bake for 20 to 25 minutes, until golden brown. Cut into 9 squares and serve with butter.

VARIATION

Cornbread Blueberry Muffins

Replace 1/2 cup of the buttermilk with 1/2 cup orange juice. Add the grated zest of 1 orange to the wet ingredients. Increase the sugar to 1/2 cup. Once you have pulsed the wet and dry ingredients together 3 times, add 1 cup blueberries to the food processor and pulse twice more—any further and the blueberries will get chopped. It's okay (ideal, really) if there are little pockets of flour. Bake for 18 minutes, until golden.

LEFTOVER LUXURIES

Tear apart leftover cornbread into large pieces (making 3 cups) and toss together with 5 beaten eggs and 1 cup milk. Pour into a baking dish and bake at 350°F until golden brown and bubbly. You've just made cornbread pudding for a crowd!

TOP SECRET

Some folks like cornbread to be delicate and others like it to be crispy. To achieve the latter, grease the baking pan (or better still, a cast-iron pan) and place in the oven to heat up. Remove, and *then* pour in the batter.

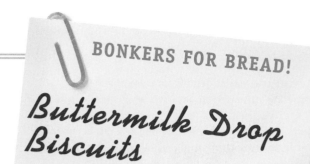

BONKERS FOR BREAD!

Buttermilk Drop Biscuits

Hot biscuits at nearly every meal are regarded by many Southerners as a birthright, and consequently many Southern ladies of a certain age can mix and bake a tray of biscuits in their sleep. It's not quite so easy if you didn't start around the age of 6, but a food processor–mixed, spoon-dropped version creates an excellent facsimile.

2 cups all-purpose flour

2 teaspoons baking powder

1/2 teaspoon baking soda

1/4 teaspoon salt

1/2 cup (1 stick) butter

1 cup buttermilk

PREP TIME: 5 minutes • **COOK TIME:** 15 minutes • **MAKES** 12 biscuits

1 Preheat the oven to 425°F. Put the flour, baking powder, baking soda, and salt in the work bowl of a food processor. Pulse once to combine, then add the butter in pieces.

2 Pulse on and off for a few seconds until the mixture makes coarse crumbs. Pour in the buttermilk all at once and pulse just enough to moisten. Do not overmix. The dough should be soft, lumpy, and wet.

3 Drop a dozen spoonfuls of dough on an ungreased baking sheet. Bake for 12 to 15 minutes, until raised and golden brown. Serve immediately.

VARIATION
Cheddar-Chive Biscuits
Add 2 tablespoons chopped fresh chives along with the flour. Cut the butter back to 1/4 cup (1/2 stick) and add 1/2 cup grated sharp cheddar cheese.

FIX IT FAST
If you don't have buttermilk, you can substitute 3/4 cup plain yogurt thinned with 1/4 cup milk. Or, make your own sour milk by blending a scant cup of milk with 2 tablespoons lemon juice. Stir well and let sit 10 minutes. It will achieve a thick consistency very like commercial buttermilk.

TOP SECRET
Traditionalists will scoff, but the food processor is the baker's best friend...if you know how to use it. The key to making great baked goods (biscuits especially) in the food processor is to not overpulse. Instead, always make sure to pulse just to the point where the ingredients resemble large, coarse crumbs.

Spiced Pumpkin Muffins

An excellent way to get a little more fiber and nutrition-rich pumpkin into your diet, these muffins are tasty enough for a regular morning breakfast and festive enough, with their topping of a few pumpkin seeds, to accompany a traditional Thanksgiving dinner.

1 1/2 cups unbleached flour

1/2 cup whole-wheat flour

2 teaspoons baking powder

1/2 teaspoon salt

1 teaspoon ground cinnamon

1/2 teaspoon ground ginger

1/2 teaspoon ground nutmeg

1/4 teaspoon ground cloves

1/4 cup (1/2 stick) butter, softened

1/2 cup brown sugar

1 egg

1/2 cup whole milk

3/4 cup pumpkin puree

1/4 cup roasted *pepitas* (hulled pumpkin seeds)

PREP TIME: 10 minutes • **COOK TIME:** 15 minutes • **MAKES** 12 muffins

1 Preheat the oven to 350°F and line a 12-cup muffin pan with paper liners.

2 Sift the flours, baking powder, salt, cinnamon, ginger, nutmeg, and cloves together in a medium bowl. In a large bowl, cream the butter and brown sugar together until fluffy. Add the egg, milk, and pumpkin and mix well. Stir into the dry ingredients just until combined.

3 Divide the batter among the prepared cups, sprinkle each with a few *pepitas*, and bake for 15 to 17 minutes, or until a tester comes out clean. Cool on a rack before serving.

VARIATION

Pumpkin-Cranberry Muffins

Add 1 teaspoon orange zest to the mixture along with 1/2 cup dried cranberries. Top each muffin with a few cranberries, pressing them down into the batter, instead of *pepitas*.

TOP SECRET

When it comes to cooking, pumpkin and butternut squash are completely interchangeable. In fact, butternut squash is often preferable—many pumpkins are bred to be big and round for jack-o'-lanterns, but the resulting flesh is watery and flavorless. Butternut tends to be consistently denser and richer, with a dark orange color and a deep squash flavor.

Walnut Pumpkin Loaf

This no-fail pumpkin bread is perfect for bake sales, potluck suppers, and lazy weekend breakfasts. It's moist and rich, and keeps well for several days. Not too sweet, it's an excellent accompaniment to stews and soups, and as it bakes, it breathes the essence of autumn into your kitchen.

2 cups unbleached flour

1/2 cup whole-wheat flour

1/2 cup sugar

1/2 cup brown sugar

2 teaspoons baking powder

1 teaspoon baking soda

1/2 teaspoon salt

1 teaspoon ground cinnamon

1 teaspoon ground ginger

1/2 teaspoon ground nutmeg

1/4 teaspoon ground cloves

1 can (15 ounces) pumpkin purée

1/2 cup milk

2 eggs, beaten

1/4 cup (1/2 stick) butter, melted

1/2 cup chopped walnuts

PREP TIME: 8 minutes • **COOK TIME:** 1 hour, 10 minutes
MAKES 1 loaf (9-inch), about 12 slices

1 Preheat the oven to 350°F and grease a 9-inch loaf pan.

2 In a large bowl, stir together the flours, granulated sugar, brown sugar, baking powder, baking soda, salt, cinnamon, ginger, nutmeg, and cloves. In a medium bowl, whisk together the pumpkin, milk, eggs, and butter. Fold the pumpkin mixture into the flour, stirring just to combine. Fold in the walnuts.

3 Spoon into the prepared pan and bake for 1 hour and 10 minutes, or until a knife inserted in the center comes out with a few crumbs clinging to it. Cool completely on a wire rack before cutting.

VARIATION

Pumpkin-Cranberry Bread with White Chocolate
Leave out the walnuts and instead stir in 3/4 cup dried cranberries and 1/2 cup white chocolate chips.

LEFTOVER LUXURIES

Moist vegetable breads like this and zucchini bread freeze particularly well. Wrap the loaf in heavy-duty foil, crimping the seal tightly, then place in a heavy-duty ziplock bag to keep it fresh. To reheat, remove from the plastic and place the foil-wrapped bread directly on the oven rack in a 350°F preheated oven for 20 minutes, until warm and fragrant.

TOP SECRET

If your brown sugar is as solid as a brick, there's no need to run to the store: Combine 2 tablespoons dark molasses with 1 cup white sugar for light brown sugar. For dark brown sugar, combine 1 tablespoon blackstrap molasses with 1 cup white sugar.

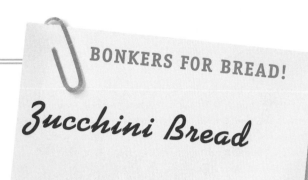

Zucchini Bread

At the height of summer, when zucchini season rolls on and on and your garden won't stop producing and your neighbors sneak by to leave *their* zucchini on your back step at night, there's nothing to do but throw up your hands and bake zucchini bread. What's disappointing is recipes that only call for 1/2 cup grated zucchini. That's no way to get rid of the stuff. This recipe is.

3 cups
grated zucchini

2 cups brown sugar

3 eggs, beaten

1 cup vegetable oil

2 teaspoons
vanilla extract

3 cups flour

3 teaspoons
ground cinnamon

1/2 teaspoon
ground nutmeg

1 teaspoon
baking soda

1 teaspoon
baking powder

1 teaspoon salt

1 cup
chopped pecans

PREP TIME: 10 minutes • **COOK TIME:** 1 hour • **MAKES** 2 loaves (8-inch)

1 Preheat the oven to 350°F and liberally grease two 8-inch loaf pans.

2 In a large bowl, stir together the zucchini, brown sugar, eggs, oil, and vanilla. In a medium bowl, combine the flour, cinnamon, nutmeg, baking soda, baking powder, and salt.

3 Pour the dry ingredients into the wet, add the pecans, and mix until just combined, leaving a few streaks of flour. Pour into the prepared pans.

4 Bake for 1 hour, until a knife poked in the center comes out with a few crumbs clinging to it.

VARIATION

Chocolate Chip Zucchini Bread
Knock the zucchini down to 2 1/2 cups and add 1 cup chocolate chips to the batter.

TOP SECRET

Zucchini is packed with water, and the trick to making a light-as-air quick bread (as opposed to one that can be used as a doorstop) is to grate the vegetable, place it in a clean kitchen towel, and wring it out two or three times before proceeding with the recipe. If the zucchini is small, there's no need to.

BONKERS FOR BREAD!

Oatmeal Yeast Rolls

This recipe is a good way to get your feet wet if you're not used to baking with yeast. Because of the short rising time, it doesn't work well in a loaf pan but it makes excellent dinner rolls. The heat of the oven makes the little rolls puff up just enough, not as light as fully risen rolls, but warm and slathered with butter, they're delicious.

1 cup hot water (about 110°F)

1 envelope active dry yeast

1 teaspoon sugar

3 tablespoons melted butter

1 teaspoon salt

2 1/2 cups flour

1/2 cup rolled oats

Milk, for brushing

PREP TIME: 15 minutes • **COOK TIME:** 15 minutes • **MAKES** 12 rolls

1. Preheat the oven to 400°F. Place the water in the work bowl of the food processor and sprinkle the yeast over it. Add the sugar and leave it for 10 minutes, until the yeast is fully dissolved and slightly foamy.

2. Add the butter, salt, flour, and oats and pulse to form a soft dough. Scrape the dough out onto a floured surface, dip your hands in flour, and roll the dough into a cylinder about 18 inches long. Cut it into 12 pieces and lightly roll each into a ball.

3. Lay the rolls on an ungreased baking sheet and cover lightly with a clean kitchen towel. Allow to rise for about 20 minutes in a very warm corner of the kitchen (on top of the preheating oven is a good place).

4. Remove the kitchen towel and lightly brush the rolls with milk. Bake for 15 to 20 minutes, until lightly browned. Remove from the oven and let them cool for about 10 minutes before eating. If you cut into them while piping hot, they'll be too doughy.

TOP SECRET

If your kitchen is too cold or you just want a faster rise, after the dough is mixed in the food processor, turn it into a lightly oiled glass bowl and microwave on the lowest setting for about 3 minutes. Leave the bowl sitting in the microwave for 20 to 30 minutes, until doubled in size. Divide the dough into rolls as instructed and let rise on the baking sheet for 10 minutes.

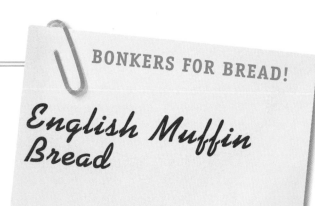

BONKERS FOR BREAD!

English Muffin Bread

What we call English muffins are a version of what the English call crumpets, and the hallmark of this little yeasty cake is that it's full of big bubbles, which toast up crunchy and trap melting butter in little golden pools. Trouble is, each crumpet is individually cooked in a special metal ring on a griddle. This loaf, bakes up pale with a cornmeal crunch and lots of bubbles inside thanks to all the yeast and baking soda.

2 cups milk

1/2 cup water

2 tablespoons sugar

2 envelopes active dry yeast

Cornmeal

4–5 cups unbleached flour

2 teaspoons salt

1/4 teaspoon baking soda

Butter, for serving

PREP TIME: 10 minutes • **COOK TIME:** 50 minutes • **MAKES** 2 loaves (8-inch)

1 Heat the milk, water, and sugar in a small pan over medium-low heat to 110°F on a digital instant-read thermometer. Stir in the yeast and let it sit for 10 minutes, until frothy. While the yeast is working, liberally grease two metal 8-inch loaf pans and sprinkle the bottom and sides thickly with cornmeal, shaking to distribute evenly.

2 In a large bowl, blend the flour, salt, and baking soda. Add the yeast mixture and stir, adding more flour, if needed, to make a soft dough.

3 Divide the dough in half and turn into the prepared pans. Lightly grease two pieces of plastic wrap and put the plastic, greased side down, over each pan. Let rise in a warm place for about 1 hour, until doubled in size.

4 About 45 minutes into the rising, preheat the oven to 375°F. Sprinkle cornmeal on the top of each loaf and bake for 25 to 30 minutes, until lightly browned and pulling away from the sides of the pan. Cool completely on a wire rack before slicing. Toast each slice before buttering and eating.

VARIATION

Honey Whole-Wheat Muffin Bread

Stir 3 tablespoons honey into the milk in place of the sugar. Replace 1 1/2 cups of the flour with 1 1/2 cups whole-wheat flour.

TOP SECRET

Cornmeal is the baker's best friend. If you're after a crispy crust on virtually anything—be it pizza dough or a quick bread—dust the surface of the pan lightly with cornmeal, and you'll be thrilled with the result.

Parker House Rolls

Airy yeast rolls are immensely rewarding because they look like something straight out of a bakery, yet require so little effort by comparison. What's more, you can bake the rolls for 10 minutes until they just hold their shape and have begun to lightly brown, then freeze the parbaked little morsels so that you can bake a few hot rolls for supper whenever you like.

3/4 cup (1 1/2 sticks) butter

1 cup whole milk

1/4 cup sugar

2 envelopes active dry yeast

2 eggs

1/2 teaspoon salt

4–5 cups flour

PREP TIME: 15 minutes • **COOK TIME:** 20 minutes • **MAKES** 2 dozen rolls

1 Melt 1 stick of the butter in a small pan over medium-low heat, being careful not to brown. Add the milk and heat to 110°F on a digital instant-read thermometer. Stir in the sugar until dissolved, then remove from the heat. Stir in the yeast with a fork to dissolve, and let sit until frothy, about 10 minutes.

2 Beat the eggs in the bottom of a large mixing bowl. Pour the yeast mixture over the eggs, mixing constantly, then add the salt, stirring to dissolve. Add the flour, starting with 4 cups and slowly mixing in as much of the additional cup needed to make a soft dough.

3 Turn onto a floured surface and knead for about 5 minutes, until smooth and satiny. Oil the mixing bowl and put the dough back in the bowl, turning to coat with the oil. Cover with plastic wrap and let rise in a warm place for about 1 1/2 hours, until doubled in size.

4 Divide the dough in half and make 12 balls of dough out of each, laying them on two lightly greased baking sheets. Cover each sheet with a clean kitchen towel and leave in a warm place to rise for about 45 minutes, until doubled. After 30 minutes of rising, preheat the oven to 350°F. Bake the rolls for 20 minutes, until golden. Melt the remaining 1/2 stick of butter and brush the rolls with it as they emerge from the oven.

TOP SECRET

If you're making any yeast-raised bread, make it work to your schedule. The dough can be mixed and left to rise overnight in the refrigerator, or even left there for several days. The cold won't kill the yeast, it will just slow it right down, and the bread will continue to rise. When ready to bake, remove from the fridge, punch it down, and let it rise again for another 30 to 45 minutes, then bake. An added benefit to subduing yeast to your schedule is that very slowly raised bread develops a much better flavor.

Orange-Honey Rolls

Hearty with a lot of body and only mildly sweet, these orange-perfumed rolls are perfect for breakfast or for accompanying a bowl of warm soup. They also make wonderful ham and cheese sandwiches.

1 cup milk

Zest and juice of 1 orange

3/4 cup (1 1/2 sticks) unsalted butter

3 tablespoons honey

1 envelope active dry yeast

1 egg, beaten

3 1/2 cups unbleached flour

1 cup whole-wheat flour

1/2 teaspoon salt

PREP TIME: 15 minutes • **COOK TIME:** 25 minutes • **MAKES** 20 rolls

1 In a small saucepan over medium heat, combine the milk, orange zest and juice, 1/2 stick of the butter, and the honey until the butter melts and the mixture is about 110°F on a digital instant-read thermometer. Stir in the yeast and let sit for 10 minutes, until frothy. Stir in the egg.

2 In a large bowl, combine the flours and salt. Pour in the yeast mixture and beat well with a wooden spoon (you can also do this in a mixer and beat with a dough hook for 5 minutes). The dough will be sticky and soft.

3 Lightly grease two pieces of plastic wrap and put the plastic, greased side down, over the bowl. Let rise in a warm place until doubled in size, about 1 1/2 hours. About 15 minutes before the end of rising, preheat the oven to 350°F and lightly grease two 9-inch round cake pans.

4 Using a metal spoon, drop 10 spoonfuls of dough evenly into each cake pan, leaving room between each dollop. Bake for 25 minutes, until the rolls are golden. Remove from the oven and transfer to wire racks. Melt the remaining 1/2 stick of butter and brush it on the rolls as they emerge from the oven. Cool before eating.

VARIATION
Swedish Rye Rolls
Leave out the honey and replace it with 1 tablespoon brown sugar. Replace 1 cup of the unbleached flour with 1 cup rye flour, and add 1 teaspoon caraway seeds. The orange-scented rolls are similar to *limpa*, a Swedish rye bread that's often served with split pea soup and is wonderful for sandwiches.

TOP SECRET
Save those waxy butter wrappers when you're done with a stick, instead of throwing them out. They're perfect for greasing pans with a minimum of mess. When you're done using them, toss them in the trash.

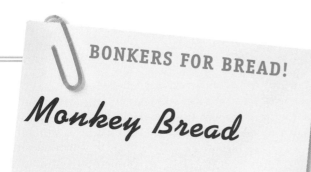

BONKERS FOR BREAD!

Monkey Bread

Staple snack of a thousand summer camps, *monkey bread* is the term for balls of dough dipped in butter and cinnamon-sugar and baked with the rolls packed on top of each other, so they rise up into a delicious, sticky mass that you pull apart with your fingers. It's not a fussy recipe, and it's surprisingly easy to make from scratch.

ROLLS
1/4 cup (1/2 stick) unsalted butter

3/4 cup milk

1/4 cup sugar

1 envelope active dry yeast

2 eggs, lightly beaten

1/2 teaspoon salt

2 1/2 cups flour

TOPPING
5 tablespoons butter, melted

1/2 cup sugar

1 teaspoon cinnamon

PREP TIME: 20 minutes • **COOK TIME:** 30 minutes • **SERVES:** 8–10

1 *For the rolls:* In a small saucepan over medium-low heat, melt the butter in the milk until the mixture reaches 110°F on a digital instant-read thermometer. Off the heat, stir in the sugar and sprinkle the yeast over the surface. Stir to dissolve with a fork and leave for 10 minutes, until frothy.

2 Pour the mixture into the bowl of a stand mixer fitted with a dough hook. With the mixer running at low speed, add the eggs and salt and then gradually add the flour. Turn up the mixer and knead with the dough hook for 5 minutes, until dough is smooth and elastic. Form into a ball and put in an oiled bowl, turning to coat evenly. Cover with plastic wrap and let rise in a warm place until doubled, about 1 1/2 hours.

3 *For the topping:* Put the melted butter in a small bowl; combine the sugar and cinnamon in another small bowl. Divide the dough into 30 pieces, rolling each into a ball. Lightly grease a Bundt pan or 12-cup tube pan. Dip each piece of dough in the butter, then in the cinnamon-sugar, and mound them evenly around the pan. Lightly grease a piece of plastic wrap and put the plastic, greased side down, over the pan. Let rise for 1 hour, until doubled in size.

4 Preheat the oven to 450°F. Bake the bread for 25 to 30 minutes, until puffy and golden brown. Turn the pan onto a serving plate immediately so all the buttery sugar runs down over the rolls. Eat while still warm.

TOP SECRET

If you're longing for that rosy hue that many professional-quality baked goods have, dissolve the yeast in carrot juice rather than water. The result will also add an additional hit of sweetness.

White Sandwich Loaf

Every kitchen needs a recipe for a no-nonsense sandwich bread, and here's a real keeper—firm for slicing, moist enough to be tender. It also makes the best cinnamon toast and French toast ever.

1 tablespoon sugar

1/2 cup hot water (about 110°F)

1 envelope active dry yeast

3 1/2 cups flour

2 teaspoons salt

PREP TIME: 15 minutes • **COOK TIME:** 35 minutes • **MAKES** 1 loaf (9-inch)

1 Stir the sugar into the water and sprinkle the yeast over the top. Stir with a fork to dissolve, and leave for 10 minutes, until frothy.

2 Stir the flour and salt together in a large mixing bowl and make a well in the center. Add the yeast mixture all at once and stir with a wooden spoon to make a dough. Turn onto a well-floured surface and knead for 6 to 7 minutes, until smooth and elastic.

3 Oil the bowl and put the dough back in the bowl, turning to coat. Cover with plastic wrap and let rise until doubled, about 2 hours. Turn onto the floured surface again and pat into a rectangle.

4 Fold in three like a letter and lay, seam side down, in a buttered 9-inch loaf pan. Cover with a clean kitchen towel and let rise for 45 minutes. After 30 minutes of rising, preheat the oven to 400°F. When the dough is doubled in size, bake for 30 minutes, until well-browned.

VARIATION

Whole-Wheat Sandwich Loaf

Replace 1 cup of the flour with whole-wheat flour. Sprinkle the inside of the greased baking pan with a tablespoon of whole-wheat flour, tapping to coat the bottom and sides, then turn over and discard any excess.

TOP SECRET

Here's a way to make sure your bread is done: Use oven mitts and a clean kitchen towel to take the bread out of the pan at the end of the suggested cooking time, when it looks golden brown, then *return* it to the oven, upside down for 5 minutes. The underside will cook golden brown as well, and you'll ensure there's no doughy center. Brush with butter when you remove it the second time, to keep the crust tender for sandwiches.

TOP 8 USES FOR LEFTOVER BREAD

It doesn't matter how big your family is, or whether you prefer quick breads, yeast breads, or Wonder bread, you will almost always have a few straggler pieces left over. Don't throw them out! You can find a number of yummy uses for them, like these.

1 Make bread salad
Called *Panzanella* in Italy and *Fattoush* in Egypt, this delectable dish requires nothing more than torn up leftover bread and a toss with chopped fresh tomatoes and light vinaigrette.

2 Make breadcrumbs
Toast leftover bread on a cookie sheet at 275°F, crumble into a food processor, and whir until fine. Store in an airtight container for up to 3 months.

3 Soften brown sugar
Stick a piece of bread in a bag of hard brown sugar for 48 hours and seal. The result? Softened sugar.

4 Thicken pureed soups and spreads
Slice stale bread and put it in a food processor with soup. Puree, and voilà! Thick and luscious.

5 Make breadsticks
Slice stale bread into long thin strips, brush with butter or olive oil, sprinkle with sesame seeds, and bake until crispy in a 300°F oven.

6 Make mini-tart crusts
Slice stale, sweet quick breads, soak them in beaten egg, and press them into mini-tart tins. Bake at 300°F for 5 minutes, remove the pan from the oven, cool, fill, and then rebake.

7 Make Apple Brown Betty
Layer slices of stale bread in a deep pie dish, top with slices of peeled apple, cinnamon, sugar, and butter, and repeat. Sprinkle with breadcrumbs, dot with butter, and bake until golden at 300°F.

8 Make bull's-eye eggs
Using a juice glass, pop out a small circle in slices of stale white bread. Sauté in a hot, buttered nonstick pan, and break an egg into the circle. Cook until the white is firm, flip, and remove when the yolk is cooked to your liking.

BONKERS FOR BREAD!

Whole Whole-Wheat Bread

In general, chefs know that a bread made with all whole-wheat flour will be heavier and much denser than bread made with half whole-wheat, half white flour. For added fiber and health, however, sometimes a complete whole-grain loaf is exactly what you want. This one *will* be heavy and dense, but that's the point here. The small amount of yeast works over a long period to make a lighter-textured bread.

3 cups whole-wheat flour

1 tablespoon brown sugar

1 teaspoon instant yeast

2 teaspoons salt

1 1/2 cups water

2 tablespoons extra-virgin olive oil

Cornmeal, for sprinkling

PREP TIME: 3 minutes • **COOK TIME:** 1 hour • **MAKES** 1 loaf (9-inch)

1 In a large bowl, mix the flour, sugar, yeast, and salt. Stir in the water and oil to make a sticky dough. Cover the bowl with plastic wrap and leave it to rest in a warm place overnight, at least 12 hours and up to 24 hours.

2 Grease a metal 9-inch loaf pan liberally and sprinkle lightly with cornmeal. Turn the dough into the loaf pan and sprinkle the top generously with cornmeal. Cover loosely with plastic wrap and allow to rise in a warm place for 2 more hours.

3 Toward the end of the rising time, preheat the oven to 350°F degrees. Bake for 45 to 50 minutes, until golden. Allow to cool in the pan for 10 minutes, then turn onto a wire rack and cool completely before slicing.

VARIATION

Honey-Sunflower Whole-Wheat Bread

Replace the sugar with 2 tablespoons honey and stir in 1/2 cup hulled, toasted, salted sunflower seeds along with the flour.

TOP SECRET

For sweeter flavor and added lightness, mix in 1 tablespoon applesauce with the water and oil, and proceed with the recipe.

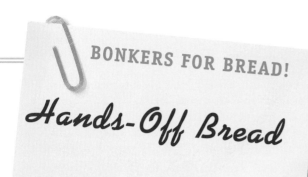

BONKERS FOR BREAD!

Hands-Off Bread

Based on a stunningly simple technique from a well-known New York City baker, Jim Lahey of Sullivan Street Bakery, this recipe uses a tiny amount of yeast and makes beautiful, crusty bread that looks like it came straight off the shelves of a fancy bakery—and it takes about 3 minutes of work. The only catch is that you have to let it sit for 18 hours (while you go about your day); then follow the baking directions exactly.

3 cups unbleached flour

1 tablespoon Kosher salt or 2 teaspoons iodized salt

1/4 teaspoon active dry yeast

1 1/2 cups water

PREP TIME: 3 minutes • **COOK TIME:** 1 hour • **MAKES** 1 large round

1 Put the flour, salt, yeast, and water in a large bowl and stir. If it doesn't combine easily, add a few more tablespoons of water. It should be a very wet dough. Cover with plastic wrap and let it sit for 18 hours, give or take an hour or two (it will rise up the sides of the bowl and be extremely bubbly).

2 Pour the dough onto a generously floured surface, and add up to another 1/2 cup of flour until it becomes workable. Fold it over several times on itself, and turn it into a heavily floured shallow dish. Coat the top generously with flour as well. Cover with plastic wrap and leave to rise another 2 hours, until doubled.

3 After 1 1/2 hours of the second rise, preheat the oven to 450°F. During the preheating, put a 6- to 8-quart lidded pot inside, empty, to heat. (Use a Dutch oven or a cast-iron or enamel-covered cast iron pot). When the dough has risen, carefully remove the hot pot from the oven. Remove the lid and tip the dough into the pot.

4 Shake the pot to redistribute if the dough tips in very crooked but don't worry if it's messy. Put on the lid and return to the oven. Bake for 30 minutes, then remove the lid and bake another 15 to 30 minutes, until the dough has a rich dark brown crust. Remove to a wire rack and cool.

TOP SECRET

One of the keys to this marvelous bread is that it bakes at a very high heat. If you're lucky enough to have a convection setting on your oven, set it to 450°F convection, which will actually push it closer to 525°F. The resulting bread will be of artisanal quality.

Super-Nutty Quick Bread

Simple, quick, and easy, this bread is also remarkably light (and even reasonably healthy), and perfect for an impromptu breakfast.

2 cups buttermilk

1 cup Grape-Nuts Cereal

1 egg, lightly beaten

3 cups all-purpose flour

1 cup sugar

1 teaspoon baking powder

1 teaspoon baking soda

1/2 teaspoon salt

PREP TIME: 10 minutes • **COOK TIME:** 30 minutes • **MAKES** 2

1 Preheat the oven to 375°F. Grease two 8 x 4-inch loaf pans.

2 In a large bowl, combine the buttermilk and cereal. Let stand for 10 minutes, then add the egg.

3 In another large bowl, combine the flour, sugar, baking powder, baking soda, and salt. Stir into the cereal mixture just until moistened.

4 Spoon the batter into the prepared pans. Bake for 30 to 35 minutes, or until a toothpick inserted near the center comes out clean. Cool for 10 minutes before removing to a wire rack.

VARIATION

Cinnamon Grape-Nuts Quick Bread

Add 1/2 teaspoon ground cinnamon to the flour mixture. Top the loaves with a handful of Grape-Nuts right before baking.

TOP SECRET

Cereal is not just for the breakfast bowl anymore. Grape-Nuts is the secret trick to adding crunch and texture to quick bread. But don't overlook cornflakes (crush them and they make a great coating for fried chicken or cutlets) or puffed rice (sprinkle them on butternut squash soup for a terrific crunchy counterpoint).

BONKERS FOR BREAD!

Grilled Cheese Bread

Deliriously rich and gooey, this is a perfect loaf to make over a campfire...or on your home grill.

1 package (3 ounces) cream cheese, softened

2 tablespoons unsalted butter, softened

1 cup shredded mozzarella cheese

1/4 cup chopped green onions

1/2 teaspoon garlic salt

1 loaf (1 pound) French bread, sliced

PREP TIME: 10 minutes • **COOK TIME:** 15 minutes • **SERVES:** 10

1 Preheat a grill to medium.

2 In a small bowl, beat the cream cheese and butter. Add the cheese, onions, and garlic salt and mix well.

3 Spread on both sides of each slice of bread and reassemble the loaf. Wrap the loaf in a large piece of heavy-duty foil and seal tightly. Grill, covered, for 8 to 10 minutes, turning once. Unwrap foil and grill for 5 minutes longer.

VARIATION

Smoky Goat Cheese Loaf

Switch things up by using goat cheese instead of cream cheese and smoked Gouda in place of the mozzarella. You can also add grated Parmesan for a spark of flavor.

TOP SECRET

Cheeses of all sorts bake and grill very well. But what gives this loaf its unbeatable silkiness is cream cheese. Often overlooked and rarely taken seriously, this wonderful secret ingredient makes for a delicious loaf. Feel free to use the low-fat variety, but not the nonfat (which will crumble, rather than melt).

12 JUST DESSERTS

SWEET FINISHING TOUCHES

The desserts in this chapter play into that primal love of sweets that so many of us share, from the best spice cake recipe you'll ever find to the greatest chocolate chip cookies ever made (very special trick included here). If you're someone who thinks "Baking is so complicated," if you're worried that your pie crusts aren't up to par or that your homemade cakes are never moist enough, then this chapter is for you. It has all the recipes you need to get your oven glowing and your sweet tooth humming. You can be the pastry chef–rock star in your own kitchen.

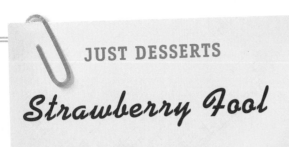

JUST DESSERTS

Strawberry Fool

Fruit fools are a classic British summer dessert, particularly gooseberry fool, a sweet and tart pudding made of cream and gooseberries. Though we don't see those in the United States too often, there's still no reason to be denied this delicious treat. Pile it into tall glasses for an elegant effect, and stick a finger of shortbread on top.

1 pound ripe strawberries, stemmed and rinsed, or frozen berries, partially thawed

1/4 cup sugar

1–2 tablespoons Grand Marnier or orange juice

2 cups heavy whipping cream

1 teaspoon vanilla extract

PREP TIME: 20 minutes • **COOK TIME:** 0 minutes • **SERVES:** 6

1 Put the fruit in a blender with the sugar and Grand Marnier or orange juice, and process until smooth. Taste and add more sugar, if necessary.

2 Using a handheld mixer, whip the cream with the vanilla in a medium bowl until it forms stiff peaks.

3 Gently fold the fruit puree into the whipped cream. Mound into serving glasses or pile into a serving dish. Chill for up to 1 hour before serving. If you make it in advance, it can be kept in the fridge for several hours, but it won't keep well overnight, as the berry puree will begin to separate a bit from the cream.

VARIATION

Rhubarb Fool

A fleeting treat, when rhubarb is ripe in spring, trim the rhubarb into small pieces and cook with 3 tablespoons orange juice and 3/4 cup sugar in a covered saucepan over medium heat for about 15 minutes, or until tender. Cool slightly and puree in a food processor or blender. Blend the whipped cream with the rhubarb, leaving some pink streaks.

TOP SECRET

To add maximum flavor to less-than-flavor-packed fruit, add a tablespoon of that fruit's juice—prepackaged—and the result will be spectacular.

JUST DESSERTS

Poached Pears

When you poach pears, the lightly spicy, winey fragrance that rises from the pan is heavenly, and the pears are marvelous served alone or with a trickle of cream, or best, with a dollop of vanilla ice cream or frozen yogurt to melt into the light syrup. Poaching is perfect for the hard pears you so often find in supermarkets. They emerge tender and succulent, as perfect as if they'd ripened on a tree.

4 large firm pears (Anjou or Bosc work well)

2 cups red wine

2 cups water

1 cup sugar

2 sticks cinnamon

1 lemon

Unsweetened whipped cream

PREP TIME: 6 minutes • **COOK TIME:** 1 hour • **SERVES:** 4

1 Peel the pears, leaving the stems on.

2 In a large saucepan, combine the wine, water, sugar, and cinnamon. Use a small knife or vegetable peeler to peel the zest off the lemon in one long strip and drop it in the water. Heat over medium-high heat, stirring until the sugar is dissolved.

3 Bring to a boil, add the pears, and reduce the heat. Cover the pan loosely and simmer for 30 to 45 minutes, turning them occasionally in the liquid, until the pears are tender. Poke them gently with the tip of a knife to check tenderness. The knife should pierce easily to the center.

4 Serve warm with a dollop of unsweetened whipped cream and extra syrup (strained) on the side, or let the pears cool in the syrup. Store in the refrigerator in the syrup.

VARIATION
Asian Spiced Poached Pears
Leave out the lemon zest and add 3 whole star anise and peeled and sliced coins from a 2-inch piece of fresh ginger, 8 whole peppercorns, and 4 whole cloves.

TOP SECRET

How do you make a round fruit sit upright for the poaching, baking, or roasting process (think baked apple)? Using a paring knife, slice the bottom of the fruit off, leaving a flat bottom. No toppling!

Cherry Clafoutis

A clafoutis (klah-FOO-tee) is a French fruit pudding, traditionally made with cherries. It's easy, too, since you can mix the batter in a blender. Serve warm and puffy, straight from the oven, when the fruit is in season—and eat cold, a bit flattened, but wonderfully tasty from the fridge for breakfast. If you don't have *real* almond extract, as opposed to the chemical, synthetic kind, leave it out.

1 1/4 cups milk

3 eggs

2/3 cup sugar

2 teaspoons vanilla extract

1/2 teaspoon almond extract

1/2 cup flour

1/4 teaspoon salt

3 cups cherries, pitted

PREP TIME: 8 minutes • **COOK TIME:** 1 hour • **SERVES:** 6

1 Preheat the oven to 350°F and butter a 2-quart baking dish.

2 In a blender, mix the milk, eggs, sugar, vanilla, almond extract, flour, and salt. Spread the cherries evenly across the bottom of the pan and pour the batter evenly over them. Sprinkle the top lightly with sugar.

3 Bake for about 1 hour, until golden and puffy. A tester poked in the center should come out clean.

VARIATION

Plum or Apricot Clafoutis

Replace the cherries with 1 1/2 pounds sweet purple plums or ripe summer apricots, halved and pitted. Skip the almond extract. Turn the fruit cut-side up in the dish and pour the batter over all. You may need to bake the clafoutis in a wider, shallower dish than when baking with cherries, so the fruit halves can fit in a single layer. Bake for 30 minutes, then check to see if the clafoutis is golden. Give it 5 or 10 minutes more, if needed.

TOP SECRET

Strange but true: The traditional version of clafoutis calls for leaving the pits in. Why? They provide an extra hit of flavor to the already delicious cherries. It may not seem proper, and it isn't for everyone (especially little kids), but if you make this for a barbecue dessert, try it. It turns a great dessert into something truly extraordinary.

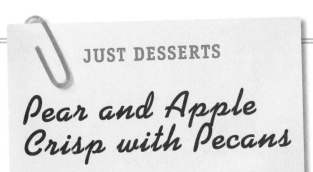

JUST DESSERTS

Pear and Apple Crisp with Pecans

This is an over-the-top crisp with a generous amount of topping and full of butter, with the crunch of pecans and succulent autumn fruits bubbling beneath. This would be a terrific dessert served warm with a spoonful of vanilla ice cream melting on top—but it's also delicious served alone, fresh from the oven.

TOPPING

2 sticks unsalted butter, softened

1 cup flour

1/2 cup sugar

1/2 cup dark brown sugar

1/2 teaspoon salt

1/2 teaspoon ground nutmeg

1 cup rolled oats

1 cup chopped pecans

FRUIT

4 cooking apples (such as Granny Smith)

4 ripe pears (try Bartlett or Bosc)

1 cup sugar

2 tablespoons cornstarch

1 teaspoon ground cinnamon

3 tablespoons fresh lemon juice

PREP TIME: 15 minutes • **COOK TIME:** 1 hour • **SERVES:** 8

1 Preheat the oven to 350°F and butter a 9 x 13-inch glass baking dish.

2 *For the topping:* In a medium bowl, using your hands, work the butter into the flour, sugar, brown sugar, salt, and nutmeg, until the mixture is in big lumps. Add the oats and pecans, tossing them through the mixture with your fingers to make clumps.

3 *For the fruit:* Peel and core the apples and pears and cut into 1-inch chunks. Toss together in the prepared dish and sprinkle with sugar, cornstarch, cinnamon, and lemon juice.

4 Distribute the topping over the whole surface and bake for about 1 hour, until golden and bubbling.

VARIATION

Cranberry Holiday Crisp

Add 1 cup fresh or frozen whole raw cranberries to the apples and pears, along with the zest of 1 orange. Replace the lemon juice with orange juice and leave out the nutmeg. Because the cranberries are so much juicier, add an additional tablespoon of cornstarch.

TOP SECRET

If your brown sugar has gone hard as a rock, slip a piece of bread into its bag, and wait for 48 hours. Remove the bread, and presto! The sugar will be usable again.

AN APPLE A DAY

You know the old expression: An apple a day keeps the doctor away. Well, this is partly true, since apples are some of the healthiest snacks around. But not all apples are equal, and many of them just do not lend themselves to cooking, while others become simply magical when baked, roasted, or sautéed. Here's a quick guide to the Garden of Eden's best-loved fruit.

Braeburn
Spicy-sweet, crisp, good for cooking and eating out of hand.

Cameo
Sweet-tart, dense, resists browning, and while good for cooking, necessitates longer baking times.

Cortland
Sweet, tender, ideal for garnishes and salads, but not for cooking.

Gala
Super-crisp, tart, and perfect for eating and cooking.

Golden Delicious
Sweet and mellow, ideal for baking.

Granny Smith
Extremely tart, perfect for snacking, baking, and saucing.

Honeycrisp
Delicious combination of honeyed sweetness and tartness, best for snacking and salads.

Idared
Tangy and crisp, great for snacking and perfect for baking, since it's one of the few apples that holds its shape under heat.

McIntosh
Soft-fleshed and tender, ideal for saucing and baking.

Red Delicious
Mild, perfect for snacking but less so for baking.

JUST DESSERTS

Perfect Chocolate Chip Cookies

Some folks like them crisp and others like them chewy, but it's tough to please everyone. This recipe, which alters the classic recipe to good effect with extra flour, gets it just about perfect.

1 cup (2 sticks) unsalted butter, softened

1 cup sugar

1 cup light brown sugar

2 eggs

2 teaspoons vanilla extract

1 teaspoon baking powder

1 teaspoon salt

3 cups flour

1 package (12 ounces) semisweet chocolate chips

3/4 cup walnuts or pecans (optional)

PREP TIME: 15 minutes • **COOK TIME:** 11 minutes • **MAKES** about 6 dozen

1 Beat the butter with the sugar, brown sugar, eggs, and vanilla until fluffy.

2 Mix in the baking powder and salt, then add the flour and mix to combine. Stir in the chocolate chips and nuts, if using. Cover tightly with plastic wrap and chill overnight.

3 Preheat the oven to 375°F. Drop the dough onto ungreased baking sheets in 2-tablespoon dollops, leaving at least 1 inch between cookies. Bake for 9 to 11 minutes, removing when the cookies are just starting to brown and still look soft, but not raw, in the center. Remove to a wire rack and cool.

VARIATION

Giant Chocolate Peanut Butter Chip Cookies

Stir 1/2 cup cocoa powder into the dough. Instead of all chocolate chips, use 1 cup chocolate chips and 1 cup peanut butter chips, plus 1/2 cup roasted, salted peanuts. Drop the dough by 1/3 cupfuls onto large ungreased baking sheets, no more than 6 cookies per sheet, leaving plenty of space between each (you should have enough for 18 cookies). Flatten the balls of dough slightly with your hands. Bake for 16 to 18 minutes (take them out sooner for fudgy, chewy cookies; leave them a bit longer for crisper cookies).

LEFTOVER LUXURIES

Odds are you won't have any leftovers. But if you do, sandwich a scoop of ice cream (use a melon baller to dip it) between two cookies; wrap in wax paper and freeze individually for a really sweet treat.

TOP SECRET

Shhh...this secret will forever change the way you make chocolate chip cookies and will leave your pals wondering what it is that you do to make them so delicious. Simple: After you mix the ingredients together, give them a rest in the fridge overnight. If you can wait even longer, 24 hours in the chill will result in absolute perfect cookies that are neither crumbly nor cakey.

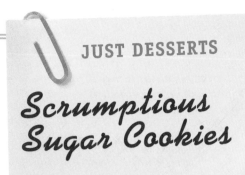

JUST DESSERTS

Scrumptious Sugar Cookies

It's difficult to find an ideal dough for rolling and cutting cookies. Here's the end of the search: a sturdy, practical dough that can be rolled and rerolled repeatedly with very little loss in quality, firm enough to transfer to baking sheets without tearing, yet bakes with a mild, delicate flavor and excellent texture. Perfect for frosting or for eating unadorned, this is likely to become your holiday classic.

1 cup (2 sticks) unsalted butter, softened

1 1/2 cups confectioners' sugar

1 tablespoon vanilla extract

1 egg

2 1/4 cups flour

1/2 teaspoon baking powder

PREP TIME: 15 minutes • **COOK TIME:** 8 minutes • **MAKES** about 3 dozen

1 Using an electric mixer, cream the butter and sugar in a large bowl until smooth, and then beat in the vanilla and the egg.

2 Sift together the flour and baking powder in a medium bowl. Blend the flour mixture gradually into the butter mixture until well-combined. Divide the dough in half, wrap each piece in plastic wrap, and chill for 30 minutes.

3 Preheat the oven to 350°F and lightly grease 2 baking sheets. On a lightly floured surface, roll out one of the dough halves to a thickness of about 1/8 inch. Cut out cookies using any cutter you like.

4 Carefully lift the cookies with a spatula and transfer them to the prepared baking sheets. Bake for about 8 minutes, just until set and not at all browned.

VARIATIONS

Drop Sugar Cookies
Blend 3 tablespoons of heavy cream or milk into the creamed sugar and butter along with the vanilla and egg. Drop dough by rounded teaspoonfuls onto prepared baking sheet. Dip the bottom of a glass in 1/2 cup sugar (mixed with 1 teaspoon cinnamon and 1/2 teaspoon cardamom, if you like) and lightly press the cookies flat.

Lemon Sugar Cookies
Add the zest of 1 lemon to the creamed sugar and butter.

TOP SECRET
Forget about flouring your work surface if it's warm out; all you'll do is wind up pressing more flour into your dough, which will give the cookie a floury taste. Instead, make a quick mixture of half flour and half confectioners' sugar and use this to dust your work surface.

Perfect Oatmeal Cookies

This is another cookie in America's repertoire for which cooks find it hard to achieve the perfect balance of chewy and crisp. Extra butter, an extra egg yolk, and a mix of plain and brown sugar helps, as does using old-fashioned rolled oats, not quick oats. Don't stint on the vanilla, either.

3/4 cup (1 1/2 sticks) unsalted butter, softened

1/2 cup sugar

1/2 cup brown sugar

1 egg plus 1 egg yolk

2 teaspoons vanilla extract

1 1/4 cups all-purpose flour

1/2 teaspoon baking powder

1/2 teaspoon baking soda

1/4 teaspoon salt

2 cups old-fashioned oats

1 cup chopped toasted pecans

PREP TIME: 15 minutes • **COOK TIME:** 12 minutes • **MAKES** about 3 dozen

1 Using an electric mixer, in a large bowl, cream the butter, sugar, and brown sugar until light and fluffy. Beat in the egg, egg yolk, and vanilla until smooth.

2 In a medium bowl, combine the flour, baking powder, baking soda, and salt. Gradually pour into the butter mixture, and fold in the oats and pecans. Cover with plastic wrap and refrigerate for at least 2 hours, or overnight.

3 Preheat the oven to 350°F. Drop the dough by 1/4 cups at least 2 inches apart on ungreased baking sheets. Bake about 12 minutes, until the centers are just set and the edges are beginning to brown. Cool on wire racks.

VARIATIONS

Chocolate Chip Oatmeal Cookies
Reduce the oatmeal by 1/2 cup and stir in a 12-ounce bag semisweet chocolate chips.

Coconut Oatmeal Cookies
Reduce the oatmeal by 1/2 cup and add 1 cup sweetened coconut flakes. Sprinkle a little coconut on top of each cookie before baking.

DID YOU KNOW?
Creaming together butter and sugar results in a perfect lemon yellow color, almost identical to the color of lemon peel. You know when it's time to stop the creaming process because this is the exact color the mixture will reach.

TOP SECRET
Crushed oatmeal cookies make the perfect filling for baked apples. When you make the cookies, make a little extra and freeze the overrun for just such a dessert.

Perfect Pie Crust

Like roast chicken and ideal omelets, pie crust is one of those super-simple recipes that can take a lifetime to master. But it also depends on your taste. If what you love is flaky pastry, use nothing but vegetable shortening, or better yet, lard. If you like a crust with real flavor, use all butter. Or split the difference and use half shortening, half butter.

2 cups unbleached flour

1 teaspoon salt

2/3 cup shortening and/or unsalted butter, chilled

1 teaspoon white vinegar

About 1/2 cup ice cold milk

PREP TIME: 10 minutes • **COOK TIME:** 10 minutes, if prebaking
MAKES 2 pie crusts (9-inch)

1 Sift the flour and salt into a large bowl, holding the sifter high over the bowl to aerate the flour. Add the shortening and/or butter and vinegar and cut it in with a fork, two knives, or a pastry blender (you can also do this step in the food processor), until it forms clumps the size of tiny peas.

2 Sprinkle 1 tablespoon of the milk over one edge of the flour. Toss to combine, then push it to one side and sprinkle another tablespoon on the next part. If the pastry looks moist enough with 5 tablespoons, stop there, but you may need as many as 7 or 8 tablespoons.

3 Dump the pastry onto a lightly floured surface and quickly press into 2 disks. Wrap in wax paper and chill in the freezer for at least 20 minutes, if you want to continue right away, or refrigerate up to a week.

4 On a lightly floured surface, roll each disk as thin as you can, about 1/8 inch, trying not to touch it much with your bare hands. To transfer to a pie plate, loosely roll the circle around the rolling pin, then unroll over the plate. Press lightly to fit and trim off overhanging edges with a paring knife. Proceed with recipe, or parbake by lining with wax paper, weighing down with 2 cups dry beans, and bake at 400°F for 10 minutes, until just browned.

TOP SECRET

Lard traditionally produces the flakiest pie crust, but chefs know another secret: the addition of white vinegar—or gin—into the mixture, added before rolling. Who knew?

TOP 8 THINGS TO STUFF INTO A PIE

Pie has been called the perfect food. The combination of crispy crust with everything from fruit to vegetables to meat to cheese makes it an unbeatable combination of flavor and texture. Make them big, make them small, fold them over and make them half-moon shaped, but however you make them, just be prepared for them to be eaten, quickly. Here are some longtime favorites.

1 Sour cherries
Blend pitted sour cherries with 1 tablespoon sugar and a sprinkling of tapioca powder, then top it with a second crust and bake.

2 Ham and cheese
Make a batter of 2 eggs and 1 cup half-and-half, and blend together with ham and cheddar, Swiss, or any combination of cheeses.

3 Chicken and vegetables
Cube leftover chicken and toss with diced carrots, celery, onions, and other vegetables. Blend in a can of prepared white sauce and season, to taste. Cover with a second crust and bake.

4 Strawberry rhubarb
Combine sliced strawberries with chopped rhubarb, 1 cup sugar, and a few tablespoons tapioca powder. Cover with a second crust, and bake.

5 Blueberry banana
Combine 1 cup blueberries with 4 sliced bananas, 1 cup sugar, and a few tablespoons tapioca powder. Cover with a second crust and bake.

6 Thanksgiving turkey and stuffing
Cube or chop turkey coarsely, then mix together with leftover stuffing and gravy. Cover with a second crust and bake.

7 Butternut squash
Cube butternut squash, drizzle with maple syrup, a pinch of ground cloves, ground cinnamon, and 1/4 cup brown sugar. Top with streusel (see page 298) and bake.

8 Sweet green tomato
Slice 6 to 8 green tomatoes, drizzle with lemon juice, ground cinnamon, sugar, 1 tablespoon cornstarch, and butter. Cover with a second crust and bake.

JUST DESSERTS

Streusel-Topped Apple Pie

A streusel topping on an apple pie is a more tender, buttery affair than the topping on a crisp, so, in general, avoid nuts in the streusel. You can, however, add 1/2 cup old-fashioned rolled oats if you like a bit of texture. Fresh-ground cloves in the filling adds new dimension to the tangy apple flavor.

TOPPING

1 cup unbleached flour

1/3 cup sugar

1/3 cup light brown sugar

1 1/2 teaspoons cinnamon

1/4 teaspoon salt

1/2 cup (1 stick) unsalted butter

FILLING

2 1/2 pounds cooking apples, such as McIntosh or Granny Smith

1 pie crust (9-inch), homemade or frozen

1/2 cup sugar

2 tablespoons flour

1 teaspoon ground cinnamon

1/4 teaspoon freshly-ground cloves

1/4 teaspoon salt

2 tablespoons fresh lemon juice

PREP TIME: 20 minutes • **COOK TIME:** 1 hour, 15 minutes • **MAKES** 1 pie (9-inch)

1 Preheat the oven to 375°F.

2 *For the topping:* Blend the flour, sugar, brown sugar, cinnamon, and salt in a medium bowl. Rub the butter in with your fingers until the mixture looks like little peas (you can also do this quickly in the food processor). Set aside.

3 *For the filling:* Peel, core, and thinly slice the apples. Mound them into the crust, heaping them a little higher in the center, and sprinkle evenly with sugar, flour, cinnamon, cloves, salt, and lemon juice—no need to toss or stir.

4 Spread the topping liberally over the apples. Place on the center rack and put a baking sheet below to catch drips and spills. Bake for 45 minutes, then reduce the temperature to 350°F and cover the topping loosely with a square of foil to prevent burning. Bake an additional 30 minutes, until the pie is bubbling and the apples are tender. Cool before slicing.

VARIATION
Double Crust Apple Pie

Roll a second disk of pastry into a 10-inch round. Brush the edges of the bottom crust with milk and gently lay the top crust on. Trim off the overhang. Brush with milk and sprinkle with sugar. Place on the center oven rack. Bake for 45 minutes at 375°F, then reduce the heat to 350°F and continue baking for about 45 minutes longer, or until the apples are tender and the crust is brown.

TOP SECRET

For the tastiest, most crispy crust around, open up the oven door in the middle of the baking process, and mist in a few drops of water with a plant mister. The steaming effect is what creates incredible crusts both on pies and on breads as well.

Coconut Cream Pie with Cookie Crust

Not all pies need a pastry crust—some fantastic ones are made with a basic cookie crust, or even with a more unusual cookie crust. The shortbread fingers used in this recipe give the crust a nubbly texture and sweet buttery bite that's totally addictive with the creamy coconut filling.

CRUST
6 ounces shortbread cookies

1/4 cup sweetened coconut flakes

1/2 cup (1 stick) unsalted butter, melted

FILLING
5 egg yolks

1/4 cup cornstarch

1 can (15 ounces) unsweetened coconut milk

2/3 cup sugar

1/4 teaspoon salt

1/2 cup sweetened coconut flakes

2 tablespoons butter, melted

1 teaspoon vanilla extract

TOPPING
1 1/4 cups heavy cream

2 tablespoons sugar

2/3 cup sweetened coconut flakes

PREP TIME: 15 minutes • **COOK TIME:** 15 minutes • **MAKES** 1 pie (9-inch)

1 Preheat the oven to 325°F.

2 *For the crust:* Put the shortbread in a ziplock bag and hit and roll with a rolling pin until fine crumbs form (you can also do this in a food processor). Pour the crumbs in the bottom of a 9-inch glass pie plate and use a fork to stir in the coconut flakes. Pour the butter over all and use the flat bottom of a cup to press the crust firmly down into the bottom and sides. Bake for 15 minutes, until lightly browned. Cool on a wire rack.

3 *For the filling:* Whisk the egg yolks and cornstarch in a small bowl. Put the coconut milk in a medium saucepan with the sugar, salt, and coconut flakes and bring to a boil, whisking just to dissolve the sugar. Pour a little of this hot mixture onto the yolks and whisk fast. When the mixture is smooth, slowly pour it into the coconut milk, whisking constantly. Cook for 2 minutes, whisking all the while, until thickened. Remove from the heat and stir in butter and vanilla. Pour immediately into the shell. Let cool for 5 minutes, then press a sheet of plastic wrap directly onto the surface. Refrigerate at least 3 hours, until firm.

4 *For the topping:* Whip the cream and sugar in a small bowl with a handheld mixer until soft peaks form. Smooth over the chilled pie and sprinkle the top with coconut flakes. Serve at once or chill for several more hours.

TOP SECRET

If your cream simply won't stand up in high, soft peaks, add a drop (and just a drop) of lemon juice, and continue beating. Like magic!

One-Pot Bittersweet Brownies

Some brownies are just too sweet—top them with ice cream and you're barely getting any chocolate flavor, just sugar and vanilla. These brownies are formulated just right for true chocolate flavor—sweet enough for kids to love, but with enough hint of strong dark chocolate to make grown-ups swoon. Best of all, you can make them in one pot. Less cleanup, more time to eat brownies.

1 cup (2 sticks) unsalted butter

1 bar (10 ounces) bittersweet chocolate or 1 1/2 cups semisweet chocolate chips

1 1/2 cups sugar

1/4 teaspoon salt

3 tablespoons flour

5 eggs, beaten

PREP TIME: 10 minutes • **COOK TIME:** 30 minutes • **MAKES** 14 brownies

1 Preheat the oven to 325°F and line an 18-cup muffin pan with paper liners. Put the butter in a large saucepan over low heat. Add broken chocolate or chocolate chips to the butter. Stir gently until the butter is melted. Even if the chocolate has a few lumps left, remove it from the heat and allow it to sit for 5 minutes, then stir again until smooth.

2 Add the sugar and salt to the chocolate and stir to dissolve. Beat in the flour and eggs.

3 Divide the batter among the prepared cups. Bake for 30 minutes, until just set in the center and not at all brown. Cool before eating.

VARIATION

Cream Cheese Marbled Brownies

In a small bowl, beat an 8-ounce package of softened cream cheese with 1/2 cup sugar, 1 egg, and 1 teaspoon vanilla. When you have divided the brownie batter among the muffin cups, drop a heaping spoonful of the cream cheese on top. Use the tip of a paring knife or a chopstick to very gently swirl the cream cheese into the chocolate mixture. Bake an additional 5 minutes, if necessary, until the centers are set.

TOP SECRET

It doesn't matter whether you're making a chocolate cake or brownies: The easiest and fastest way to get to chocolate heaven is to do two things. First, choose chocolate that is high in cacao, approximately 60 to 65 percent. This will provide the greatest hit of flavor. Second, if you're in a rush, melt the chocolate together with the butter in a microwavable dish, stirring every few seconds.

JUST DESSERTS

Chocolate Cobbler

Similar to the one-pan chocolate cakes that require no butter or eggs, Chocolate Cobbler is one of those "miracle" cakes that makes its own sauce—in this case, a hot fudge sauce that will have you returning to the pan again and again.

1 cup flour

3/4 cup sugar

1/4 cup plus 3 tablespoons Dutch-process cocoa

1 teaspoon baking powder

1/2 cup whole milk

1 teaspoon vanilla extract

1/4 cup (1/2 stick) unsalted butter, melted

1 cup chopped toasted pecans

3/4 cup light brown sugar

1 3/4 cups boiling water

PREP TIME: 10 minutes • **COOK TIME:** 35 minutes • **SERVES:** 6

1 Preheat the oven to 350°F and butter a 9 x 9-inch nonstick baking pan.

2 In a small bowl, blend the flour, sugar, 3 tablespoons of the cocoa, and the baking powder. Stir in the milk, vanilla, butter, and pecans. Pour into the prepared baking pan.

3 In a small bowl, whisk the brown sugar and remaining 1/4 cup cocoa and spoon evenly over the batter in the pan. Do not stir.

4 Very slowly, drizzle the water over the pan, trying to wet every inch of the sugar and cocoa. Do not stir! Bake for 35 to 40 minutes, until puffed.

VARIATION

Vanilla Chocolate Cobbler

Leave the cocoa out of the batter that goes in the bottom of the pan but leave it in the topping; you'll have a vanilla cake cobbled with lush hot fudge sauce.

FIX IT FAST

"Dutch-process" is a low-acid cocoa powder with smoother flavor than regular cocoa powder. The chocolate has been treated with an alkalizing agent to decrease acidity and increase solubility in liquid. Bakers like it because it bakes up with a richer color and smoother flavor. But you can alkalize any cocoa: Add 1/4 teaspoon baking soda to 1/4 cup regular cocoa to bring it to the same acidity level.

TOP SECRET

The key to toasting nuts, including pecans, is to place them in a dry pan on top of the stove, and watch them, closely. Nuts have a very high fat content and will burn much more quickly in a greased pan than in a dry pan.

JUST DESSERTS

Spice Layer Cake with Cream Cheese Frosting

Most so-called spice cakes are hesitant when it comes to the spicing, which misses the point altogether of a good spice cake. The parade of spices—allspice, ginger, cloves, nutmeg, and more—should be warm and potent. Then the rich cream cheese icing provides a creamy accent. That's what this cake does.

PREP TIME: 35 minutes • **COOK TIME:** 25 minutes • **SERVES:** 12

CAKE

2 cups flour

1 teaspoon baking soda

1 teaspoon baking powder

1 teaspoon ground ginger

1 teaspoon ground cinnamon

1 teaspoon ground nutmeg

1 teaspoon ground allspice

1/2 teaspoon ground cloves

1/2 teaspoon salt

1/2 cup whole milk

1 cup sour cream

1 stick unsalted butter

2 cups light brown sugar

4 eggs

FROSTING

2 packages (8 ounces each) cream cheese, softened

1/2 cup (1 stick) butter, softened

6 cups confectioner's sugar

2 teaspoons vanilla extract

1. Preheat the oven to 350°F. Grease three 9-inch cake pans and line the bottoms with wax paper or parchment paper.

2. *For the cake:* In a medium bowl, sift together the flour, baking soda, baking powder, ginger, cinnamon, nutmeg, allspice, cloves, and salt. In a small bowl, blend the milk and sour cream together. In a large bowl, cream the butter and brown sugar together until fluffy. Beat in the eggs one at a time. Add the flour mixture in thirds, alternating with thirds of the milk and sour cream, until blended. Divide the batter among the prepared pans and bake for 25 minutes, or until the center springs back when touched, or when a toothpick inserted in the center emerges clean. Cool in the pans for 15 minutes, then turn onto a wire rack and cool completely before frosting.

3. *For the frosting:* Beat the cream cheese and butter in a medium bowl until smooth. Blend in the sugar, continuing to beat until fluffy. Stir in the vanilla.

4. Put a dollop of frosting on the bottom of the cake plate and put the first layer on, top facing up. Top with a generous amount of frosting, smoothing it to the edges. Repeat with the remaining layers, frosting the top and sides. Chill for at least 1 hour to firm up the frosting, but remove from the refrigerator 20 minutes before serving.

TOP SECRET

To add a drop of heat to the spice cake, include 1/8 teaspoon cayenne pepper with the dry ingredients.

Ultimate Strawberry Shortcake

When it's the height of strawberry season, there's nothing like freshly made shortcake—the buttery, biscuit kind, weighted with fresh-cut fruit and softly whipped cream. This is the Cadillac of recipes, super-rich and buttery. Skip supper one summer night and just have this instead.

SHORTCAKE

2 cups all-purpose flour

1/4 cup sugar

1 tablespoon baking powder

1/2 cup (1 stick) butter

3/4 cup heavy cream

FILLING

6 cups fresh strawberries

2 tablespoons sugar

1 cup heavy cream

PREP TIME: 20 minutes • **COOK TIME:** 15 minutes • **SERVES:** 6

1 Preheat the oven to 375°F and line a baking sheet with parchment paper.

2 *For the shortcake:* Combine the flour, sugar, and baking powder in a medium bowl. Cut 6 tablespoons (3/4 of the stick) of butter into small pieces into the bowl, and work the butter and flour with a fork until the mixture has the consistency of sand. Stir in the cream and turn the dough onto a lightly floured work surface. Knead lightly, 3 or 4 times, just to bring the dough together. Pat out to a rectangle about 3/4 inch thick and cut out 3-inch rounds with a biscuit cutter or the rim of a drinking glass. (You may need to gather the scraps together and press gently to form the last shortcake.) Transfer with a spatula to the prepared baking sheet. Melt the remaining 2 tablespoons of the butter and brush the shortcakes lightly. Sprinkle with a little extra sugar, if desired. Bake for 15 minutes, until golden brown.

3 *For the filling:* Hull and slice the strawberries and toss them in a large bowl with the sugar. Whip the cream just until soft peaks form.

4 Split the shortcakes and place the bottom halves on individual serving plates. Divide the strawberries among the biscuits and top with the whipped cream. Put the tops on and serve at once.

TOP SECRET

The high fat content of rich cakes, like shortcake, means that they're not likely to stick to the parchment paper, but sometimes cakes and cookies do get stuck even on that incredibly nonstick surface. When that happens, turn the cake over very gently and brush it lightly with very hot water—not too much! You just want to pry it loose, not drench it. In 10 or 20 seconds, the wet paper will release from the cake and lift right off.

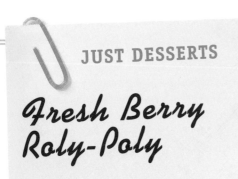

JUST DESSERTS

Fresh Berry Roly-Poly

In the height of the summer, when fresh berries of all shapes and sizes are in season, take advantage of them with this delicious, surprisingly simple dessert that's perfect for weeknight treats. But in the dead of winter, follow the trick below to breathe life back into the berries. It'll seem like summertime is right around the corner!

1 cup fresh blueberries

1 cup fresh strawberries

1 cup fresh raspberries

1 cup fresh seedless green grapes

1/4 cup grape juice or sweet red wine

Whipped cream (optional)

Fresh mint leaves (optional)

PREP TIME: 5 minutes • **COOK TIME:** 0 minutes • **SERVES:** 6

1 In a large, dry, nonstick saucepan set over medium-low heat, warm the berries and grapes gently until they begin to give off their liquid. Immediately remove them and their juice to a large bowl.

2 Add the grape juice or wine, blend carefully, and let stand at room temperature for 2 hours. Cover and refrigerate, just to chill.

3 Serve in individual bowls, topped with whipped cream and mint, if using.

VARIATION
Fresh Fruit Seviche
Combine fresh fruit with the juice of 2 limes. Add a pinch of cayenne pepper and replace the mint with basil, and omit the whipped cream.

TOP SECRET

The best way to breathe life back into fruit—fresh or frozen—is to macerate it. Cover it in an acidic liquid (alcohol will also do) for up to 2 hours, and watch the fruit plump right back up.

No-Bake Peanut Butter Cookies

What's better than a gooey and crunchy peanut butter cookie? Simple: one that you don't have to bake! This amazingly simple four-ingredient recipe will become a kitchen standard.

1 cup sugar

1 cup light corn syrup

2 cups peanut butter

4 cups cornflakes

PREP TIME: 10 minutes • **COOK TIME:** 0 minutes • **MAKES** 8 dozen

1 Place the sugar and corn syrup in a deep saucepan. Bring to a boil, then continue boiling for 1 minute, stirring constantly.

2 Add the peanut butter and stir until melted. Stir in the cereal.

3 Drop by rounded teaspoonfuls onto wax paper. Let set.

VARIATION

No-Bake Peanut Butter Chocolate Cookies

Add 2 tablespoons semisweet chocolate chips with the peanut butter.

TOP SECRET

Just like Grape-Nuts (see Top Secret, page 284), using cornflakes in baking adds remarkable crunch and sweet, corny flavor. Use them—whole or crushed— wherever you'd use breadcrumbs or wherever you want a sweet and crunch-filled coating.

Peanut Butter Chocolate Bites

If you like crispy rice treats, you'll love Peanut Butter Chocolate Bites. Rich and satisfying, they'll easily become a new favorite that you can pull together in no time.

1/4 cup (1/2 stick) unsalted butter

1 package (10 ounces) marshmallows

3/4 cup creamy peanut butter

5 cups crispy rice cereal

1 cup butterscotch chips

1 cup semisweet chocolate chips

PREP TIME: 10 minutes • **COOK TIME:** 0 minutes • **MAKES** 12

1 Grease a 9 x 13-inch pan.

2 In a large saucepan or microwavable bowl, melt the butter and marshmallows. Remove from the heat and stir in the peanut butter. Gradually add the cereal and mix until well-coated.

3 Spread and press into the prepared pan; set aside.

4 In a small microwavable bowl or the top of a double-boiler over simmering water, melt the butterscotch chips and chocolate chips. Spread over the cereal mixture, then cover and freeze for 15 to 20 minutes, or until the chocolate is set. Cut into squares or break into pieces to serve.

VARIATION
Cinnamon Peanut Treats
Add another layer of flavor by stirring 1/2 teaspoon ground cinnamon in with the peanut butter.

TOP SECRET
A campfire favorite is the perfect way to add gooey-ness to any baked good: Marshmallows melt beautifully and—miraculously—are low in calories.

JUST DESSERTS

Apple Butter Babies

Kids love these simple-to-make, yummy snack bars after school, after dinner, or anytime.

2 cups sugar

2 eggs

3/4 cup
vegetable oil

2 1/2 cups
self-rising flour

1 teaspoon
ground cinnamon

3 cups peeled,
diced tart apples

1 cup chopped
walnuts

3/4 cup
butterscotch chips

PREP TIME: 10 minutes • **COOK TIME:** 35 minutes • **MAKES** 2 dozen

1 Preheat the oven to 350°F. Grease a 9 x 13-inch baking pan.

2 In a large bowl, combine the sugar, eggs, and oil. Mix well. Stir in the flour and cinnamon (batter will be thick).

3 Stir in the apples and walnuts. Spread into the prepared baking pan and sprinkle with the butterscotch chips.

4 Bake for 35 to 40 minutes, or until golden and a wooden pick inserted near the center comes out clean. Cool before cutting.

VARIATION
Pecan Butter Babies
Swap out unsalted pecan halves for the walnuts.

TOP SECRET
Self-rising flour is the key to a cakey, rich texture without the addition of baking powder.

Peanut Butter Chocolate Sheet

Delightful as a birthday cake but wonderful any old time, this sheet cake won't last long in your house.

CAKE

2 cups all-purpose flour

2 cups sugar

2/3 cup cocoa powder

2 teaspoons baking soda

1 teaspoon baking powder

1/2 teaspoon salt

2 eggs

1 cup milk

2/3 cup vegetable oil

1 teaspoon vanilla extract

1 cup strong brewed coffee, room temperature

FROSTING

1 package (3 ounces) cream cheese, softened

1/4 cup creamy peanut butter

2 cups confectioner's sugar

2 tablespoons milk

1/2 teaspoon vanilla extract

PREP TIME: 15 minutes • **COOK TIME:** 35 minutes • **SERVES:** 12

1 Preheat the oven to 350°F. Grease a 9 x 13-inch baking pan.

2 *For the cake:* Combine the flour, sugar, cocoa powder, baking soda, baking powder, and salt in a large bowl. Add the eggs, milk, oil, and vanilla, then beat for 2 minutes. Stir in the coffee (batter will be thin).

3 Pour into the prepared baking pan and bake for 35 to 40 minutes, or until a wooden pick inserted near the center comes out clean. Cool completely on a wire rack.

4 *For the frosting:* Beat the cream cheese and peanut butter in a medium bowl until smooth. Beat in the confectioners' sugar, milk, and vanilla. Spread over the cake. Cut into 12 squares and serve.

VARIATION

Fancy Peanut Butter Chocolate Sheet

To dress up the cake, sprinkle it with miniature chocolate chips or a mixture of chocolate chips and finely chopped peanuts.

TOP SECRET

You love it hot, as your morning drink, or cold, as a warm-weather treat. But coffee has far more uses than just these! Chocolate and coffee go together beautifully, and the addition of brewed coffee into a chocolate cake (or brownies, for that matter) provides deep, incomparable, luscious flavor that can't be beat.

JUST DESSERTS

Gooey Double Peanut Pie

Peanut butter and roasted peanuts combine to create an extra-rich, salty-sweet peanut pie with a sticky texture and a deep, sweet flavor.

2 eggs

1/3 cup creamy peanut butter

1/3 cup sugar

1/3 cup light corn syrup

1/3 cup dark corn syrup

1/3 cup unsalted butter, melted

1 teaspoon vanilla extract

1 cup salted peanuts

1 unbaked pastry shell (9-inch)

PREP TIME: 10 minutes • **COOK TIME:** 30 minutes • **SERVES:** 6

1 Preheat the oven to 375°F.

2 In a large bowl, beat the eggs. Gradually add the peanut butter, sugar, light and dark corn syrup, butter, and vanilla. Mix well.

3 Fold in the peanuts and pour into the pastry shell. Bake for 30 to 35 minutes, or until set. Cool. Cut into 6 slices and serve.

VARIATION

Butterscotch Peanut Pie
Add 1/2 cup butterscotch chips to the peanut butter mixture.

TOP SECRET
In virtually every baking scenario involving peanuts, the unsalted variety is what's called for. But in this case, salted peanuts are just the ticket. Why? The saltiness of the peanuts is a perfect counterpoint to the very (very!) sweet richness of the pie.

THE CHEATING CHEF'S
BEST OF THE BASICS

Every great chef knows that the real secret to delicious food is having a stash of very basic recipes in his or her pocket. It's these wonderful things—flavorful condiments, zippy salad dressings, rich stocks—that elevate food from good to great. If you've never made, say, ketchup before, you're in for a real treat. And when that store-bought bottle is empty, you may just take it off your shopping list—permanently.

The secrets here? They're the recipes themselves.

Condiments and Spreads

Ketchup

Forget about buying this American staple— homemade is so much better and an inspired way to use up those extra tomatoes at the end of summer.

Makes 3 pints

> 4 quarts (about 24) ripe tomatoes, peeled, cored, and chopped
>
> 1 large yellow onion, chopped
>
> 1 large red bell pepper, cored, seeded, and chopped
>
> 1 1/2 teaspoons celery seed
>
> 1 teaspoon mustard seed
>
> 1 teaspoon whole allspice
>
> 1 stick cinnamon
>
> 1 cup firmly packed brown sugar
>
> 1 tablespoon salt
>
> 1 1/2 cups cider vinegar
>
> 1 tablespoon paprika

1. In a large, nonreactive saucepan or Dutch oven over moderate heat, combine the tomatoes, onion, and red bell pepper, and cook until the vegetables are soft. Using a food mill or a sieve, press the vegetables through to make a puree. Return the vegetable puree to the saucepan.

2. Over high heat, cook the vegetable puree rapidly until it is thick and the volume is reduced by about half, about 1 hour.

3. Cut a 4-inch square of cheesecloth. Place the celery seed, mustard seed, allspice, and cinnamon stick in the center, gather up the corners to form a bag, and secure with kitchen string. Add the spice bag, brown sugar, and salt to the tomato mixture. Over low heat, cook the mixture gently for 25 minutes, stirring frequently.

4. Stir in the cider vinegar and paprika. Continue to cook, stirring frequently, until the mixture is thick.

5. Spoon the ketchup into 3 hot, sterilized pint jars, leaving a 1/8-inch space between the top of the ketchup and the rim of the jar. Wipe the rims, cover, and immerse the jars for 10 minutes in water brought slowly to a boil. Cool and test for airtight seals by gently pressing the center of the lid; if the depression in the center holds, the seal is good. If it does not, store in the refrigerator and use immediately.

6. Label, date, and store in a cool, dark place for up to 1 year; the ketchup will be ready to eat in 1 week. Once a jar has been opened, store the ketchup in the refrigerator.

Cocktail Sauce

The zesty side for shrimp and other seafood. This is not only cheaper than bottled cocktail sauce, but you can mix ingredients to suit your taste.

Makes about 1 cup

> 1 cup Ketchup (above) or bottled chili sauce
>
> 1 tablespoon prepared horseradish
>
> 1 tablespoon lemon juice
>
> 1/2 teaspoon Worcestershire sauce
>
> 1/8 teaspoon hot red pepper sauce

1. In a small, nonreactive bowl, combine all the ingredients and stir until well blended. Cover the bowl and refrigerate for at least 1 hour before serving.
2. Store in an airtight container in the refrigerator for up to 1 month.

Mustard

Named for the plant that produces the seeds from which the powder is derived, this versatile condiment is easily made and adjusted to suit a particular taste or use. The basic mix includes 2 to 3 tablespoons of a liquid (vinegar, wine, water, flat beer) to about 1/4 cup dry mustard. Other additions can include turmeric (which gives a bright yellow tint), garlic, tarragon, sugar or honey, salt, and more. Use it to spice up hot dogs, hamburgers, or sandwiches, or brush over meats before grilling or roasting.

Makes about 2 cups

  1/3 cup mustard seed

  3 tablespoons dry mustard

  1/2 cup cider vinegar

  1/2 cup dark beer

  2 cloves garlic, minced

  1/4 cup firmly packed light brown sugar

  3/4 teaspoon salt

  1/2 teaspoon ground ginger

  1/4 teaspoon ground allspice

1. In a small bowl, combine the mustard seed, dry mustard, and cider vinegar. Cover the bowl with plastic wrap and let the mustard mixture stand at room temperature for 3 hours.
2. In a small saucepan, combine dark beer, garlic, brown sugar, salt, ginger, and allspice. Stir in the mustard mixture. Over moderate heat, bring the mixture to a boil; reduce the heat to low and simmer for 5 minutes, stirring occasionally.
3. Spoon the mustard into a hot, clean canning jar and seal tightly. Let the mustard cool to room temperature. Store in a cool, dark place and in the refrigerator after opening.

Mayonnaise

Homemade mayonnaise tastes so good that it improves all the salads and sandwiches it gets into. Our version is boiled, eliminating any fear of salmonella contamination from raw eggs. You can experiment with lemon juice for the vinegar and different oil. You also might try cayenne for the white pepper.

Makes 2 1/3 cups

  4 egg yolks

  2 tablespoons water

  1 tablespoon white-wine vinegar

  1 1/2 cups vegetable oil (or a combination of vegetable and olive oils)

  Pinch ground white pepper

1. In the bowl of a food processor or blender, combine the egg yolks, water, and vinegar, and whirl just until the ingredients are combined. With the motor running, drizzle in the oil very slowly; if the oil is added too quickly, it will become a liquid dressing.
2. Transfer the egg mixture to the top of a double boiler and cook until a thermometer placed in the sauce registers 160°F. Stir in the white pepper. Store in the refrigerator for up to 5 days.

Tartar Sauce

Once you've tasted a homemade version of this classic fish accompaniment, you won't waste your money on prepared tartar sauces.

Makes 1 1/4 cups

  1/2 cup Mayonnaise (above)

  1/2 cup reduced-fat sour cream

  6 scallions, minced

  1/4 cup chopped Bread-and-Butter Pickles

  2 tablespoons lemon juice

  1 tablespoon capers, drained

  1 tablespoon minced parsley

  1 tablespoon Dijon mustard

1. In a medium bowl, combine all the ingredients and stir until well blended.
2. Cover the bowl and refrigerate for 2 hours or overnight before using. Store in the refrigerator for up to 5 days.

Peanut Butter

This American staple can really eat up your budget. Surprisingly, peanut butter is not only cheaper to make at home, but healthier, too.

Makes 1 cup

4 cups shelled, salted dry-roasted peanuts

1 tablespoon plus 1 teaspoon safflower or other mild-flavored vegetable oil

1. *For creamy-style peanut butter:* Using a food processor or blender, and working in batches, process the peanuts and the oil until the desired consistency is reached. Stop and scrape down the sides of the processor container as needed.

2. *For chunky-style peanut butter:* Using a food processor or blender, coarse chop about 1/3 of the peanuts; set aside. Working in batches, process the remaining peanuts with the oil until the desired consistency is reached. Scrape down the sides of the processor container as needed. Stir in the chopped peanuts.

3. Scrape the peanut butter into a clean container with an airtight lid. Store in the refrigerator for up to 1 month.

Salad Dressings

Classic Vinaigrette

The classic salad dressing that can be (and should be) whipped up just before serving, then used sparingly over the freshest mixed greens. Since all the ingredients used in vinaigrette are pantry staples, this is a gourmet touch that is quick and easy to make and not costly at all.

Makes 1/4 cup

1/4 cup extra-virgin olive oil

4 teaspoons vinegar (white-wine, red-wine, tarragon, etc.) or fresh lemon juice

1/2 teaspoon salt

Freshly ground black pepper, to taste

In a small, nonreactive bowl, whisk together all the ingredients until well blended. Use immediately.

Herb Vinaigrette

Fresh herbs give a heightened taste to this vinaigrette that you will never get from a bottled version.

Makes 1/4 cup

1/4 cup extra-virgin olive oil

4 teaspoons vinegar (white-wine, red-wine, tarragon, etc.) or fresh lemon juice

1 tablespoon minced fresh herb, such as tarragon, basil, chives, or parsley

1/2 teaspoon salt

Freshly ground black pepper, to taste

In a small, nonreactive bowl, whisk together all the ingredients until well blended. Use immediately.

Mustard Vinaigrette

This is a classic dressing often served in good French restaurants.

Makes 1/4 cup

1/4 cup extra-virgin olive oil

4 teaspoons vinegar (white-wine, red-wine, tarragon, etc.) or fresh lemon juice

1 teaspoon Dijon mustard

1/2 teaspoon salt

Freshly ground black pepper, to taste

In a small, nonreactive bowl, whisk together all the ingredients until well blended. Use immediately.

Seasonings

Bouquet Garni

This famous combination uses either fresh herb sprigs or dried leaves. It can be added to soups, stews, and any moist-heat cooked meat and poultry dishes.

1/2 bay leaf

2 sprigs parsley

1 sprig thyme

1. Cut a piece of cheesecloth about 4-inches square. Lay the herbs in the center of the cheesecloth, then bring the corners of the cloth together to form a bundle around the herbs. Tie the top of the bundle with kitchen string.

2. Add herb bundle to soup or stew. Once the cooking is finished, the bundle can easily be removed and discarded.

Herbes de Provence

This popular French mixture can be sprinkled over meats, fish, or poultry before grilling; stirred into rice, couscous, or other grain mixtures; added to omelets or scrambled eggs; or whisked with oil and vinegar for a lovely salad dressing.

6 teaspoons dried oregano, crumbled

3 teaspoons dried basil, crumbled

3 teaspoons dried sweet marjoram, crumbled

3 teaspoons dried thyme, crumbled

1 1/2 teaspoons dried mint, crumbled

1 1/2 teaspoons dried rosemary, crumbled

1 1/2 teaspoons dried sage leaves, crumbled

1 teaspoon fennel seed, crumbled

1. In a mortar, blender, or food processor, combine all the herbs. Crush or pulse-chop them to the consistency desired.

2. Place the herb mixture in a ziplock bag or airtight container, label, and date. Keep in a dry place at room temperature. Use within 3 months.

Italian Herb Blend

This well-loved herb mix is almost essential in pasta dishes and sprinkled on pizza. It is also delicious with chicken or firm fish.

6 tablespoons dried basil, crumbled

3 tablespoons dried oregano, crumbled

2 tablespoons dried parsley, crumbled

2 tablespoons dried thyme, crumbled

1 teaspoon dried garlic

1. In a ziplock bag or airtight container, combine all the ingredients.

2. Label, date, and store in a dry place at room temperature. Use within 3 months.

Chili Powder

You don't have to pay fancy prices for fancy spice mixes. Make your own and then slowly start adding a little more of one ingredient or a little less of another until you have your own favorite variation.

Makes about 1/4 cup

3 tablespoons ground chile peppers or paprika

1 tablespoon ground cumin

1 teaspoon ground turmeric

1 teaspoon dried oregano, finely crumbled

1 teaspoon garlic powder

1/8–1 teaspoon ground cayenne pepper

1/4 teaspoon salt

1/4 teaspoon ground black pepper

1. Combine all the ingredients in an airtight container. Shake until all the spices are well blended.

2. Store in a cool, dark place for up to 6 months.

Southwest Seasoning Mix

Sprinkle this taste of the Southwest over meats or seafood before grilling, over veggies, or over freshly popped popcorn. Stirring 1 tablespoon of this seasoning mix into 1 cup sour cream, then chilling, makes a fabulous dip.

Makes 1 cup

1/4 cup chili powder

1/4 cup onion powder

2 tablespoons ground cumin

2 tablespoons ground coriander

2 tablespoons dried oregano, crumbled

2 tablespoons dried basil, crumbled

1 tablespoon dried thyme, crumbled

1 tablespoon garlic powder

1. Combine all the ingredients in a container with a tight-fitting lid. Shake until all the spices are well blended.

2. Store in a cool, dark place for up to 6 months.

Cooking Stocks

Beef Stock

At the heart of every great soup, there is a great stock. Although canned broth is convenient, it is really not as flavorful as your own stock. Plus, when you make your own, you have the satisfaction of knowing exactly what goes into it—and what doesn't. When you buy the beef for this rich-tasting stock, ask the butcher to break up the bones into pieces small enough to fit into your stockpot or Dutch oven. This will be cheaper, tastier, and far less salty than most canned broths.

Makes 3 quarts

    4 pounds meaty beef bones, including marrow and shinbones, or knucklebones

    2 yellow onions, thickly sliced

    2 carrots, thickly sliced

    2 stalks celery with leaves, sliced

    6 sprigs fresh parsley

    2 small bay leaves

    1 sprig fresh thyme or 1/2 teaspoon dried thyme, crumbled

    10 black peppercorns

    1 tablespoon salt

HELPFUL HINT

How to Clarify Stock

To have stock that is beautifully clear and tantalizing, you must clarify it after cooking. There are two methods for clarifying stock: The first will yield fairly clear results; the second method will be very clear.

STRAINING: Line a fine sieve with cheesecloth and pour the stock through; this will remove any small solids in the stock.

EGG-WHITE METHOD: Separate 2 eggs and whisk together the whites; crush the eggshells. Add the whites and shells to the stock and slowly bring to a simmer, uncovered. When the whites begin to set, pour the stock through a cheesecloth-lined sieve or colander; any particles will be trapped in the egg.

---

1. Preheat the oven to 400°F. Place the beef bones, onions, and carrots in a roasting pan and roast until the bones turn a rich brown, for 30 to 45 minutes.

2. Transfer the mixture to a large stockpot or Dutch oven. Add the celery, parsley, bay leaves, thyme, peppercorns, and salt. Add enough water to cover the bone mixture (about 5 quarts).

3. Add a little water to the roasting pan and stir to scrape up the browned bits. Pour the liquid and bits into the stockpot.

4. Place the stockpot over moderately high heat, and slowly bring the mixture to a boil, using a slotted spoon to skim off and discard any fat or scum that rises to the surface. Reduce the heat, partly cover the stockpot, and simmer gently for 3 to 4 hours.

5. Line a fine sieve with cheesecloth and set it over a large bowl. Slowly pour the stock through the sieve; discard the solids. Let the stock cool to room temperature. Pour the stock into serving-size, airtight containers; cover, label, and date. Store the stock in the refrigerator for a week or freeze for up to 6 months. If fat congeals on top of the stock while refrigerated or frozen, remove and discard before using the stock.

Chicken Stock

You can use the same technique to make turkey stock with your leftover holiday bird.

Makes 2 quarts

    5 1/2-pound stewing hen or 2 pounds chicken wing tips, necks, and backs

    3 stalks celery, sliced

    1 large carrot, sliced

    1 large onion, quartered

    1 leek, sliced

    6 sprigs fresh parsley

    1/2 teaspoon dried thyme

    1 bay leaf

    1 teaspoon salt

    1/2 teaspoon black peppercorns

1. In a large stockpot or Dutch oven, combine all the ingredients. Add enough water to cover the chicken mixture (about 10 to 12 cups). Over moderately low heat, bring the mixture slowly to a boil, using a slotted spoon to skim off and discard any fat or scum that rises to the surface.

2. Reduce the heat, partly cover the saucepan, and simmer gently until the stock is well flavored, about 3 hours. The longer you simmer the stock, the richer the flavor.

3. Line a fine sieve with cheesecloth and set it over a large bowl. Slowly pour the stock through the sieve; discard the solids. Let the stock cool to room temperature. Pour the stock into serving-size, airtight containers; cover, label, and date. Store the stock in the refrigerator for a week or freeze for up to 6 months. If fat congeals on top of the stock while refrigerated or frozen, remove and discard before using the stock.

Vegetable Stock

A creative way to use vegetable peelings, leftover vegetables, or parts full of nutrition but not generally served with the vegetables, such as mushroom stems, broccoli and cauliflower stalks, and celery tops. It's what makes homemade vegetable stock very economical and much better than vegetable cubes.

Makes about 3 quarts

1/4 cup (1/2 stick) unsalted butter

5 onions, peeled and chopped

2 leeks, halved lengthwise, cleaned, and sliced

2 whole cloves garlic

4 carrots, chopped

4 stalks celery with leaves, chopped

6–8 dried mushrooms

1 small bunch fresh parsley

1 sprig fresh thyme or 1/2 teaspoon dried thyme, crumbled

1 tablespoon salt

1/2 teaspoon ground allspice

Pinch nutmeg or mace

4 quarts cold water

1 tablespoon red-wine vinegar (optional)

1 fresh red chile, halved and seeded (optional); wear gloves when handling—chiles burn

HELPFUL HINT

Make Your Own Bouillon Cubes

No one can deny the convenience of bouillon cubes, but you don't have to spend your hard-earned money to have them on hand. When cooking a pot of stock, occasionally cook the liquid down to 2 cups—it will be thick and intense in both flavor and color. Let the reduced stock cool completely, then pour it into ice-cube trays and place the trays in the freezer. When the stock cubes are solid, remove them from the ice-cube trays, wrap each in foil, and store the cubes in a labeled and dated ziplock freezer bag. Each cube will make 1 cup of soup.

1. In a large stockpot over moderate heat, melt the butter. Add onions, leeks, and garlic, and cook, until the onions are golden, 5 to 8 minutes. Add the carrots, celery, mushrooms, parsley, thyme, salt, allspice, nutmeg or mace, and cold water.

2. Bring the mixture slowly to a boil, using a slotted spoon to skim off and discard any fat or scum that rises to the surface. Reduce the heat, partly cover the saucepan, and simmer gently for 2 hours, adding more water as needed to maintain the level at about 3 quarts. If using, add the red-wine vinegar and red chile, and simmer for 30 minutes longer.

3. Line a fine sieve with cheesecloth and set it over a large bowl. Slowly pour the stock through the sieve, gently pressing with a wooden spoon to squeeze all the liquid from the solids; discard the solids and the red chile. If desired, clarify the stock (see "How to Clarify Stock," page 314). If a thicker stock is desired, do not discard the solids when straining; puree about 1/2 cup of the cooked vegetables and stir the puree back into the stock. Let the stock cool to room temperature. Pour the stock into serving-size, airtight containers; cover, label, and date. Store the stock in the refrigerator for a week or the freezer for up to 6 months.

Dry Mixes

Biscuit and Pancake Mix

This mix will quickly make many favorite breakfast treats—not only biscuits and pancakes but also scones and waffles.

Makes about 8 cups

6 cups all-purpose flour (or 3 cups all-purpose flour and 3 cups whole-wheat flour)

3 1/2 tablespoons baking powder

1 cup instant nonfat dry milk

1 tablespoon salt

1 cup vegetable shortening

1. In a large bowl, combine the flour, baking powder, powdered milk, and salt, and stir until well mixed. Using a pastry blender or 2 knives, cut in the shortening until the biscuit mix resembles coarse meal.

2. Put the mix into a ziplock bag, label, date, and refrigerate for up to 6 weeks.

Basic Cake Mix

Don't purchase cake mix—make your own. This basic mix can be stored for 10 to 12 weeks. It's so flexible that you'll quickly develop your own recipes to fill your family's needs.

Makes 16 cups

8 cups all-purpose flour

6 cups sugar

1/4 cup baking powder

1 1/2 teaspoons salt

2 1/4 cups (1-pound can) vegetable shortening

1. In a large bowl, sift together the flour, sugar, baking powder, and salt. Stir until all the ingredients are well blended.

2. Add the vegetable shortening and, using a pastry blender or 2 knives, cut the shortening into the flour mixture until it resembles very coarse crumbs.

3. Place the mix in a large, airtight container or a ziplock bag. Label and date, and store the mix in a cool, dry place or in the refrigerator for 10 to 12 weeks.

HELPFUL HINT

Make Your Own Real Vanilla Extract

Every kitchen needs a bottle of vanilla extract—one of the most used flavorings—but as you know, it can be expensive. While imitation vanilla costs less, you pay a big price in the loss of that real vanilla flavor. What to do? Make your own.

Place a vanilla bean in a small, clean jar. Pour 3 tablespoons of plain vodka over the vanilla bean. Close the lid tightly and let the mixture stand for 4 weeks. Remove and discard the vanilla bean before using the extract.

SWAPS AND **SUBSTITUTIONS**

The lesson for home cooks to learn is that the absence of a particular ingredient isn't necessarily a shipwreck. A chef goes with the flow, rolls with the punches, takes it in stride—any cliché you like to describe the professional attitude to cooking. The show must go on, and dinner must be served even if the kitchen suddenly ran out of milk.

If you have to make a substitution, there's no question that your finished product will be different from the recipe's original intent, but that's okay. Giving yourself permission to move ahead with a recipe, even if you have to use a few tablespoons of ketchup instead of the tablespoon of tomato paste you need, your stew will be just as tasty.

The substitutions below offer some food for thought: "If I'm vegetarian, what could I put in this stew besides beef?" as well as replacements for common allergens (such as peanuts) and replacements for alcohol. They vary from highly specific (baking powder, for example, which is a combination of cream of tartar and baking soda) to the more general (Need some white wine in a recipe? Try a little apple juice with white-wine vinegar). If you find a substitution in the "Baking" category, don't try to use it for anything other than a baking recipe (i.e., a substitute for sour cream can go in a cake but not on your mashed potato).

When measurements are given, follow them carefully to achieve a better result. When they're not, play it by ear. That's what a chef would do.

Baking

Baking powder, 1 teaspoon:
1/3 teaspoon baking soda and 1/2 teaspoon cream of tartar
....
1/4 teaspoon baking soda and 1/2 cup sour milk or buttermilk (decrease liquid in recipe by 1/2 cup)
....
1/4 teaspoon baking soda and 1/2 teaspoon vinegar or lemon juice used with milk to make 1/2 cup (decrease liquid in recipe by 1/2 cup)

Buttermilk, 1 cup:
1 cup yogurt
....
1 cup milk plus 2 tablespoons lemon juice (let sit 10 minutes)
....
1 cup milk plus 2 tablespoons white vinegar (let sit 10 minutes)

Chocolate chips, 1 ounce semisweet:
1 ounce sweet cooking chocolate

Chocolate, 1 ounce semisweet:
1 ounce unsweetened chocolate and 3 tablespoons sugar
....
3 tablespoons cocoa and 1 tablespoon oil or butter and 3 tablespoons sugar

Chocolate, 6 ounces semisweet chips, melted:
2 squares unsweetened chocolate, 2 tablespoons shortening, and 1/2 cup sugar

Chocolate, unsweetened, 1 ounce:
3 tablespoons cocoa and 1 tablespoon oil or butter

Chocolate, white, 1 ounce:
1 ounce milk chocolate

Cocoa, 1/4 cup:
1 ounce (1 square) baking chocolate (decrease fat in recipe by 1 teaspoon)

Coconut, 1 1/2 tablespoons dried flakes:
3 tablespoon fresh grated coconut

Coconut cream, 1 cup:
1 cup whipping cream plus 1/2 teaspoon coconut extract
....
1 cup whipping cream

Coconut milk, 1 cup:
1 cup whole milk plus 1/2 teaspoon coconut extract
....
1 cup whole milk

Confectioner's sugar, 1 cup:
1 cup granulated sugar plus 1 tablespoon cornstarch ground to a powder in a food processor

Cornmeal, self-rising, 1 cup:
7/8 cup flour, 1 tablespoon baking powder, and 1/2 teaspoon salt

Corn syrup, 1 cup:
1 cup sugar and 1/4 cup liquid from recipe
....
1 cup honey

Cream of tartar, 1/2 teaspoon:
1 1/2 teaspoons lemon juice or vinegar

Flour, all-purpose, 1 cup:

1 cup and 2 tablespoons cake flour

1 1/2 cups fine breadcrumbs

1 cup rolled oats

1 cup quick oats

1/3 cup cornmeal or soybean flour and 2/3 cup all-purpose flour

1/2 cup cornmeal, bran flour, rice flour, rye flour, or whole-wheat flour and 1/2 cup all-purpose flour

3/4 cup whole-wheat flour or bran flour and 1/4 cup all-purpose flour

1 cup rye flour or rice flour

1/4 cup soybean flour and 3/4 cup all-purpose flour

Flour, cake, 1 cup:

1 cup minus 2 tablespoons sifted all-purpose flour

Flour, self-rising, 1 cup:

1 cup minus 2 tablespoons all-purpose flour, 1 teaspoon baking powder, and 1/2 teaspoon salt

Honey, 1 cup:

1 1/4 cups sugar and 1/4 cup liquid in recipe

Lemon juice, 1 teaspoon:

1/2 teaspoon cider vinegar

Maple sugar, 1/2 cup:

1 cup maple syrup

Maple syrup, 2 cups:

2 cups sugar boiled with 1 cup water and 1/2 teaspoon maple flavoring

Marshmallows, 10 large:

1 cup mini marshmallows

1 cup marshmallow fluff

Molasses, 1 cup:

3/4 cup light or dark brown sugar in 1/4 cup hot water or recipe liquid

3/4 cup sugar plus 5 tablespoons additional recipe liquid (decrease recipe's baking soda by 1/2 teaspoon and add 2 teaspoons baking powder)

3/4 cup sugar plus 1 1/4 teaspoons cream of tartar and 5 tablespoons additional recipe liquid

1 cup honey

1 cup dark corn syrup

1 cup maple syrup

Nuts, 1 cup:

1 cup rolled oats, toasted in a dry skillet until lightly browned

Shortening, 1 cup:

1 cup minus 2 tablespoons lard

1 1/8 cups butter (decrease salt in recipe by 1/2 teaspoon)

1 1/8 cups margarine (decrease salt in recipe by 1/2 teaspoon)

Sour cream, 1 cup:

1 cup plain yogurt

1/2 cup milk and 1 tablespoon white vinegar or lemon juice (let sit for 10 minutes) and 1/3 cup melted butter

Sugar, brown, 1 cup:

1 cup granulated sugar

1 cup granulated sugar plus 1/4 cup molasses

1/2 cup liquid brown sugar

Sugar, 1 cup:

1 cup corn syrup (decrease liquid in recipe by 1/4 cup; don't replace more than 1/2 cup sugar with corn syrup)

1 1/3 cups molasses (decrease liquid in recipe by 1/3 cup)

1 1/4 cups powdered sugar

1 cup brown sugar, firmly packed

1 cup honey (decrease liquid in recipe by 1/4 cup)

1 3/4 cups confectioners' sugar, packed

Vanilla bean, 1:

1 tablespoon vanilla extract

1 teaspoon vanilla paste

Cooking

Arrowroot, 1 tablespoon:

1 tablespoon flour

1 teaspoon cornstarch

Breadcrumbs:

crushed soda crackers

crushed cornflakes

crushed potato chips

Chili sauce, 1 cup:

1 cup tomato sauce, 1/4 cup brown sugar, 2 tablespoons vinegar, 1/4 teaspoon ground cinnamon, 1/8 teaspoon ground cloves, 1/8 teaspoon ground allspice, and a dash of hot sauce

1 cup ketchup, 1/4 teaspoon ground cinnamon, dash of hot sauce, dash of ground cloves, and dash of allspice

Flour, 1 tablespoon, for thickening:

1 1/2 teaspoons cornstarch

1 1/2 teaspoons arrowroot

1 1/2 teaspoons potato starch

1 tablespoon granular tapioca

1 tablespoon rice flour

1 tablespoon cornstarch

1 1/2 teaspoons whole-wheat flour and 1/2 teaspoon all-purpose flour

Garlic, 1 clove:

1/8 teaspoon garlic powder

1/2–1 teaspoon garlic salt

Ketchup, 1 cup:

1 cup tomato sauce, 1/4 cup brown sugar, and 2 tablespoons vinegar

Mayonnaise, 1 cup:

1/2 cup yogurt and 1/2 cup mayonnaise

1 cup sour cream

1 cup cottage cheese pureed smooth in blender

Mustard, Dijon, 1 tablespoon:

3 teaspoons prepared mustard, pinch of sugar, and 1 teaspoon white-wine vinegar

Mustard, dry, 1 teaspoon:

1 tablespoon prepared mustard

1/2 teaspoon mustard seeds

Mustard, prepared, 1 tablespoon:

1 teaspoon dry mustard plus 2 teaspoons vinegar

Olive oil, 1/4 cup (for frying or adding to a recipe, not for dressings):

1/4 cup melted butter

1/4 cup bacon fat

1/4 cup shortening

1/4 cup lard

Onion, 1 small:

1 1/3 teaspoons onion salt

2 tablespoons instant minced onion

1 teaspoon onion powder

Pepper, white, 1 teaspoon:

1 teaspoon black pepper

Rice, raw, 1 cup:

1 cup raw converted rice

1 cup raw brown rice

1 cup raw wild rice

1 cup cooked bulgur or pearl barley

Sour cream, 1 cup:

3/4 cup sour milk and 1/3 cup butter or margarine

3/4 cup buttermilk and 1/3 cup butter or margarine

1/3 cup buttermilk, 1 tablespoon lemon juice, and 1 cup pureed cottage cheese

1 cup plain yogurt

3/4 cup milk, 3/4 teaspoon lemon juice, and 1/3 cup butter or margarine

Tomatoes, canned, 1 cup:

1 1/3 cups diced tomatoes simmered for 10 minutes

Tomatoes, fresh chopped, 2 cups:

1 can (16 ounces) chopped tomatoes with juice

Tomatoes, packed, 1 cup:

1/2 cup tomato sauce plus 1/2 cup water

Tomato juice, 1 cup:

1/2 cup tomato sauce and 1/2 cup water

1 cup vegetable juice

Tomato paste, 1 tablespoon:

2 tablespoons ketchup plus 1 teaspoon soy sauce

Tomato sauce, 2 cups:

3/4 cup tomato paste plus 1 cup water

Tomato soup, 1 can (10 3/4 ounces):

1 cup tomato sauce plus 1/4 cup water

Vinegar, 1 teaspoon:

2 teaspoons lemon juice

Wide egg noodles:

Broken fettuccine

Worcestershire sauce, 1 teaspoon:

1 teaspoon steak sauce

Dairy

Butter, 1 cup:

7/8 cup shortening and 1/2 teaspoon salt

7/8 cup lard and 1/2 teaspoon salt

1 cup margarine

Cream, half-and-half, 1 cup:

7/8 cup milk and 1/2 tablespoon butter or margarine

1 cup evaporated milk

1/2 cup coffee cream plus 1/2 cup milk

Cream, heavy, 1 cup (for cooking or baking):

3/4 cup milk and 1/3 cup melted butter or margarine

Cream, light, 1 cup:

3/4 cup milk and 3 tablespoons melted butter or margarine (for cooking or baking)

1 cup evaporated milk

Cream, whipped:

1 can evaporated milk, chilled for 12 hours, blended with 1 tablespoon lemon juice

nondairy dessert topping

Egg, large, 1:

2 1/2 tablespoons dry whole egg powder and 2 1/2 tablespoons warm water

2 yolks and 1 tablespoon water (for baking)

2 yolks (for stovetop cooking such as custards)

1/2 teaspoon baking powder, 1 tablespoon vinegar, and 1 tablespoon recipe liquid (for baking)

1 tablespoon cornstarch (for baking; don't replace more than 1 egg for every 3 eggs with cornstarch)

dissolve 1 tablespoon gelatin in 3 tablespoons cold water, add 1 tablespoon boiling water, cool and beat frothy (reduce recipe liquid by 2 tablespoons)

1/4 cup commercial egg substitute

Milk, buttermilk, 1 cup:

1 cup minus 1 tablespoon milk and 1 tablespoon lemon juice or vinegar (let sit for 10 minutes)

1 cup milk and 1 3/4 teaspoons cream of tartar

Milk, evaporated, 1 cup:

1/2 cup cream plus 1/2 cup water

1 cup whole milk

Milk, skim, 1 cup:
4–5 tablespoons nonfat dry milk and 1 cup water

Milk, sweetened condensed, 1 can (14 ounces):
dissolve 1 cup sugar and 3 tablespoons butter or margarine in 1/2 cup warm evaporated milk

Milk, whole, 1 cup:
1 cup reconstituted nonfat dry milk and 2 teaspoons melted butter or margarine

1/2 cup evaporated milk and 1/2 cup water

1/4 cup whole dry milk and 1 cup water

1 cup fruit juice (for baking)

1 cup potato water (for baking)

1/4 cup nonfat dry milk and 2 teaspoons melted butter or margarine and 7/8 cup water

1 cup soy milk

1 cup almond milk

1 cup water plus 1 1/2 teaspoons butter (for baking)

1 cup buttermilk and 1/2 teaspoon baking soda (decrease recipe's baking powder by 2 teaspoons)

Sour cream:
plain yogurt

Yogurt, plain, 1 cup:
1 cup buttermilk

1 cup cottage cheese blended until smooth

1 cup sour cream

Herbs and Spices

Allspice:
cinnamon

nutmeg

mace

cloves

Aniseed:
fennel seed

few drops of anise extract

Basil:
oregano

thyme

Cardamom:
1/2 teaspoon ground cinnamon and 1/2 teaspoon ground ginger

Chervil:
tarragon

parsley

Chili powder:
oregano, cumin, and a dash of hot pepper sauce

Chives:
scallions

onions

leeks

Cilantro:
parsley

Cinnamon:
nutmeg

allspice

Cloves:
allspice

cinnamon

nutmeg

Cumin:
chili powder

Ginger:
allspice

cinnamon

mace

nutmeg

Italian seasoning:
1 teaspoon dried oregano leaves, 1/2 teaspoon dried basil leaves and 1/2 teaspoon dried thyme leaves

Mace:
allspice

cinnamon

ginger

nutmeg

Marjoram:
basil

thyme

savory

Mint:
basil

marjoram

rosemary

Nutmeg:
cinnamon

ginger

mace

Oregano:
thyme

basil

Parsley:
chervil

cilantro

Poultry seasoning:
sage and a bit of either thyme, marjoram, savory, or rosemary

Pumpkin pie spice:
1/2 teaspoon ground cinnamon plus 1/4 teaspoon ground ginger, 1/4 teaspoon ground nutmeg, and 1/8 teaspoon ground cloves

Red pepper:
black pepper

hot sauce

Rosemary:
thyme

tarragon

savory

Saffron:
turmeric

Sage:
poultry seasoning

savory

marjoram

rosemary

Savory:

thyme

marjoram

sage

Tarragon:

chervil

fennel seed

dash of aniseed

Thyme:

basil

marjoram

oregano

savory

Low-Fat Swaps

Butter:

canola oil

olive oil

applesauce

pureed prunes

Chocolate, 1 ounce:

3 tablespoons cocoa

Cottage cheese, full-fat, 1 cup:

1 cup low-fat cottage cheese, 2 tablespoons skim milk, and 1 tablespoon lemon juice

Cream, whole milk (for baking):

skim milk

low-fat milk

Cream cheese (for baking):

low-fat ricotta cheese

yogurt

yogurt cheese

Neufchâtel (light cream cheese)

Crème fraîche:

yogurt cheese

low-fat or nonfat yogurt

low-fat or nonfat sour cream

Egg, large, 1:

2 egg whites

Eggs, 2:

1 egg and 2 whites

egg substitute

Oil (for baking):

applesauce

mashed bananas

pureed stewed prunes

Oil (for basting):

fruit juice

low-fat stock

Oil (for frying):

vegetable stock

wine

vinegar

Ricotta cheese, full-fat:

1/2 whole-milk ricotta cheese and 1/2 part-skim ricotta cheese

low-fat cottage cheese

nonfat cottage cheese

Salad dressing:

lemon or orange juice whisked with pureed roasted red peppers, carrots, onions, and garlic

Sour cream:

plain yogurt

low-fat yogurt

nonfat yogurt

Sour cream (for adding to soups and sauces):

yogurt cheese

soy milk

roasted vegetables, pureed

cooked rice, pureed

Whipped cream or ice cream (as dessert topping):

frozen yogurt

low-fat yogurt

low-fat ice cream

Whipped cream, 1 cup (in dessert recipes):

3 egg whites beaten stiff

1 cup yogurt cheese

Whipping or heavy cream, 1 cup:

1 cup evaporated skim milk

2 teaspoons cornstarch or 1 tablespoon flour whisked into 1 cup nonfat milk (for cooking, not whipping)

White sauce:

pureed white beans

Wine and Spirits

Amaretto:

almond extract

Beer, dark:

beef stock

mushroom stock

Beer, light:

chicken stock

ginger ale

white grape juice

nonalcoholic beer

Brandy or eau-de-vie:

fruit juice, such as apple, apricot, cherry, grape, peach, raspberry

flavored extracts (only for small amounts)

Calvados:

apple juice concentrate or juice

Chambord:

raspberry juice, syrup, or extract

Champagne:

sparkling white grape juice

ginger ale

white wine

Claret:

nonalcoholic wine

currant or grape juice

Cognac:

Scotch

whiskey

peach, apricot, or pear juice

Cointreau:

orange juice or concentrate

Crème de menthe:
water or fruit juice and spearmint extract or oil

Curaçao:
orange juice or concentrate

Framboise:
raspberry juice or syrup

Frangelico:
almond extract

Galliano:
licorice extract

Grand Marnier:
orange juice or concentrate

Grappa:
grape juice

reduced red wine

Grenadine:
pomegranate molasses, juice, or syrup

Hard cider:
apple cider or juice

Kahlúa:
strong coffee or espresso with a dash of cocoa

Kirsch (Kirchwasser):
black cherry, raspberry, boysenberry, currant, or grape juice

Red Burgundy:
nonalcoholic wine

red-wine vinegar

grape juice

Red wine:
nonalcoholic wine

pomegranate juice

beef or chicken stock

water with red wine or balsamic vinegar

red grape juice with red-wine or rice-wine vinegar

tomato juice

Rum, dark:
molasses thinned with pineapple juice and almond extract

rum extract

Rum, light:
pineapple juice with almond extract

rum extract

Sake:
rice-wine vinegar

Schnapps:
extract such as peppermint or peach

Sherry:
orange or pineapple juice

Southern Comfort:
cider vinegar and peach nectar or juice

Tequila:
cactus nectar or juice

Triple sec:
orange juice or concentrate

Vermouth, dry:
nonalcoholic white wine

white grape juice

white-wine vinegar

Vermouth, sweet:
nonalcoholic sweet wine

apple or grape juice and balsamic vinegar

White Burgundy:
nonalcoholic wine

white grape juice or apple juice with white-wine vinegar

White wine:
nonalcoholic wine

chicken stock

water with white-wine vinegar or cider vinegar

white grape juice or apple juice with white-wine vinegar

ginger ale

Ethnic Cooking
Asian

Bok choy (Chinese white cabbage):
beet greens

kale

Swiss chard

Chinese cooking wine:
dry sherry

Chinese five-spice powder:
aniseed or star anise, fennel seed, cinnamon, black peppercorns, and cloves

Galangal (Thai ginger):
fresh ginger

Lemongrass:
lemon zest

Lotus root:
jicama

water chestnuts

Mirin (Japanese rice wine):
sweet white wine

Nam pla (Thai fish sauce):
soy sauce and lime juice

Rice-wine vinegar:
Cider vinegar

white-wine vinegar

Sesame oil:
1 tablespoon sesame seeds fried in 1/2 cup vegetable oil

Thai basil:
Italian basil

Water chestnuts:
jicama

Indian

Atta (chapati flour):
1/2 cup all-purpose unbleached flour plus 1/2 cup sifted whole-wheat flour

Chana dal:
split yellow peas

Curry powder:
ground ginger, cumin, coriander, fenugreek, turmeric, and fennel

Garam masala:
1 teaspoon cardamom seeds, 1 tablespoon cumin seeds, 1 tablespoon coriander seeds, 2 teaspoons black peppercorns, 1 teaspoon ground cinnamon, 1 teaspoon ground cloves, and 1 teaspoon ground nutmeg

Jaggery (coarse palm sugar):
date sugar

brown sugar

Toor dal, urad dal, moong dal:
red lentils

Mediterranean

Broccoli rabe:
broccoli plus arugula or dandelion greens

Cannellini beans:
Great Northern beans

navy beans

red kidney beans

Fava beans:
lima beans

butter beans

Fennel:
celery plus some fennel or aniseed

Parmesan cheese:
any hard, aged grating cheese such as Asiago, Romano, or aged Monterey Jack

Pine nuts:
walnuts

walnuts and almonds

Vegetarian

Buttermilk, 1 cup:
1 cup soy milk mixed with 2 teaspoons lemon juice or white vinegar

Cheese:
soy or nut cheeses

Egg, 1 large (replacements best for baking):
1 mashed banana

1/4 cup applesauce, 1 tablespoon agar flakes and 1 tablespoon water

1 tablespoon ground flaxseeds soaked 2 minutes in 3 tablespoons boiling water

commercial egg substitute

Gelatin:
agar agar

arrowroot

guar gum

xanthan gum

Mayonnaise:
soy or olive oil mayonnaise

Milk:
almond milk

rice milk

soy milk

Meat:
beans

cheese

seitan (wheat meat)

tempeh (cultured soybeans)

TVP (textured vegetable protein)

tofu

Meat stock:
vegetable stock

water from cooking beans, pasta, or vegetables

mushroom or vegetable bouillon cubes

miso (soybean paste) with water

Ricotta or cottage cheese:
crumbled tofu

Sausage or smoked meats:
canned chipotles in adobo

roasted vegetables

toasted nuts

smoked tofu

smoked cheeses

Allergies

Butter:
olive oil

untoasted sesame oil

clarified butter (no milk solids)

Chocolate:
carob

Cow milk:
almond milk

goat milk

soy milk

rice milk

Cow milk cheese:
goat cheese

sheep cheese

soy cheese

nut cheese

Peanut butter:
almond butter

sunflower seed butter

soy nut butter

Peanuts:
almonds

sunflower seeds

Wheat flour (for baking):
flour from barley, buckwheat, corn, kamut, oats, rice, rye, or spelt

Wheat pasta:
pasta from corn, spelt, kamut, quinoa, rice

INDEX